Total E-mail Marketing

Total E-mail Marketing

Dave Chaffey

BUTTERWORTH
HEINEMANN

OXFORD   AMSTERDAM   BOSTON   LONDON   NEW YORK   PARIS
SAN DIEGO   SAN FRANCISCO   SINGAPORE   SYDNEY   TOKYO

Butterworth-Heinemann
An imprint of Elsevier Science
Linacre House, Jordan Hill, Oxford OX2 8DP
200 Wheeler Road, Burlington MA 01803

First published 2003

British Library Cataloguing in Publication Data
A catalogue record for this book is available from the British Library

Library of Congress Cataloguing in Publication Data
A catalogue record for this book is available from the Library of Congress

ISBN 0 7506 5754 5

For information on all Butterworth-Heinemann publications
visit our website at www.bh.com

Typeset by Keyword Typesetting Services Ltd
Printed and bound in Great Britain

Contents

Preface

Effective e-mail marketing is not just about great creative. E-mail marketing is becoming an essential, integral part of e-marketing and indeed marketing. So, in writing this book I wanted to create a comprehensive guide that not only covers how to create great campaigns and creative, but also describes a strategic approach to integrate e-mail into the communications mix. *Total E-mail Marketing* covers:

- how to use e-mail to support all stages of the customer lifecycle of customer relationship management (CRM): selection, acquisition, retention and extension

- using e-mail for a range of marketing applications: as a promotional tool, regular communications tool (e-newsletters), conversion tool (multistage e-mail), referral tool (viral marketing), research tool and customer support tool

- lists: building and maintaining house lists and selecting rented lists

- campaign design from strategy, through conversion modelling to creative and testing

- how to manage not only outbound e-mail, but also inbound e-mail

- resourcing e-mail, looking at the best options for outsourcing, and in-house management using software packages

- integrated e-mail marketing with the web site, with direct mail, advertising, public relations and word-of-mouth.

To illustrate the power of e-mail marketing I also wanted to draw on a range of examples and experiences from different practitioners. So, in each chapter you will find detailed case studies for business-to-consumer (B2C), business-to-business (B2B) and not-for-profit, and viewpoints from a range of e-mail practitioners. To help you to improve your e-mail marketing I have also included a series of checklists that can be used to plan future campaigns and highlighted key insights that are factors for success.

HOW IS THE BOOK STRUCTURED?

Total E-mail Marketing has been developed for fast, efficient learning. It is structured around eight major topics that are of concern to marketers.

Chapter 1 Introduction

Chapter 1 highlights the power of e-mail marketing. It looks at the success factors in e-mail marketing and compares it with traditional direct marketing, highlighting its benefits and disadvantages.

Chapter 2 E-mail marketing fundamentals

Permission marketing, customer relationship management, legal and ethical constraints, and the foundation of e-mail marketing are covered in Chapter 2.

Chapter 3 E-mail campaign planning

Key stages and issues in developing an e-mail marketing strategy and campaign plans are described in this chapter.

Chapter 4 E-mail for customer acquisition

This chapter discusses how to use online marketing to acquire new customers and migrate existing offline customers online. This includes building a house list through the capture of e-mail addresses and profiling and using e-mail to support online customer acquisition.

Chapter 5 Using e-mail for customer retention

How to use e-mail to develop customer relationships and techniques to keep visitors returning to a web site and making repeat purchases.

Chapter 6 Crafting e-mail creative

This practical chapter highlights the different options for developing e-mail creative from the e-mail attributes (message headers), the structure, style and tone of the message body, and its form (HTML and text).

Chapter 7 E-mail marketing management

This chapter is about making it happen. It looks at the best way to implement your plans by discussing how to resource e-mail marketing in terms of partners, purchasing software and managing inbound enquiries.

Chapter 8 E-mail marketing innovation

This chapter looks at the future of e-mail marketing. Issues covered include combating SPAM, the use of wireless access devices such as personal digital assistants (PDAs) and mobiles, and the opportunities for using rich media such as video streaming.

WHO IS THIS BOOK FOR?

Marketing and business professionals

This book has been developed as a resource to support a range of professionals involved with e-marketing:

- *marketing managers* responsible for defining an e-marketing strategy, implementing strategy or maintaining the company web site alongside traditional marketing activities

- *e-marketing specialists* such as new media managers, e-marketing managers and e-commerce managers responsible for directing, integrating and implementing their organisation's e-marketing

- *senior managers and directors* seeking to identify the right e-business and e-marketing approaches to support their organisation's strategy

- *information systems managers* also involved in developing and implementing e-marketing and e-commerce strategies

- *technical project managers or web masters* who may understand the technical details of building a site, but want to enhance their knowledge of e-marketing.

Students

This book will also be of relevance to students studying e-marketing, including professionals studying for awards from professional bodies such as the Chartered Institute of Marketing and the Institute of Direct Marketing; postgraduate students on specialist masters degrees in electronic commerce, electronic business or e-marketing and generic programmes in Marketing Management, MBA, Certificate in Management or Diploma in Management Studies which involve modules or electives for e-business and e-marketing; and undergraduates on business programmes that include marketing modules on the use of the digital marketing.

LEARNING FEATURES

A range of features has been incorporated into *Total E-mail Marketing* to help the reader to get the most from it. They have been designed to assist understanding, reinforce learning and help readers to find information easily. The features are described in the order in which they are found.

At the start of each chapter

- *Chapter at a glance*, including an overview, main learning points and the chapter topics.

In each chapter

- *E-mail marketing excellence boxes*: real-world examples of best practice approaches referred to in the text.

- *Campaign checklist boxes*: lists to help you to plan e-mail marketing and campaigns.

- *E-mail marketing insight boxes*: highlight factors critical to effective e-mail marketing.

At the end of each chapter

- *References*: these are references to books, articles or papers referred to within the chapter.

- *Web links*: these include all resource sites mentioned within the chapter and significant sites that provide further information on the concepts and topics of the chapter.

At the end of the book

- *Index*: all keywords and abbreviations referred to in the main text.

Acknowledgements

This book has been created using insights and case studies provided by many professionals who are closely involved with e-mail marketing. I would like to thank all the following for helping to give the book a range of different viewpoints and opinions:

Jeremiah Budzik, DoubleClick
William Corke and Rory Teeling, Harvest Digital
Mark Davies, Context Partners
Maddie Davis, Butterworth-Heinemann, Elsevier Science
Philippa Edwards and Robert Perrin, Anderson Baillie Marketing
Stephen Groom, Marketing Law
David Hughes, E-mail Vision
Glenn Jones, glue London
Bill Kaplan, FreshAddress
Matthew Kelleher, Claritas Interactive
Martin Kiersnowski, Interactive Prospect Targeting
Derek Mansfield, Bold Endeavours
Richard Mayer, Befocused
David Mill, MediaCo
Ollie Omotosho, Commontime
Andrew Petherick, Mailtrack
Caroline Piggins, Corpdata
David Reed, European Centre for Customer Strategies
Duncan Smith, Ashton Court Consultants
Paul Smith, MultimediaMarketing Consortium
Stephen Spelman, Altum
Tara Topliff and Naomi Broad, Virgin Atlantic
Sue Ward, Chartered Institute of Marketing, What's New in Marketing
Rhian Whitehead, Elsevier Science
John Woods, Site Intelligence

Dave Chaffey

Chapter

1

Introduction

CHAPTER AT A GLANCE

Overview

This chapter highlights the power of e-mail marketing. E-mail marketing is evaluated in comparison with traditional direct marketing and its benefits and disadvantages are shown.

Chapter objectives

By the end of this chapter you will be able to:

- assess the benefits and risks of e-mail marketing;
- describe the typical structure and metrics of an e-mail campaign;
- outline the different types of e-mail marketing and how they integrate with other forms of marketing and e-marketing.

Chapter structure

- Introduction: typical e-mail marketing questions
- Modelling and measuring e-mail marketing effectiveness
- Why e-mail marketing matters
- Why e-mail marketing beats direct mail
- Why e-mail marketing beats web site-based marketing
- Why 'total e-mail marketing'?
- Meeting the challenges of total e-mail marketing
- Why e-mail marketing is not so different from direct mail

INTRODUCTION: TYPICAL E-MAIL MARKETING QUESTIONS

'What success rate can I expect for an e-mail-shot to 20 000 prospects from a vendor list rented from a vendor, where the e-mail contains a hyperlink to a web site?'

'We have collected e-mail addresses for 20% of our customer base. We are looking to start using e-mail newsletters and promotions to encourage repeat business. Which factors will govern the success of our e-mail campaigns?'

These are typical questions from marketers keen to run e-mail campaigns, but unsure of the results that they are likely to achieve. We have all heard campaign success stories with response rates in double figures, but at the same time we all receive an ever-increasing amount of e-mail into our inbox. As Internet users receive thousands of e-mail messages every year, much of it unsolicited, how can we maximise our response rate?

Think about the factors that will govern the response rate to an e-mail campaign. One factor that you may have identified is how well targeted the campaign is to the interests and needs of the recipients: are the e-mails relevant to the audience? The offer made to encourage clickthrough to the site is another key factor. You may also have considered the quality of the creative: is it enticing in drawing the recipient in? How well does the copy explain the offer? These are very similar to the factors that govern the success of traditional postal mail. You may also have considered some factors that are specific to e-mail marketing: have the people on the lists agreed or opted in to receive e-mail communications? The characteristics of the message are also important: what is the subject line of the e-mail? At what time and on which day of the week did it arrive? Who is it from? Is it a plain text message or an HTML page including images? Finally, you may have mentioned the importance of the web page to which recipients clickthrough: is the design of this page effective in encouraging further action? So a whole host of factors is involved, some familiar to direct marketers and some new.

Total E-mail Marketing will give you detailed guidance on all these factors to enable you to devise powerful e-mail campaigns that maximise response. To start this process, the range of critical factors needed to develop successful e-mail promotions may be summarised by using the mnemonic 'CRITICAL'. CRITICAL is a checklist of questions to ask about your e-mail campaigns. It stands for:

- *Creative*: this assesses the design of the e-mail, including its layout, use of colour and image and the copy.

- *Relevance*: do the offer and creative of the e-mail meet the needs of the recipients?

- *Incentive* (or offer): The WIFM factor or 'What's in it for me' for the recipient. What benefit does the recipient gain from clicking on the hyperlink(s) in the e-mail? For example, a prize draw is a common offer for business-to-consumer (B2C) brands.

- *Targeting and timing*: targeting is related to the relevance. Is a single message sent to all prospects or customers on the list, or are e-mails with tailored creative, incentive and copy sent to the different segments on the list? Timing refers to when the e-mail is received: the time of day, day of the week, point in the month and even the year; and it may relate to particular events. There is also the relative timing – when is it received compared with other marketing communications – this depends on the integration.

- *Integration*: are the e-mail campaigns part of your integrated marketing communications? Questions to ask include: are the creative and copy consistent with my brand? Does the message reinforce other communications? Does the timing of the e-mail campaign fit with offline communications?

- *Copy*: this is part of the creative and refers to the structure, style and explanation of the offer together with the location of hyperlinks in the e-mail.

- *Attributes* (of the e-mail): assess the message characteristics such as the subject line, from address, to address, date/time of receipt and format (HTML or text).

- *Landing page* (or microsite): this is the page, or pages, reached after the recipient clicks on a link in the e-mail. Typically, on clickthrough, the recipient will be presented with an online form to profile or learn more about them. Designing the page so that the form is easy to complete can affect the overall success of the campaign.

MODELLING AND MEASURING E-MAIL MARKETING EFFECTIVENESS

Further common questions from marketers starting out with e-mail marketing are:

'How do I decide on the size of list used to meet my objectives?'

and

'How do I assess the success of my campaign?'

One of the great benefits of e-mail, in common with other forms of direct marketing, is its accountability. This book presents a simple Excel spreadsheet-based model that you can use for setting objectives and comparing the effectiveness of different tests or campaigns. Figure 1.1 shows the framework used for this model.

To evaluate the success of different e-mail campaigns, the following variables may be considered.

- *Number of e-mails sent*: how many e-mails are sent to list members.
- *Clickthrough rate* (%): the percentage of recipients that respond to the e-mail by clicking on a link.
- *Completion rate on landing page* (%): the percentage of the recipients who clickthrough that go on to complete form.
- *Conversion rate to action*: direct marketing campaigns are always aimed at achieving a response. Those that complete the landing page have responded, but we often have an additional aim, which is to convert this response into an action or a marketing outcome. Such outcomes include gaining a customer through achieving an initial sale or a repeat sale. To achieve these outcomes there will often need to be a follow-up. For example, a sales representative who has used e-mail marketing to gain a qualified lead will aim to convert the recipient into a customer. This could be achieved through follow-up e-mails combined with phone-calls and meetings.

By modelling different combinations of number of e-mails sent, clickthrough rates, completion rates and conversion rates, it is possible to set more realistic objectives for a campaign. Figure 1.2 shows a best and worst case for a typical e-mail campaign which is well targeted and has a relevant, appealing offer. Such scenarios can be discussed with your e-mail marketing agency to help agree a realistic target. The actual results can then also be compared against the forecast, as shown.

Obtaining the spreadsheet

This spreadsheet is available free at www.weboutcomes.com/total-email. The spreadsheet has been devised to enable 'What-if' objective setting. For example, it is possible to work back to the number

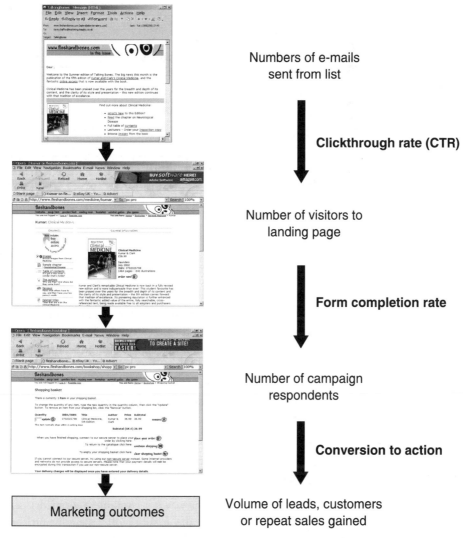

Numbers of e-mails
sent from list

Clickthrough rate (CTR)

Number of visitors to
landing page

Form completion rate

Number of campaign
respondents

Conversion to action

Marketing outcomes

Volume of leads, customers
or repeat sales gained

Figure 1.1 A simple model for objective setting for e-mail marketing. With permission of Elsevier Science

of e-mails that need to be sent to achieve the desired number of outcomes with a given click-through, completion rate and conversion rate, as shown in Figure 1.2.

E-MAIL MARKETING INSIGHT

Conversion-based modelling

Use conversion-based modelling to set realistic objectives and to help learn for future campaigns.

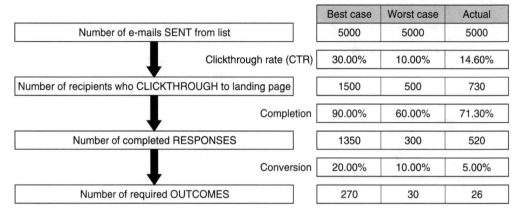

	Best case	Worst case	Actual
Number of e-mails SENT from list	5000	5000	5000
Clickthrough rate (CTR)	30.00%	10.00%	14.60%
Number of recipients who CLICKTHROUGH to landing page	1500	500	730
Completion	90.00%	60.00%	71.30%
Number of completed RESPONSES	1350	300	520
Conversion	20.00%	10.00%	5.00%
Number of required OUTCOMES	270	30	26

Figure 1.2 Part of spreadsheet model showing best case and worst case scenarios for an e-mail campaign against the actual campaign result

But what about . . .?

You may well have noticed that we have started with a simplified version of campaign metrics. For instance, it is assumed here that all e-mails sent will be received. In Chapter 3, it will be seen that a fair proportion of e-mails, perhaps more than 10%, will be bounced back to the sender since the e-mail addresses are no longer valid ('gone-aways'). Further measures of success, such as the open rate, which can be evaluated for HTML e-mails, are also considered in Chapter 3. The model is also extended to include all the different cost elements of an e-mail campaign and an estimate of campaign value is use to calculate return on investment.

WHY E-MAIL MARKETING MATTERS

The marketing potential of e-mail can be clearly seen by the way it is rivalling other media as a form of direct communication. In the UK, in January 2002, the number of e-mails being sent and received by UK households exceeded domestic letters by 300 million (550 million e-mails compared with 258 million domestic letters, according to NetValue, 2002). E-mail has become an accepted method of communicating for both consumers and businesses. E-mail has now overtaken post in many countries. Think about your own use of e-mail and the web. How much time do you spend reading and responding to business e-mails and how much time do you spend using the web? If you are typical, you will spend more time with your e-mail than using the web.

The success of early adopters of e-mail marketing has encouraged many other companies. Targeted campaigns to opt-in lists can achieve double-figure responses, at a lower cost than traditional direct marketing. Research shows that US e-mail advertising revenue is projected to reach $1.26 billion in 2002, up from $948 million in 2001 (Gartner G2, 2002). By 2005, e-mail advertising revenue is forecast to total $1.5 billion. Of course, this is a long way short of the direct mail market, even though the report is entitled 'E-mail savings threaten a $196.8 billion direct mail market'. The report states that direct mail has reached its peak and will account for less than 50% of mail received by US households by 2005, down from 65% in 2001. Denise Garcia, research director at Gartner said: 'as e-mail use, familiarity and trust increases, consumers will become more comfortable with accepting advertisements through their computer'.

WHY E-MAIL MARKETING BEATS DIRECT MAIL

E-mail offers many practical benefits over traditional direct mail. Its lower cost means it is possible to send more, better targeted, messages to each recipient as part of the campaign, which can be used to convert more of the audience to respond. E-mail can be used to send reminders about a sales promotion and messages offering further benefits can be sent to those who fail to win. Figure 1.3 gives an example of a campaign structure that achieved double-digit response. It shows that following an initial e-mail (1) with different creative for four segments offering entry into a prize draw, a reminder (2) was sent to those who had not entered. Those entering the prize draw had the opportunity to provide the e-mail addresses and names of friends or colleagues who were sent an e-mail offering them the opportunity to take part in the campaign (3). This is a viral referral (see Chapter 4 for more on viral marketing). Finally, an e-mail was sent to losers (4) which offered participation in a further draw. Clearly, such a campaign structure can achieve a better response than traditional direct marketing where sending this many communications is usually impractical because of cost.

It can be seen that e-mail gives more options for converting the audience to action. It is even possible to follow-up losing contestants with the option of further competition. Finally, the e-mail is not a one-way communication: feedback from customers via the landing page about their buying behaviour and positioning of products was also incorporated into the campaign to inform market research.

The many benefits to e-mail marketing in comparison with traditional direct marketing have been analysed by Gartner G2 (2002). According to these analysts, e-mail marketing offers:

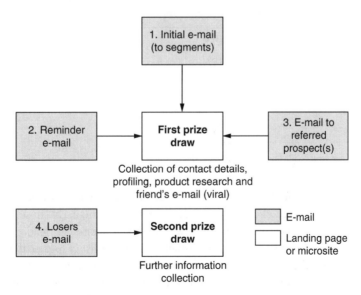

Figure 1.3 Example e-mail campaign structure. Supplied by UK-based e-mail marketing specialists Harvest Digital (www.harvestdigital.com)

- *Higher response rates*: on average, response rates are between 6 and 8% for permission-based e-mail, a significantly higher figure than the majority of direct marketing campaigns.

- *A shorter duration for campaign creation*: Gartner G2 estimates that e-mail campaigns are completed in 7–10 business days on average, compared with 4–6 weeks for direct mail.

- *A more rapid response*: Gartner G2 reports that responses to e-mail accumulate in an average of 3 days, while direct mail requires an average response time of 3–6 weeks.

- *A faster overall cycle–cycle time*: Gartner G2 suggests that the overall cycle time of an e-mail campaign from creation to delivery and response is one-tenth the time of traditional direct mail.

- *Lower costs*: it is estimated that current e-mail costs range from $5 to 7 per 1000, compared with $500 to $700 per 1000 for direct mail.

In addition, we can use viral campaigns effectively to increase response rates further, we can use e-mail for market research and the medium is accountable, in that open rates show how many people respond to the medium.

Claritas estimated the differences between e-mail and direct mail costs for 60 000 prospects as shown in Table 1.1. It is evident that while the list cost may be higher, this is offset by the reduced print, postage and fulfilment costs. A more detailed budget model for campaign planning is presented in Chapter 3. One advantage provided by the lower costs is the opportunity to communicate more frequently with customers. Take the example of a travel company: late-breaking holiday details can be e-mailed to customers who are looking for a last-minute deal. Figure 1.4 shows a weekly newsletter from Advantage Travel Centres.

Table 1.1 Cost estimate comparing a direct mail campaign with an e-mail campaign for 60 000 prospects

Cost item	Direct mail campaign	E-mail campaign
List cost	£5k	£15k
Design	£5k	£5k
Print	£6k	£0k
Postage	£13k	£0k
Fulfilment	£7.5k	£2.5k
Total	£35.5k	£22.5k

Source: Claritas Interactive (www.claritasinteractive.co.uk)

We have to give a word of caution on costs. As has been experienced with banner adverts, there has been a decline in the average clickthrough rate for e-mail, particularly those from rented lists. Combining a high cost per thousand with the low clickthrough rate can lead to a high cost per sale. Table 1.2 shows that the cost per sale for e-mail to a rented list is higher than that for direct mail to a rented list since the response rate is higher in the latter case. However, a retention e-mail to a house list of customers is the most cost-effective form of marketing in Table 1.2. We have to ask, though: how useful are cross-industry averages? The cost-effectiveness critically depends on clickthrough and the conversion rates, and these depend on the skills of the marketer

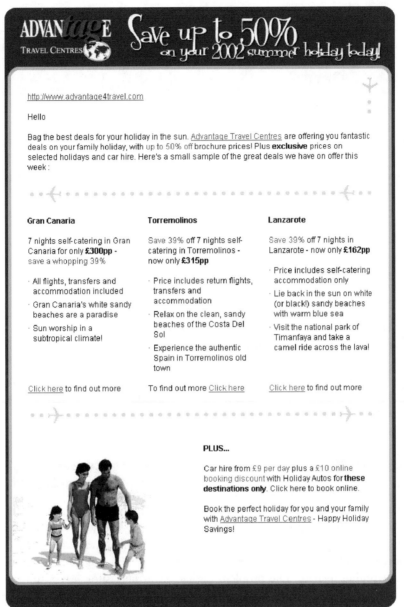

Figure 1.4 E-mail newsletter from Advantage Travel Centres (www.advantage4travel.com) (Source: David Mill, MediaCo (www.media.co.uk)

in defining their targeting, timing, offer and creative such that these can vary dramatically. The data in Table 1.2 suggest that it is never worthwhile e-mailing to a rented list. The Virgin Atlantic case study later in this chapter and many other successful campaigns show that it is still definitely worthwhile to undertake campaigns to an opt-in list. Looking at it the other way, it is still possible to produce a campaign to a house list that is not cost-effective if the campaign planning is wrong.

Table 1.2 Comparative costs and responses for different forms of direct communication

Type of campaign	Cost per thousand (CPT)	Clickthrough	Conversion to sale	Cost per sale
E-mail to rented list	$150	0.4%	3%	$1250
Banner ads	$10	0.5%	3%	$67
Direct mail to rented list	$875	n/a	1.2%	$73
Retention e-mail to house list	$5	15%	3.7%	$1
Direct mail to house list	$761	n/a	3.9%	$20

Source: Cross-industry average from Forrester (2001).

n/a: not applicable.

So, to summarise, e-mail offers many advantages as a communications tool: it offers immediacy, targeting and accountability, and is relatively cheap. It is also more cost-effective to target niche groups. For example, a bank could e-mail an 18–25-year-old female customer, who reads a particular newspaper, has a credit card and has responded to an e-mail campaign within the last 6 months. Such precision targeting is known as using multiple selects. For rented lists the cost per thousand is increased for multiple selects.

WHY E-MAIL MARKETING BEATS WEB SITE-BASED MARKETING

E-mail marketing is a vital part of the e-marketing communications mix. It is arguably as important as or more important than the web site itself. How can we justify this statement? Well, a web site's greatest strength is also its greatest weakness. A major benefit of the web site is that the audience of the web site is self-selecting. They are mainly attracted, or pulled to the web site, by the content on offer, which is indicated by search engine listings or links from other sites (or pushed using offline media). The problem is that once the visitor leaves the site, they may never return. This is where e-mail wins: it is a push medium. If the visitor's e-mail can be captured on their visit to the site, the e-mail can be used to remind the visitor about the company and its products, together with incentives to visit the web site. This is part of permission marketing, which is described in Chapter 2.

Since e-mail is a push medium, this makes it a great medium for time-critical information. E-mail alerts are the obvious application. Time-critical market information available from Newswire services provides up-to-the-minute information about the way in which a company and its competitors are featured in the media.

Less frequent e-mail alerts can also be of value: weekly and monthly alerts can be used for less critical knowledge. Such alert information can be added-value information in e-mail newsletters: you act as a source of knowledge for your customers.

E-mail is also better than the web site for targeted communications. It is superior since you, not the visitor, choose who sees what information. Web site designers have to cater for a range of audiences. This can make it difficult for customers in any segment to find the communications that have been developed for them. Similarly with special offers, which often have to be highlighted by a space little bigger than a postage stamp: it is better to use the space provided by an e-letter. With e-mail the customers who are to receive the communications are chosen using standard database marketing selects. For example, Boots the Chemist used e-mail to target customers within 30 minutes' drive time of a new range of opticians: try doing that using a web site!

Customers can also choose the information they need and when they need it. Advanced e-mail services give customer choice, over what information is delivered and when it is delivered. This and other forms of personalisation are discussed in more detail in Chapter 2.

The web site does work better in some areas; for example, providing a depth of information is only possible through multiple web pages. Here, the e-mail is best used in combination with the web, to direct customers to the more detailed information.

So, e-mail marketing does not beat web site marketing in all respects; rather, the two are perfect partners.

WHY 'TOTAL E-MAIL MARKETING'?

Much that has been written about e-mail marketing is limited to creating e-mail campaigns based on buying lists to gain new customers. This misses the value of e-mail in supporting all aspects of the buying process and entire customer lifecycle. Total e-mail marketing:

- Includes building and maintaining house lists as well as renting lists
- Covers using e-mail for the entire customer lifecycle from customer selection, acquisition, retention and extension
- Is integrated with the web site and other direct communications
- Uses a range of different e-mail types, from e-mail offers and regular e-newsletters, to multistage and viral e-mails
- Includes management of inbound communications to improve customer satisfaction.

The impact of total e-mail marketing on the modern organisation is significant. Iconocast (2001) reported that Dell Computer achieves more than $1 million in revenue per week through e-mail marketing campaigns. Considering inbound communications, each month in 2000, Dell received 50 000 e-mail messages and 100 000 order-status requests.

E-mail marketing: it's not just e-newsletters

Many marketers immediately think of e-newsletters and sales promotions as the main opportunities for deploying e-mail, but the opportunities are much greater. Think about how many of the following techniques you could deploy.

- *Acquisition tool*: here, e-mails are sent to members of a bought-in list to acquire new customers. Alternatively, you could advertise in an established e-newsletter to drive traffic to your web site.

- *Conversion tool*: many sites use offers to capture leads in the form of e-mail addresses. E-mails can then be sent to customers aimed at converting leads to customers. Multistage e-mails can be automated to encourage conversion to a sale.

- *Retention tool*: this is the classical e-newsletter or promotional e-mail sent to your house list of customers. It is aimed at keeping your company at 'front-of-mind' and achieving repeat purchases through offers delivered by e-mail. Automated multistage e-mails can also be used to retain customers at renewal; for example, for insurance or utility services.

- *Brand-building tool*: e-mail is used to increase the frequency and depth of communications with customers. For example, Pepsi UK use e-mail as their main e-marketing tool to deliver news about celebrity endorsers and the latest competitions and games.

- *Research tool*: many marketers do not immediately think of e-mail as a way of learning more about prospects and customers, but research is straightforward to build into e-newsletters and e-promotions. Questionnaires within the e-mail itself do not work well so are not widely used, but using e-mail to encourage customers to participate in a web site survey or focus group does work and is more widespread.

- *Viral tool*: viral e-mail does not only mean shock videos for the 18–30s. It is more widely applicable for using e-mail to encourage acquisition of new customers by referrals from existing customers: the classical 'member-get-member' approach.

- *Service delivery tool*: many customers prefer queries answered via e-mail as a way of avoiding the 'our call is important to you' holding systems of phone support. Many organisations are now receiving tens of thousands of e-mail enquiries. Managing these in a cost-effective manner which improves, rather than damages the brand is a major challenge for e-marketers.

MEETING THE CHALLENGES OF TOTAL E-MAIL MARKETING

Although the potential for e-mail marketing is clear, it presents a steep learning curve for marketers. These are some of the solutions that will be proposed in this book.

Permission challenges

SPAM, unsolicited commercial e-mail, is the main barrier to the acceptance of e-mail marketing, and is well-known and reviled. Likewise, the need for a permission-based approach is well-recognised. Rather than taking up too much space repeating these well-known problems, we will concentrate on giving detailed guidance on how to achieve permission marketing. What exactly does this mean when you are designing an online form for collecting customer needs? What are the options: which are legal, which are ethical and which will result in the highest response rates?

Permission marketing is covered in Chapter 2. In Chapter 8 we look at the future of e-mail given the ever-increasing wave of SPAM and measures taken by governments, the industry and consumer organisations to combat it.

E-mail marketing strategy

Rather than concentrating on individual campaigns which encourage an approach of moving from one campaign to another without focus, we describe an integrated approach to e-mail strategy that links marketing objectives and e-marketing objectives to different forms of e-mail marketing.

Campaign design strategies

E-mail marketing gives the potential for more complex e-mail campaigns. How can we develop the best form of campaign to achieve our objectives?

Campaign design strategies for customer acquisition are described in Chapter 4 and for customer retention in Chapter 5.

Buying lists

If you are familiar with buying lists for direct marketing, what are the similarities and differences for buying e-mail lists? How can you tell whether a list meets your needs? What are the questions to ask list brokers or list owners when purchasing lists?

E-mail marketing also provides new challenges for marketers. Managing lists, producing a new form of creative, response rates and privacy issues all need to be considered as they do for conventional direct marketing.

Buying lists is covered in more detail in Chapter 4.

Developing creative

The response rates for e-mail campaigns can be impressive, but what is the best design practice to achieve these? What are your different alternatives for the subject line? Why is the 'From' address important? How should a promotional e-mail be structured? How do you write compelling copy? Where and how should the call-to-action link to the web site?

Developing creative is covered in Chapter 6.

Testing and measurement

E-mail marketing gives the marketer a much clearer view of how their campaigns are performing, but the detail may obscure the critical points. We describe approaches to testing and ask: which are the measures that matter? What options should reporting systems contain?

Testing and measurement are covered in Chapters 2 and 7.

List fulfilment and e-mail management

For your initial forays into e-mail marketing, you may decide to use a specialist e-mail fulfilment house. However, those companies that dispatch e-mails from in-house can achieve big cost savings.

There are many pitfalls for the unwary when dispatching e-mails. List fulfilment and e-mail management are measured in Chapter 6.

WHY E-MAIL MARKETING IS NOT SO DIFFERENT FROM DIRECT MAIL

We end this chapter by summarising the benefits of e-mail marketing and we find that the e-mail marketing is not so different from direct mail. This is unsurprising given that they are both forms of direct marketing. The trick is either to use them together or to use them selectively where one is better. E-mail marketing builds on many of the benefits of direct mail. E-mail marketing is:

- *accountable*: unlike advertising or PR we can readily calculate the cost of customer acquisition and return on investment for each campaign; a tool for calculating this is examined in Chapter 5

- *precisely targeted*: although targeting using segmentation such as age and gender is still possible using e-mail marketing, opt-in offers more

- *cheap*: costs of acquisition and retention are often cheaper than for direct mail.

Table 1.3 summarises the benefits of e-mail discussed in this section.

Table 1.3 E-mail benefits

Characteristic	E-mail benefits
Targeting	Possible to target smaller niches since cost is lower
Cost	Cost is lower owing to lower printing and distribution costs
Campaign creation	Faster
Campaign response	Faster
Response rate	Higher
Accountability	Greater: can measure the open rate of messages. Easy to track the response from different parts of the campaign

Total e-mail marketing aims to equip you with the background knowledge to make a flying start to exploiting these opportunities for e-mail. The case study below illustrates how a powerful offer and high-impact creative can achieve a successful acquisition campaign. A successful viral element was also included. Finally, it illustrates how e-mail marketing can integrate different forms of offline and online media. Figure 1.5 shows one of the e-mails used in the campaign.

E-MAIL MARKETING EXCELLENCE

Virgin Atlantic Fly Free For Life

The campaign

To celebrate the launch of Virgin Atlantic's new web site, a viral campaign was launched offering one customer the chance to Fly Free For Life (paying applicable passenger taxes). A competition and game were used to encourage people to visit a microsite and provide their e-mail address. This campaign was promoted via cold e-

Figure 1.5 E-mail creative for the Virgin Atlantic Fly Free For Life campaign

mails to bought-in lists (Figure 1.5), banners on various sites, the flying club newsletter, a radio campaign and poster site driving traffic to a specially built microsite. To maximise exposure, it was expected that the campaign would take off virally (i.e. the game would be forwarded by e-mail to friends to play, and they would forward it on, etc.). The main objective of the campaign was to sign up customers to the site-registered base, to receive e-mail alerts on Virgin Atlantic offers and news.

The microsite

Once at the microsite (Figure 1.6), customers had to answer a simple question (Who is the chairman of Virgin Atlantic Airways?) to gain entry into the competition. The microsite offered customers the choice of three types of entry:

- enter the competition only (for people who may already have joined up to the flying club, were already site registered or who were just competition 'junkies')
- enter the competition and site register (to receive e-mail alerts on special offers and news)
- enter the competition and enrol in the flying club.

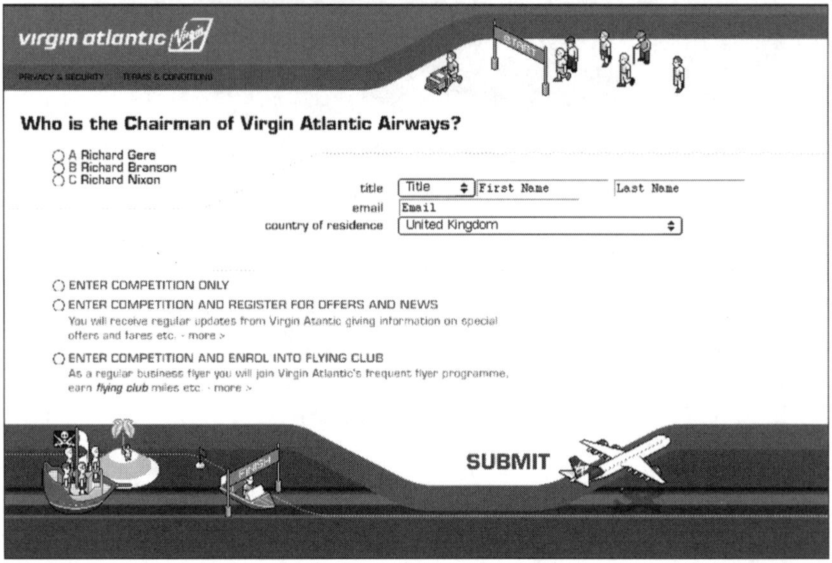

Figure 1.6 Landing page competition creative for the Virgin Atlantic Fly Free For Life campaign

To gain a further entry into the competition, entrants also had the opportunity to play the interactive game on the microsite.

This game was called 'Globetrotter' and was based on visitors navigating their way around the world (depicted by icons of Virgin's network, e.g. Statue of Liberty, palm trees) within a time limit and being chased by a pack of 'wannabe mates' (who have come out of the woodwork to go on holiday with you now you have won this fantastic prize!). If the players bumped into anything they slowed down and their mates had a chance of catching them up, therefore sending them back to the beginning.

The ability to send the game to a friend was present throughout. If the game was forwarded to a friend, it contained a score to beat (time taken to complete/fail game), to provide a challenge aspect. Once the game was completed users were given the option of playing again and prompted to refer friends. Users were also prompted to visit the new web site.

For each friend who went on to enter the competition, the original entrant (who forwarded the game in the first place) received another entry into the competition, thereby increasing their chances of winning.

As well as launching in the UK, the campaign launched in the USA, Hong Kong, India and South Africa, offering free flights for life to London. The 'Lovin' London' game was specific to the UK, with icons and landscapes of the UK to navigate through.

E-mail lists

The e-mail lists and the relevant selects used for this campaign were:

TheMutual.net	HTML and text	10 000	30+, £40k+, have clicked on travel offers
Doubleclick	HTML and text	15 000	Economy, professional
Claritas	HTML and text	15 000	Economy travellers, non-European destinations
Guardian newsletter	Text	5 × 35 000	Long-haul travellers
Virgin Wines database	HTML and text	90 000	

These lists were selected primarily on the audience being long-haul, leisure economy travellers who had expressed an interest in travel.

Results

The total traffic from all online advertising and all e-mail activity was 241 460 visits.

Delivered	190 523	
HTML open rate	82 686	43%
Clickthrough	53 939	31%
Clickthrough from opened e-mails		65%
Pass along (e-mail referrals)	2932	1.53%

Banner advertising delivered 10 296 clickthroughs with an average clickthrough rate of 0.63%.

In addition to e-mail passalongs, the viral contribution of the campaign was successful with, on average, just under one e-mail per visitor being sent from the site to friends to spread the word about the site. It resulted in 200 000 additional e-mails being delivered from the site: the main source of visitors. Clickthrough for opened e-mails was extremely high, averaging around 80%, suggesting that the offer and creative were compelling.

Over 100 000 registrants with e-mail addresses available for future campaigns were achieved, breaking down as follows:

Registration online	Globetrotter	Lovin' London	Total
Competition only	67 138	29 906	97 044
Site registered	70 508	27 661	98 169
Flying club	8891	4763	13 654
Total			208 867

(Case courtesy of Tara Topliff and Naomi Broad at Virgin Atlantic and Glenn Jones at glue London.)

REFERENCES

Forrester (2001). E-mail marketing press release, November.

Gartner G2 (2002). Gartner G2 says e-mail marketing campaigns threaten traditional direct mail promotions. Gartner G2 press release, 19 March.

NetValue (2002). Record e-mail usage signals last post for letters. Press release, 13 March. NetValue UK (www.netvalue.com).

WEB LINKS

Clickz (www.clickz.com) has great columns on e-mail marketing, e-mail marketing optimisation and e-mail marketing case studies.

Conversion Marketing objectives spreadsheet (www.weboutcomes.com).

DM News (www.dmnews.com): updates on e-mail campaigns and new practices.

EMMA – E-Mail Marketing Association (www.emmacharter.org), formed in July 2001 to support best practice amongst agencies and clients; charter gives best practice guidelines on e-mail marketing.

Opt-in News (www.optinnews.com): an online magazine focusing on permission-based e-mail marketing. Also has columns similar to ClickZ.

Chapter

2

E-mail marketing
fundamentals

CHAPTER AT A GLANCE

Overview

This chapter looks at what the concepts of permission marketing and customer relationship management mean in practice. What does permission marketing mean beyond 'opt-in'? Under what legal constraints do e-mail marketers operate?

Chapter objectives

By the end of this chapter you will be able to:

- identify all the characteristics of permission marketing
- assess the legal constraints on e-mail and know sources to keep updated
- evaluate how e-mail marketing can be used to support customer relationship management.

Chapter structure

- Introduction
- Permission marketing
- Legal constraints
- Customer relationship management
- CRM: a health warning
- Online CRM
- Personalisation and mass customisation
- An integrated e-mail marketing approach to CRM

INTRODUCTION

In this chapter we lay the foundations for detailed guidelines in later chapters which describe approaches for developing and implementing e-mail strategies. The well-established concepts underpinning e-mail marketing described in this chapter are permission marketing and customer relationship management (CRM).

Permission marketing, or gaining consent for marketing communications to be received, is fundamental to successful e-mail marketing. We will explore the development of the permission marketing concept and ask what it means in practice. For example, how do opt-in and opt-out relate to permission marketing and what are the legal constraints on e-mail marketing? Meanwhile, the concept of CRM has proved popular as an approach to improving customer focus and customer loyalty. Companies have found that the customer lifecycle of customer acquisition, retention and extension provides a useful framework for bringing focus to creating different marketing strategies and tools. If you are already familiar with the permission marketing and CRM concepts, you may want to fast-forward to Chapter 3, where we look at the specifics of developing an e-mail marketing strategy. However, in this chapter we challenge some of the conventional wisdom about permission marketing and CRM and also explain how e-mail can be used in conjunction with the web site and traditional communications.

PERMISSION MARKETING

Permission marketing is an integral part of e-mail marketing. Permission marketing is a term popularised by Seth Godin, formerly a VP of marketing at Yahoo!. Godin (1999) argues that there is a need for permission marketing since there is an ever-increasing number of marketing communications bombarding consumers. He notes that while research shows that we used to receive 500 marketing messages a day, with the advent of the web and digital TV this has now increased to over 3000 a day! From the marketing organisation's viewpoint, this leads to a dilution in the effectiveness of the messages: how can the communications of any one company stand out? From the customer's viewpoint, time is seemingly in ever-shorter supply; customers are losing patience and expect reward for their attention, time and information. Godin refers to the traditional approach as interruption marketing.

The typical, expected reaction to interruption marketing is evident from qualitative research conducted by Evans et al. (2000). When consumers were asked about unsolicited mail, these were typical reactions:

> *'... I would prefer it if I didn't see anything in the post unless I had specifically requested it' (Female, 25–34).*

> *'... Personally, if I've got something that I want to do financially, I would look into it and go to my own people. I would search them out myself rather than look at something that came through on the carpet because generally you just pick it up and throw it away' (Female, 25–44).*

> *'... It's just it's annoying to be sent things that you are not interested in. Even more annoying when they phone you up... If you wanted something you would go and find out about it' (Female, 45–54).*

Such customers want to exert control over communications and this is what permission marketing can provide. Permission marketing involves seeking the customer's permission before engaging them in a relationship and providing something in exchange for initiating the relationship. The classic exchange is based on incentives such as information, entertainment or monetary value. In a web site context, a business-to-business (B2B) site may offer a free report in exchange for a customer sharing their e-mail address, which will be used to maintain a dialogue, a while a business-to-consumer (B2C) site may offer access to a game or entry into a prize draw. Further details on the types of offer available are provided in Chapter 3.

Such an approach can reduce the frustrations of consumers referred to above, since communications following opt-in are expected, not unsolicited, and can be better targeted by profiling during and following opt-in.

However, direct marketers have criticised the permission marketing approach in that it is not an entirely new, radical approach. Ross (2001) says:

the large number of direct marketers who start the selling process with an ad offering information and take it from there with a graduated programme of data collection and follow-ups will wonder how it is that they have been practising permission marketing for all this time without knowing.

Ross also notes that in order to achieve permission, it is necessary to gain the attention of prospects, and this is, of course, only possible using ... interruption marketing.

Although consumers' perceptions are often negative, research shows that direct mail is continuing to grow in terms of volume and expenditure, even as advertising expenditure falls. For example, in the UK, DMIS (2002) reports that volume increased by 4.5% and expenditure by 5.9% compared to the previous year. This can only be happening if marketers are satisfied with the cost-effectiveness of direct mail. Note that much of this mail is not permission based, but it is still engaging consumers. The same research shows that:

- the average household receives 12.4 items of direct mail every 4 weeks
- business managers receive an average of 14 items of direct mail per week
- 75% of consumer direct mail is opened, 53% is opened and read and 26% is kept to be read later or passed on to somebody else
- business managers open 83%, 9% is redirected to a colleague and 16% is filed or responded to
- response rates for business mailings average 6.2% for product mailing and 6.2% for services mailings. Over 77% of marketers were satisfied with the results
- overall, 6.2% of direct mail is requested by customers
- the average consumer spends about £440 through direct mail each year.

It seems that interaction with and response to the direct mail medium is significant, and it will be interesting to see whether e-mail marketing can continue to achieve higher response rates for exceptional campaigns, given the ever-increasing tide of SPAM.

A further implication of permission marketing is that by providing choice, you will, in all likelihood, be reaching fewer people with your communications. Research by Evans et al. (2000) found a continuum between consumers who recognised that to receive targeted communications they had to provide their details, and those who felt that there was an invasion of privacy. Typical comments from the former group about collection of personal data include:

'I'm not particularly bothered about that. I've nothing terrible to hide! It doesn't really bother me, I'm just mildly interested to know how they get hold of your name sometimes' (Female 45–54).

'It's more targeted' (Female 45–54).

'Don't mind if a company wants to know more about me' (Male 18–24).

Comments from those more concerned about their personal details include:

'I think it's quite unnerving really what people might know. How much detail they do actually have on you regarding income and credit limits. I don't know what details are stored' (Female 25–34).

'... Junk mail, God. I give to one charity and the next thing I know I've got 10 charities coming in daily. They've obviously sold it on for profit' (Female, 45–54).

Clearly, those consumers in the second group are unlikely to enter into a permission-based relationship unless their privacy concerns and worries about data sharing between organisations are overcome. Advocates of permission marketing argue, however, that if consumers opt out of communications, it is not a bad thing. The cost of communications with such consumers is avoided and they may have a low propensity to buy.

Incentivisation

Incentives are not only used at the outset of a relationship, but can be used throughout the customer lifecycle. This process is often likened to dating someone. Godin (1999) suggests that dating the customer involves:

1. offering the prospect an *incentive* to volunteer

2. using the attention offered by the prospect, offering a curriculum over time, teaching the consumer about your product or service

3. reinforcing the *incentive* to guarantee that the prospect maintains the permission

4. offering additional *incentives* to get even more permission from the consumer

5. over time, leveraging the permission to change consumer behaviour towards profits.

Notice the importance of incentives at each stage. Which incentives have you or your partner offered during your relationship? In the context of e-mail marketing, the incentive is used initially to gain a prospect or customer's e-mail address and profile them. E-mail is then vital in permission marketing to maintain the dialogue between company and customer, and to offer further incentives and learning about the customer through stages 1–5.

Of course, likening customer relationship building to social behaviour is not new, as O'Malley and Tynan (2001) point out; the analogy of marriage has been used since the 1980s at least, particularly for B2B marketing. They also note that this concept also rests uneasily with the customer. Many do not want a continuous relationship with their supplier. They may prefer a discontinuous relationship based more on exchanges. They perceive the B2C relationship quite differently from that with friends or family. O'Malley and Tynan debunk much of the relationship marketing mythology by stating that:

> *They [consumers] continue to trade with organisations that use information about them to get the offer right, but they do not consider this false intimacy an interpersonal relationship. It is not driven primarily by trust, commitment, communication and shared values, but by convenience and self-interest.*

Opt-in and opt-out

Permission e-mail marketing is synonymous with opt-in. Opt-in means that a prospect or customer proactively agrees to receive future marketing communications, including e-mail. By checking a box on a web form they indicate that they agree to receiving further communications from a company.

For many companies this is preferable to opt-out, the situation where a customer must proactively ask not to receive further information, by unchecking a box.

Opt-out has an additional meaning: as described above it refers to the start of a relationship, it means opting out of an e-mail marketing dialogue before it has started. However it can also refer to the end of a relationship: here opting out refers to the customer deciding to end an ongoing e-mail marketing dialogue. If, for example, you have been receiving a monthly e-mail newsletter or promotional e-mails for a few months, but find that they are not delivering value to you, you can tell the company that you no longer wish to receive further e-mails. The opt-out process is usually referred to as unsubscribing. It can be achieved by replying to an e-mail with the word 'unsubscribe' in the subject line of the e-mail or clicking through to an opt-out page. No further e-mails should then be received. I say 'should', since many companies are not effective in making this process work. Opt-out is also part of the overall permission marketing concept: you are withdrawing your permission.

See Chapter 4 (page 115) for practical recommendations on how to obtain opt-in from web-site enquirers and a why using an opt-out approach may be better in some circumstances. We also look at some refinements of the technique such as double opt-in and notified opt-in.

CAMPAIGN CHECKLIST

Permission marketing: it's more than opt-in

To summarise this section, a checklist is provided of what permission marketing means in practice. Check it to see to what extent you practise permission marketing:

1. Permission marketing is an alternative approach to interruption marketing ☐.

2. The prospect or customer agrees to receive information. This is opt-in, i.e. it is not SPAM ☐.

3. Incentives are usually used to achieve opt-in ☐.

4. The customer is usually profiled when they opt in, or order to place them in a segment and understand their future needs from the relationship ☐.

5. Subsequent communications are tailored in-line with customer needs, based on the initial profiling ☐.

6. Incentives are used for continued dialogue: customer needs are researched as further data is collected throughout the customer lifecycle. The aim is to increase the level of permission by collecting more detailed information and responding accordingly ☐.

7. The customer can also decline receipt of information, effectively ending the relationship. This is opt-out ☐.

The battle against SPAM

For many, all e-mail marketing is SPAM. They do not know about the concept of 'permission marketing', only the annoyance of unwanted e-mail. Understanding SPAM can help the e-mail marketer to avoid the risk of being classified as SPAM. The customer can be reassured that what you are offering is not SPAM. Potential customers can be reassured that they will not be spammed. SPAM is formally referred to by the e-mail industry as unsolicited commercial e-mail (UCE). The term originally refers to the 'spiced ham' that US GIs contracted to SPAM during the Second World War. It has been said that today, SPAM stands for 'Sending Persistent Annoying E-mail'. You will know it as the instantly identifiable 'Get rich quick' offers that flood into your e-mail inbox. Later, we will review how to make your e-mail easily distinguishable from SPAM. Fortunately, perhaps incredibly, despite the problem of SPAM, permission-based e-mail marketing still works (see Figure 2.1).

See Chapter 4 (page 115) for a detailed discussion of alternatives for how to obtain opt-in from web site enquirers to avoid SPAM. Here, a discussion of different degrees of SPAM is presented. Chapter 8 also looks at the future for SPAM: is it possible to win the battle against SPAM?

LEGAL CONSTRAINTS

Nowhere is the maxim 'consult a lawyer' more relevant than for e-mail marketing, since new legislation and case law mean that it is frankly impossible for a marketer to keep up to date with the details of legislation. In fact, the maxim should read 'consult a specialist lawyer'. Legal constraints on e-mail marketing naturally vary by country. Here, we concentrate on European legislation, which is arguably the most advanced in the world. E-mail marketers operating in European countries are subject to several existing laws and there are also emerging laws. Of the existing laws, the most pertinent are the EU Data Protection Directive, and local advertising standards and telecommunications laws. Of the new laws the European Union (EU) Electronic Communications

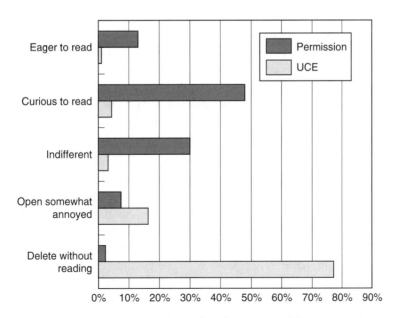

Figure 2.1   Responses to permission-based e-mail and SPAM according to IMT Strategies, September 2001, quoted in eMarketer report

directive, which was being finalised at the time of writing, is the most important. Refer to Marketing Law (www.marketinglaw.co.uk) for updates on the application of the act in different European countries.

Legal Notice

This information provides a summary interpretation of current and emerging law. It is not intended as legal advice or counsel, and is not represented as such by the author or publisher. The author or publisher makes no warranties regarding the legal acceptability of the information provided. It is advised that legal counsel is sought to ensure compliance with legislation.

Data protection legislation is there to protect the individual; to protect their privacy and to prevent misuse of their personal data. Indeed, the first article of EU directive 95/46/EC, on which legislation in individual European countries is based, specifically refers to personal data. It says:

> ... *Member states shall protect the fundamental rights and freedoms of natural persons, and in particular their right to privacy with respect to the processing of personal data.*

So what is personal data, from a marketing point of view? Well, they can simply be the name, address or e-mail address of an individual; or the sales history of the customer, the record of all communications with a person (outbound marketing or inbound e-mails where they ask a question or express an opinion). Personal data can also refer to a person's use of the web site as found in website logs, or to a server placing a cookie on an individual's PC.

Note that this clause refers to personal data regardless of whether the person is a consumer (B2C) or an individual working for an organisation (B2B). Natural person refers to the individual rather than the organisation for which they work. The implication of this is that e-mailing to generic addresses such as info@company.com or support@company.com is not subject to data protection legislation, but the moment you contact a named individual then data protection legislation does apply. So, an e-mail address 'dave.chaffey@marketing-insights.co.uk' is personal data, as are all the facts, opinions or behaviour that you record about the customer.

An organisation's data protection or information management policy must cover all aspects of processing personal data that are shown in Figure 2.2. It shows that we must start by considering the perception of the individual before they have even entered any data. They must be clear about the future uses to which their data will be put, such as whether it will be used for marketing purposes or whether it will be shared with any third parties. Sharing data with third parties is a key concern of the e-mail-receiving public, so you can increase the number of registrants if you explicitly declare: 'we will not sell your data to third parties under any circumstances'. This may be good, in the short term, but, have you considered all the circumstances? What if an opportunity arises to sell your list to a third party? What if your company is taken over by another company that does have opportunities to pass on to a third party?

For example, if a prospect opts in to an e-newsletter, this does not mean that they have agreed to receive other communications that are aimed at converting them from a prospect to a customer. In

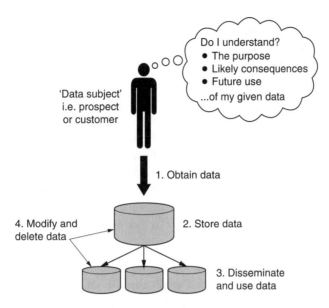

Figure 2.2 Stages in processing of personal data

this case, there should be an opt-in to the type of information that will be received and the channel through which it will be used.

So, your future use of data statement should cover:

- recipient's options: opt-in or opt-out for
- form of communication, e.g. newsletter or other promotional e-mail
- channel of communication, e.g. e-mail, phone, fax or direct mail
- whether you will share data with third parties.

It follows that the form of words, position or size of text for an opt-in is vital since this will govern whether the data subject understands the use to which their data will be put. You will want to avoid an expensive reconsenting exercise where it is necessary to contact customers because you are unsure what use of data they have consented to in the past. If you do need to reconsent you will have to do this in such a way that it is not piggy-backing on the back of an existing campaign. If the design of the data collection tool, whether it is on screen, on paper or verbal, is such that the user is being misled, then this breaks the data protection laws. Further issues follow at each of the other stages of processing personal data. For example, we must ensure the data is secure at stage 2, and that if it is disseminated in the organisation (3) it can still be modified or deleted (4) if this is required.

When developing an organisation's data protection or information management policy, you should assess whether you are using personal data 'lawfully, ethically and profitably'. Following a strict interpretation of the law may not always be in the customers' best interests and may not be profitable. For example, the law may indicate an expensive reconsenting exercise to make sure that you have permission from your customers to use their data for direct marketing purposes. If you have regular and transparent dialogue with customers, this allows informed judgements about what they seek from you in a 'privacy relationship'. Finding this balance will ultimately prove more profitable than 'blind adherence' to legislation which is open to interpretation, and which is in a constant state of flux.

The following principles are important to understanding e-mail marketing laws.

- *Personal data*: the Data Protection Directive and the UK Data Protection Act 1998 were essentially created to protect personal data. The Act defines 'personal data' as: 'data which relates to a living individual who can be identified: from those data; or from those data and other information which is in the possession of, or is likely to come into the possession of, the data controller.' This begs the question: is an e-mail address personal data? Since personal data is deemed to identify an individual uniquely, the answer is yes even if it is a generic address such as dave@yahoo.co.uk.

- *Sensitive personal data*: additional protection is given for these data, which include personal details such as religious beliefs, political affiliations, gender, health information and racial origins. Such data cannot be processed or used in any way on anything other than an 'opt-in' basis.

E-MAIL MARKETING INSIGHT

EMMA guidance on e-mail marketing

In March 2002, the chair of the E-mail Marketing Association (EMMA) attacked the practice of non-members using 'permission-based' to refer not to opt-in lists, but to 'opt-out' lists where individual members on a list had failed to opt-out of such use being made of their personal details. However, at the time of writing, the UK's Direct Marketing Association (DMA) allows its members to collect and use e-mail addresses for marketing purposes on an 'opt-out' basis. This is consistent with the law provided the data is not sensitive personal data.

Such sensitive personal data, the 1998 Act provides, cannot be processed or used in any way on anything other than an 'opt-in' basis. If an organisation has not collected sensitive personal data, therefore, the EMMA position is 'best practice' as some might see it, as opposed to strictly required by current laws.

Remember that if you decide to collect data on an 'opt-out' basis since it is still legal currently, then if opt-in becomes law in the future, you may not be able to use this data: the opt-in law may be retrospective. For this reason, many companies are deciding to use opt-in now to protect their contact database for the future.

E-MAIL MARKETING INSIGHT

By using opt-in now, you are allowing for future changes in the law to an opt-in-only regime.

CAMPAIGN CHECKLIST

Staying within the law

What are the implications for e-mail marketers arising from these emerging laws? We can make these guidelines:

1. The short-term view is that it is acceptable to use an opt-out approach now provided 'sensitive personal data' are not involved. This may result in more business in the short term, but at the risk of alienating some prospects or customers who believe they have not opted-in to these communications.

2. The longer term view is that when collecting data it may be best to start an opt-in approach now, for when the future law comes into place.

3. When buying e-mail lists, care should be taken to ask exactly how those on the list were asked whether they wished to opt-in or opt-out. This may even require assessing the form of the question (see Chapter 4, page 115).

4. Be aware of and counter the possibility of a spammer using your server for spamming. It can be hijacked if you do not have adequate security measures in place. If this does happen your server could be suspended by the ISP.

5. When devising campaigns, ensure that:

    (a) the e-mail is clearly a marketing communication: this should be the case if the offer and sender are clear

    (b) the originator of the e-mail is clear: provide a statement of origination for clarity

    (c) opt-out lists are respected

    (d) there is a clear privacy statement

    (e) on-line promotional competitions or discounts are clearly identifiable as such, and conditions easily accessible and presented clearly and unambiguously

    (f) all price indications on-line are clear and unambiguous, and indicate whether inclusive of packaging and delivery costs.

E-MAIL MARKETING INSIGHT

Always use a statement of origination so it is clear why the recipient has received the e-mail.

The implementation of the new Electronic Communications Directive from the European Community seems likely to suggest that different forms of consent to future e-mail marketing communications will be required according to the form of relationship between the marketing organisation and the individual or the data subject. Three different forms of relationship and the likely consent requirements can be identified:

1. *Individual unknown to organisation. Opt-in required.* This is the situation if an e-mail list is purchased from a third-party list owner. It seems likely that only opt-in lists can be used legally, i.e. all individuals on the list must have opted in to receive marketing communications.

2. *Individual is a prospect or suspect. Opt-in required.* If you have acquired a lead from the web site or through other offline means, then it seems likely that e-mail communications will only be legal on an opt-in basis.

3. *Individual is a customer of the organisation. Opt-out required.* It is likely that if there is an established relationship starting with a sale, then e-mail marketing communications will be legal provided the customer is given the opportunity to opt out of future communications.

This situation arises since the new directive distinguishes quite clearly that opt-out will only be acceptable for customers that have previously purchased directly from the company.

To future-proof, you should collect opt-in, but also record the different acceptable forms of communications to the customer (phone, fax, direct mail, e-mail), the date and time the data was collected and the form of consent given, i.e. opt-in or opt-out. The record should even reference the form of privacy statement in force at the time of registration.

Questions for list brokers

Some list brokers state that their lists are opt-in, when they are not. If you use such a list, you may be breaking data protection laws, have an unsatisfactory response rate and receive complaints that tarnish your brand. So, with all list brokers or vendors, you should initially ask whether the list is opt-in and find out the exact form of the opt-in, what text was used and what the source was. One list vendor in the UK has a privacy statement that states that the recipient's address was collected at a conference, via a magazine subscription or direct mail. This is not sufficiently specific. Some individuals will want to know exactly where their data was collected.

If the form and source of opt-in are not known then there can be no reassurance that you are not spamming and damage to your brand will result. You should ask that it is written into the contract that the list is warranted for use in direct marketing under current data protection legislation. This will be useful if you later receive a complaint from a recipient. You are unlikely to be prosecuted under the Data Protection Act or Telecommunications Act if you have shown due diligence in checking that your supplier is using an opt-in list.

You can also check whether the list owner is on the List Warranty Register (which was originally developed for direct mail). This is a central database of list owner and list user warranties. There are four types of warranty: consumer list owner, consumer list user, business list owner and business list user. Warranties are renewed every year. By signing a warranty the signee agrees to comply with the DMA's Code of Practice and in case of a complaint to be bound by the decisions of the DMA.

CUSTOMER RELATIONSHIP MANAGEMENT

Building long-term relationships with customers has always been essential for any sustainable business. However, for many years, marketing theory and practice suggested an emphasis on a short-term approach concentrating on achieving transactions rather than building customer life-time value. A shift from transactional marketing thinking to relationship marketing thinking was highlighted by Regis McKenna, who suggested a change:

from manipulation of the customer to genuine customer involvement; from telling and selling to communicating and sharing knowledge (McKenna, 1991).

This change has been facilitated by advances in technology enabling customers to be profiled in more detail and their needs assessed through market research. The Deutsche Bank example shows that even an international company with a large customer base can use this approach.

E-MAIL MARKETING EXCELLENCE

Customer profiling and analysis at Deutsche Bank

Technology enables Deutsche Bank to manage its customers on an amazing scale. Deutsche Bank has 73 million customers, of which 800 000 are on-line and 190 000 use its on-line brokerage service, it has nearly 20 000employees, 1250 branches, 250 financial centres and three call centres.

To manage customer data, the DataSmart infrastructure was created on four levels: to provide a technical infrastructure across the company, consolidate data, enable data analyses and segmentation, and manage multichannel marketing campaigns.

According to Jens Fruehling, head of the marketing database automation project, for every customer, over 1000 fields of data are now held. These allow the bank to understand customers' product needs, profile, risk, loyalty, revenue and lifetime value. For each customer, there is also a range of statistical models, such as affinity for a product and channel, profitability overall and profitability by type of product. External data such as Mosaic from Experian are also used where there is less information, such as for new prospects in every household: the type of house, the number of householders, status, risk, lifestyle data, financial status and age.

Models are run monthly so time-series analysis can be performed to see whether the profitability of an existing customer is falling or at risk, so a mailing can be targeted at them.

For customer acquisition the bank's customer acquisition programme, called AKM, uses up to 30 mailings per year with as many as 12 different target groups and very complex selection criteria. The bank is looking to move to a higher communications frequency so that every customer receives a relevant offer.

Customer opinion polls are also run frequently, aiming to assess customer satisfaction twice a year.

Source: ECCS (2001) (Available at European Centre for Customer Strategies, www.eccs.uk.com).

Customer relationship management is an approach to marketing that seeks to increase customer loyalty, resulting in greater customer lifetime value. O'Malley and Tynan (2001) refer to the need for this to be a win–win approach where the relationship is characterised by trust, commitment, communication and sharing, resulting in the mutual achievement of goals. To introduce CRM, many organisations use a simple framework to develop various CRM initiatives. This is the customer lifecycle, divided into stages of customer selection, retention and extension, which are related as shown in Figure 2.3.

The consequence of moving the customer between different stages of the customer lifecycle is shown in schematic form in Figure 2.3. As the customer moves from the different stages from acquisition, through extension, to retention, the loyalty of the customer and their value to the organisation increase. Attempts to build customer loyalty at each stage of the customer lifecycle will start with identifying segments and then deciding which to target.

Benefits of relationship marketing

As we have seen, relationship marketing is aimed at increasing customer loyalty, which has a number of benefits. As Reicheld (1996) explained, loyalty or retention within a current customer base is a highly desirable phenomenon since not only does it result in more transactions from each customer, but these transactions are more profitable. This occurs for several reasons:

- there are no acquisition costs (which are usually far higher than 'maintenance' costs)
- there is less need to offer incentives such as discounts, or to give vouchers to maintain their custom (although these may be desirable)
- loyal customers are less price sensitive, enabling premium pricing to be used (loyal customers are happy with the value they are getting)
- loyal customers will recommend the company to others ('referrals')
- individual revenue growth occurs as trust increases.

Failure to build long-term relationships in this way largely caused the failures of many dotcoms following huge expenditure on customer acquisition. Research summarised by Reicheld and Schefter (2000) shows that acquiring online customers is so expensive (20–30% higher than for

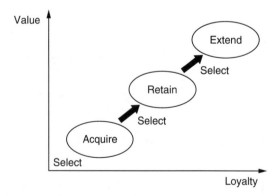

Figure 2.3 Relationship between the customer selection, acquisition, retention and extension phases of the customer lifecycle, and loyalty and customer value

traditional businesses) that start-up companies may remain unprofitable for at least 2–3 years. The research also shows that by retaining just 5% more customers, online companies can boost their profitability by 25–95%. They say:

> *but if you can keep customers loyal, their profitability accelerates much faster than in traditional businesses. It costs you less and less to service them.*

We will now examine each of the stages of the customer lifecycle in a little more detail to provide a background for later chapters.

Customer selection

Customer selection needs to occur at each stage of CRM. This relates CRM to segmentation and target marketing. Figure 2.4 shows that customer selection starts with identifying customer characteristics through profiling and understanding their product needs. For e-mail marketing, we may want to identify those customer groupings that have the best propensity for forming an online relationship. Once these have been identified, a suitable proposition and campaign plan will be developed for each segment.

Once alternative segments have been identified, we will want to target the segments with the best online potential, as resources are limited. Think about which of these categories of customer identified by Chaffey et al. (2003) may be suitable for you to target online:

- *the most profitable customers*: using the Internet to provide tailored offers to the top 20% of customers by profit may result in more repeat business and cross-sales

Figure 2.4 Segmentation and target marketing approach for e-marketing planning. LTV: lifetime value

- *larger companies (B2B)*: an extranet could be produced to service these customers and increase their loyalty

- *smaller companies (B2B)*: large companies are traditionally serviced through sales representatives and account managers, but smaller companies may not warrant the expense of account managers. However, the Internet can be used to reach smaller companies more cost-effectively. The number of smaller companies that can be reached in this way may be significant, so although the individual revenue of each one is relatively small, the collective revenue achieved through Internet servicing can be large

- *particular members of the buying unit (B2B)*: the site should provide detailed information for different interests which supports the buying decision, e.g. technical documentation for users of products, information on savings from e-procurement for information systems or purchasing managers, and information to establish the credibility of the company for decision makers

- *customers who are difficult to reach using other media*: an insurance company looking to target younger drivers could use the web as a vehicle for this

- *customers who are brand loyal*: services to appeal to brand loyalists can be provided to support them in their role as advocates of a brand, as suggested by Aaker and Joachimstahler (2000)

- *customers who are not brand loyal*: conversely, incentives, promotion and a good level of service quality could be provided by the web site to try and retain such customers.

Alternatively, if a customer is unprofitable there may not be a proactive approach to retention, i.e. special offers will not target unprofitable customers.

Smith and Chaffey (2001) refer to ideal customers. They say:

> *Who are your ideal customers? You have good and bad customers. Bad ones continually haggle about prices, pay late, constantly complain, grab all your promotions and leave you as soon as another company comes along. The ideal customers, on the other hand, are the ones that pay on time, give you as much notice as possible, share information, become partners giving you useful feedback.*

So, customer selection involves understanding the ideal customer's profile: who they are, where they are, what they want and what they spend. Simple analytical tools for assessing this include: calculation of customer lifetime value, recency, frequency, monetary value (RFM) and category analysis (see box).

We can then target these segments by using fields within the database to identify to which segment customers belong and then using mass customisation and personalisation to tailor offers to these customers, as described in the following section.

E-MAIL MARKETING INSIGHT

RFM analysis

An RFM analysis can be applied for targeting using e-mail according to how a customer interacts with an e-commerce site. Values could be assigned as follows.

Recency:
0: Not known
1: Within last 12 months
2: Within last 6 months
3: Within last 3 months
4: Within last 1 month

This could be purchase frequency or, as here, recency of a visit to the web site.

Frequency:
0: Not known
1: Every 6 months
2: Every 3 months
3: Every 2 months
4: Monthly

This could be purchase frequency or, as here, visits to the web site.

Monetary value:
0: Less than £10
1: £10–50
2: £50–100
3: £100–200
4: More than £200

This could be total purchase value or, as here, average purchase value.

Customer acquisition

Customer acquisition involves techniques used to form relationships with new customers leading to a sale. It involves using marketing communications to convert potential customers into actual customers. Figure 2.5 shows the well-known funnel model applied to web marketing. This model, which applies particularly well to B2B permission marketing, shows how e-marketing is used to gain new customers. The web site is at the heart of this model as a lead-generation tool. Lead generation happens as prospects become registered site visitors in response to offers on site, such as a free newsletter or web seminars in return for providing their contact details and profile information. For this lead-generation tool to work to maximum effect, it first needs as many targeted visitors as possible. This is where a range of e-marketing techniques is used to drive suspects to the site. Once on site, the site design and offers should be constructed to maximise capture of customer details. A combination of traditional sales and e-mail follow-up is used to convert leads into sales.

Customer acquisition can have two meanings in an e-mail marketing context. The obvious meaning is the use of the web site to acquire new customers for a company as qualified leads that can be converted into sales. However, organisations should also actively encourage *existing* customers to engage in online dialogue. Many organisations concentrate on the former, but where acquisition is well-managed, campaigns will be used to achieve conversion or migration of offline customers to

Figure 2.5 The funnel model applied to e-marketing

online customers. The online dialogue referred to, in practice, means encouraging customers to use web-site services and also encouraging communications by e-mail. There are several benefits in converting existing offline customers to online customers. First, services and communications delivered online will be cheaper. For example, American Express developed a 'Go Paperless' campaign to persuade customers to receive and review their statements online rather than by post. Phone bank First Direct uses call-centre representatives to persuade customers of the benefits of bypassing them by reviewing their statements online and communicating using a secure messaging service. Customers also gain a service with better rates. Secondly, it can be argued that once online customers are using what are hopefully more convenient online services, there will be some degree of lock-in. Once you have learned how to use one online service, why go to the bother of learning another unless there are some serious failings in your current service. Finally, we can also argue that online customers will have initiated permission marketing, so they will have agreed to receive communications, and these should be more relevant to the customers' requirements.

> ### E-MAIL MARKETING INSIGHT
>
> Customer acquisition involves both acquiring new customers and converting existing customers to online customers.

Obtaining e-mail addresses of prospects

To obtain e-mail addresses of prospects there are two approaches:

1. *Purchase of opt-in bought-in lists.* Here, as for conventional postal direct marketing, the company will contact a list broker or list owner and purchase e-mail addresses of individuals who have agreed to receive marketing e-mails. They will rent a list of e-mail addresses which will be used to run the campaign. Potential customers may have agreed to receive e-mails if they are subscribers to a magazine, or have entered an online competition on a web site such as E-mail Inform (www.emailinform.com), which is owned by Claritas interactive and has been

used to obtain around approximately 1 million e-mail addresses in return for entry into a prize draw.

2. *Building a house list*. A house list can be built using a company web site combined with permission-based marketing opt-in techniques. A relevant incentive, such as free information or a discount, is offered in exchange for a prospect providing their e-mail address by filling in an online form. Further best practice in e-mail capture is contained in the box. Careful management of e-mail lists is required since, as the list ages, the addresses of customers and their profiles will change, resulting in many bounced messages and lower response rates. Data protection law also requires the facility for customers to update their details.

In Chapter 4 we explore in more detail how e-mail lists of prospects can be purchased or rented. We will also consider how e-mail newsletters can be used for advertising encouraging a web site visit in order to gain a customer. E-mail can also be a powerful conversion tool: a follow-up message after site registration can be used to persuade customers to place their first order.

Customer retention and extension

Customer retention refers to the strategies and actions that an organisation uses to keep existing customers or to reduce churn. For e-marketers, an important aspect of retention is continuing the customer dialogue using e-mail to encourage repeat visits to a web site. Retention also involves learning more about the customers through their behaviour or through marketing research.

Once an e-mail address has been collected, the e-mail can be used to communicate with the customer in a variety of ways. While using a campaign to a house list to encourage repeat sales is typical, e-mail can also be used to inform customers about new products and events, and also to learn by inviting them to participate in online surveys.

We will review in detail in Chapter 4 how e-mail techniques such as e-newsletters can be used to assist customer retention.

The phase of customer extension refers to increasing the depth or range of products that a customer purchases from a company. For example, an online bank may initially acquire a customer through the use of a credit card. The relationship will be extended if the customer can be persuaded to purchase other financial services such as loans or insurance.

We summarise this section on the customer lifecycle by reviewing the guidance provided by Peppers and Rogers (1993) in *The One-to-One Future* on how to prioritise activity in different phases of the customer lifecycle. They say:

* Focus on share of the customer as well as market share: this means increasing the revenue from each customer as far as possible.

* Focus on customer retention, which is more cost-effective than acquisition.

* Concentrate on repeat purchases by cross- and up-selling; these also help margins increase.

* To achieve the above use dialogue at all stages to listen to customer needs and then *respond to them* in order to build trusting and loyal relationships.

CRM: A HEALTH WARNING

Many organisations have bought into the CRM concept, and over the past few years many large-scale CRM programmes have been initiated. Not all have been as successful as that for Deutsche Bank, however: estimates suggest that 70–80% fail.

Many of these failures can be explained away by difficulties in implementation: failure is common-place for many large-scale, IT-enabled projects, requiring changes in existing processes. A survey by PricewaterhouseCoopers (2001) of chief information officers in 'Top 500' companies in the UK, the USA and Australia showed that one-third of companies had experienced a delay in or scrapping of a new information system. However, such is the volume of failed CRM projects that not all can be ascribed to failures in implementation. Many are questioning whether there is a more funda-mental problem with the CRM concept. This is beginning to affect practice, the scrapping of the Safeway supermarket loyalty scheme in favour of a sales promotion approach being a good example.

As noted in the section on permission marketing, many customers do now want to be managed and cynics would suggest that 'customer relationship management' is simply 'customer management'. With customer management there is a focus on customer profitability and lifetime value. This implies efforts to reduce costs and maximise the number of products purchased by the customer, leading to increased 'share of wallet'. In this case, the relationship seems to favour the company rather than the customer.

Given this, a change in perspective is suggested. If CRM becomes CMR, a customer-managed relationship, then the balance shifts somewhat in favour of the customer. The web site provides relatively low-cost tools to enable customers to manage the relationship in terms of communica-tions received. Figure 2.6 shows how the retailer Dabs.com enables customers to choose the nature of communications with them.

ONLINE CRM

Peppers and Rogers (1998) and Peppers et al. (1999) have suggested the IDIC framework as an approach for using CRM and using the web effectively to form and build relationships (Figure 2.7). In an e-marketing context, IDIC can be related to these stages of relationship building:

1. *Customer Identification.* This stresses the need to identify each customer on their first visit and subsequent visits. Common methods for identification are the use of cookies or asking a customer to log on to a site. In subsequent customer contacts, additional customer information should be obtained using a process known as drip irrigation. Since information will become out of date with time, it is important to verify, update and delete customer information.

2. *Customer Differentiation.* This refers to building a profile to help to segment customers. Appropriate services are then developed for each customer. Examples of such segments include the top customers, non-profitable customers, major customers who have ordered less in recent years and customers who buy more products from competitors.

3. *Customer Interaction.* These are interactions provided on the web site, such as customer service or creating a tailored product. More generally, customers should listen to the needs and experiences of major customers. Interactions should be through the customer-preferred chan-nel, e.g. by e-mail, by phone or by post.

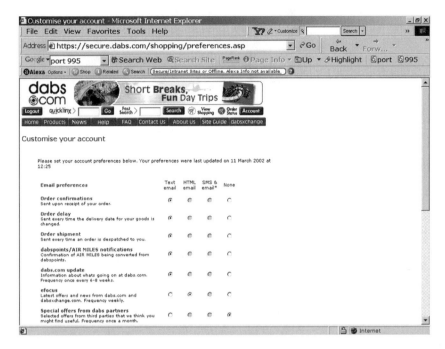

Figure 2.6   Dabs.com customer communication options

4. *Customer Customisation*. This refers to dynamic personalisation or mass-customisation of content or e-mails according to the segmentation achieved at the acquisition stage. Approaches to personalisation are explained in the section on retention. This stage also involves further market research to find out whether products can be further tailored to meet customers' needs.

PERSONALISATION AND MASS CUSTOMISATION

Personalisation and mass customisation can be used to tailor information content on a web site, and opt-in e-mail can be used to deliver it to add value and at the same time to remind the customer about a product. Personalisation and mass customisation are terms that are often used interchangeably. In the strict sense, personalisation refers to customisation of information requested by a site customer at an *individual* level. Mass customisation involves providing tailored content to a *group of individuals* with similar interests. It uses technology to achieve this at an economic level. An example of mass customisation is when Amazon recommends similar books according to what others in a segment have offered, or when it sends a similar e-mail to customers who had an interest in a particular topic, such as e-commerce.

Mass customisation can range from minor cosmetic choices made by the customer (e.g. the choice of colour, trim and specification available to the customer via the multimedia kiosks in Daewoo's car showrooms) to a collaborative process facilitated by ongoing dialogue. Peppers and Rogers (1993) give the example of Motorola, which could manufacture pagers to any of over 11 million different specifications.

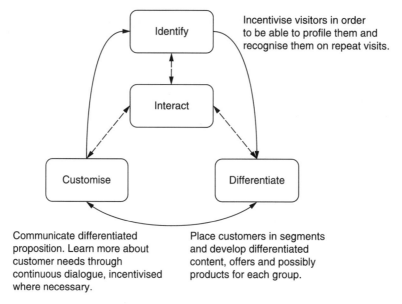

Incentivise visitors in order to be able to profile them and recognise them on repeat visits.

Communicate differentiated proposition. Learn more about customer needs through continuous dialogue, incentivised where necessary.

Place customers in segments and develop differentiated content, offers and possibly products for each group.

Figure 2.7 The IDIC model of customer relationship management

For e-mail marketing, there is a range of options for personalisation, which include variation according to:

- *the salutation*: this is the most basic level of personalisation and should be offered in all customer communications. It is not generally used for newsletters

- *the content*: for newsletters and alerts, this can be varied according to user selection. For example, Silicon.com, a news service for IT professionals, enables a range of items to be offered. These can be selected by checking boxes for the type of content. A further method of content personalisation is keyword based. This is offered by analysts such as Gartner, where particular keywords such as 'metrics' can be selected. Forbes.com has offered a keyword-based e-mail service which alerts recipients when a particular company name is covered. For e-mail promotions the content can be personalised for different segments, although it will rarely be personalised on an individual level

- *the offer*: the offer can be varied according to past behaviour such as amount spent

- *the landing page*: the landing page of the web page can be personalised if e-mails have been targeted for different segments. Content can also be personalised for individuals if they are already registered on a site. The landing page can use cookies to tailor information to an individual.

CAMPAIGN CHECKLIST

Setting your level of mass customisation

Figure 2.8 summarises the options available to organisations wishing to use the Internet for mass customisation or personalisation. You should start by considering the vertical axis. What level of profiling information do you collect about each pro-spect or customer? Increasing levels of information collection are indicated by how many of these boxes you can tick:

☐ E-mail address
☐ Name
☐ Postal address
☐ Company details (B2B)
☐ Personal characteristics: demographics (B2C), position in decision-making unit (B2B)
☐ Buying intentions
☐ Buying behaviour and sales histories
☐ E-mail campaign response characteristics
☐ Loyalty
☐ Advocacy

Turning now to the horizontal axis, this refers to the extent to which the information you collect can be applied. To what extent do you personalise e-mails or web site content, according to information collected?

If there is little information available about the customer and it is not integrated with the web site then no mass customisation is possible (A). To achieve mass customisa-tion or personalisation, the organisation must have sufficient information about the customer. For limited tailoring to groups of customers (B), it is necessary to have basic profiling information such as age, gender, social group, product category interest or, for B2B, role in the buying unit. This information must be contained in a database system that is directly linked to the content management system used to produce web site content. For personalisation on a one-to-one level (C), more detailed infor-mation about specific interests, perhaps available from a purchase history, should be available.

You can use Figure 2.8 to plan and explain your e-marketing relationship marketing strategy. The symbols X_1 to X_3 show a typical path for an organisation. At X_1 informa-tion collected about customers is limited. At X_2 detailed information is available about customers, but it is in discrete databases that are not integrated with the web site. At X_3 the strategy is to provide mass customisation of information and offers to major segments, since it is felt that the expense of full personalisation is not warranted.

Of course, how far you want to progress to the top-right quadrant of this diagram will depend on the balance between costs and reward. To move in this direction will require expenditure on personalisation systems that may be difficult to recoup. Many companies identify major customer segments rather than operating on a true one-to-one basis. In the case study mentioned earlier in this chapter, Deutsche Bank used 12 segments. Dell uses the following segments on their web site, e-mail and offline marketing communications:

● home or small office (< 5 employees)

- small and medium enterprise (5–500 employees)
- preferred accounts division (500–5000 employees)
- large corporate accounts (< 5000 employees)
- public sector.

Remember that profiling is not a one-off operation: one of the aims of permission marketing is to continue learning about the customer. Ideally, this should be made as unobtrusive as possible. The watchword could be summarised as 'Watch, don't ask'. As shown in Chapter 3, it is possible to learn about recipient behaviour with regard to e-mail campaigns by recording their propensity to open, clickthrough and respond to e-mails. Campaigns can then be devised in line with these behaviours.

E-MAIL MARKETING INSIGHT

Take a staged view of data gathering: 'Watch, don't ask'.

AN INTEGRATED E-MAIL MARKETING APPROACH TO CRM

Bringing together all the concepts covered in this chapter, I now present an overall process model for online relationship building (Figure 2.9) which shows how the web site, e-mail marketing, direct mail and other forms of marketing communications can fit together.

Stage 1 in building the relationship is visitor acquisition through traditional or new media, as detailed in Chapter 4. Once the visitor is on-site it is essential to start a dialogue through permission marketing. This is usually achieved by providing incentives to convert a visitor into a prospect by obtaining their e-mail address, permission to contact and profile information (stage 2). Direct marketing in the form of e-mail (stage 3) and direct mail (stage 4) then follows to encourage repeat visits to the site to interact with the brand, leading to additional purchases as part of customer retention and extension.

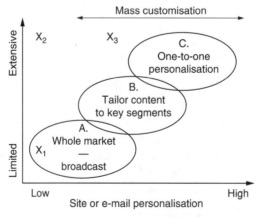

Figure 2.8 Options for mass customisation using the web site and e-mail

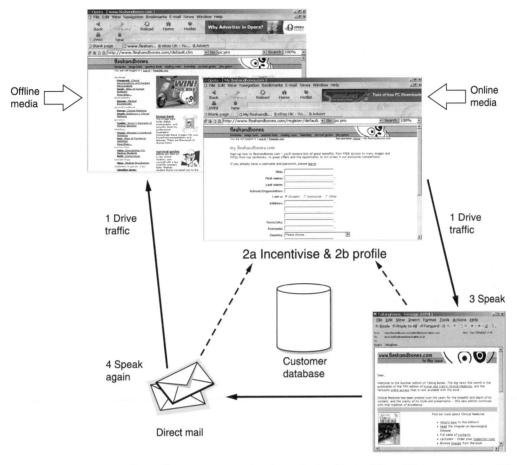

Figure 2.9 Summary of an effective process of online relationship building. With permission of Elsevier Science

We will now look at each stage in more detail.

Stage 1: Attract new and existing customers to site

The strategy for achieving online CRM should start with consideration of how to acquire customers who want to communicate in this way. These may be either new or existing customers. For new customers, the goal is to attract them to the site using a range of methods of site promotion such as search engines, portals and banner advertisements. These promotion methods should aim to highlight the value proposition of the site; for example, incentives such as free information or competitions. To encourage new users to use the one-to-one facilities of the web site, information about the web site or incentives to visit it can be built into existing direct marketing campaigns such as mailshots.

Stage 2a: Incentivise visitors to action

The first time a visitor arrives at a site is the most important, since if he or she does not find the desired information or experience, the visitor may not return. We need to move from using the customer using the Internet in pull-mode, to the marketer using the Internet in push-mode through e-mail and traditional direct mail communications. The quality and credibility of the site must be sufficient to retain the visitor's interest so that he or she stays on the site. To initiate relationship building, offers or incentives must be prominent on the home page. Many sites are unsuccessful in engaging visitors, so it can be argued that converting unprofiled visitors to profiled visitors is a major design objective of a web site. Many incentives can be used to achieve this. Offers are discussed in more detail in Chapter 3.

Stage 2b: Capture customer information to maintain relationship

Once the user has decided that the incentive is interesting he or she will click on the option and will then be presented with an online form. The user will be prompted to provide various items of information. The crucial information that must be collected is a method of contacting the customer. Ideally this will be both an e-mail address and a real-world address. The real-world address is important since from the post code or zip code it may be possible to deduce the likely demographics of that person. Some companies take the attitude that the e-mail address is the only piece of information that needs to be collected since this can be used to maintain the one-to-one relationship online. Apart from the contact information, the other important information to collect is a method of profiling the customer so that appropriate information can be delivered to him or her. For example, RS Components asks for:

- industry sector
- purchasing influence
- specific areas of product interest
- how many people you manage
- total number of employees in company.

A company must decide carefully on the number of questions asked. This must be a balance between the time taken to answer the questions and the value of the offer to the customer. If the offer is relevant and targeted, the customer is more likely to fill in a questionnaire accurately. The practical issues in designing such forms are described in Chapter 4.

Other methods of profiling customers include collaborative filtering and monitoring the content they view. With collaborative filtering, customers are openly asked what their interests are, typically by checking boxes that correspond to their interests. A database then compares the customers' preferences with those of other customers in its database, and then makes recommendations or delivers information accordingly. The more information a database contains about an individual customer, the more useful its recommendations can be. An example of this technology in action can be found on the Amazon web site (www.amazon.com), where the database reveals that customers who bought book 'x' also bought books 'y' and 'z'.

Figure 2.10 gives an example of a registration page used to capture customer information. The incentive in this case is seminar attendance. Full details of the case study are given in Chapter 3.

Stage 3: Maintain dialogue using online communication

To build the relationship between company and customer there are three main Internet-based methods of physically making the communication:

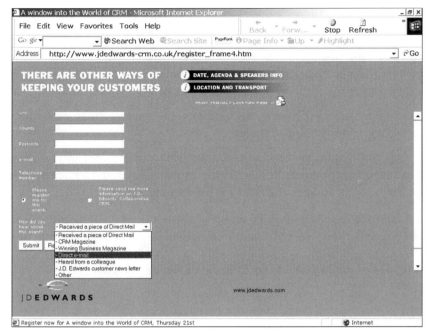

Figure 2.10 Registration page for JD Edwards (Source: Philippa Edwards and Robert Perrin, Anderson Baillie Marketing)

1. Send an e-mail to the customer with a hyperlink through to a microsite.

2. Display specific information on the web site when the customer logs in. This is referred to as personalisation. This can be combined with (1), and has been referred to as 'web response' (Hughes, 1999).

3. Use push technology to deliver information to the individual.

Information on these techniques of maintaining dialogue is given in subsequent sections. Dialogue will also be supplemented by other tools such as mailshots, phone calls or personal visits, depending on the context. For example, after a customer registers on the RS Components web site, the company sends out a letter to the customer with promotional offers and a credit card-sized reminder of the user name and password to use to log in to the site.

As well as these physical methods of maintaining contact with customers, many other marketing devices can be used to encourage users to return to a site. These include:

- loyalty schemes: customers will return to the site to see how many loyalty points they have collected, or convert them into offers. An airline such as American Airlines, with its Advantage Club, is a good example of this

- news about a particular industry (for a B2B site)

- new product information and price promotions

- industry-specific information to help the customer to do his or her job. Snap-on Tools, a manufacturer of professional-grade tools for automobile repair businesses, adds new value for its customers by supplying them with regulatory information about subjects such as waste disposal, at no fee. This strengthens Snap-on's relationship with its customers. Synetix provides technical information for chemical-plant designers to help with their day-to-day design work

- personal reminders: 1-800-Flowers has reminder programmes that automatically remind customers of important occasions and dates

- customer support: Cisco's customers log on to the site over one million times a month to receive technical assistance, check orders or download software. The online service is so well-received that nearly 70% of all customer enquiries are handled online.

While adding value for their customers by means of these various mechanisms, companies will be looking to use the opportunity to make sales to customers by, for example, cross- or up-selling.

Stage 4: Maintain dialogue using offline communication

Here, direct mail is the most effective form of communication since this can be tailored to be consistent with the user's preference. The aim here may be to drive traffic to the web site using offers such as news or online competitions.

REFERENCES

Aaker, D. and Joachimstahler, E. (2000). *Brand leadership*. New York, NY: Free Press.

Chaffey, D., Mayer, R., Johnston, K. and Ellis-Chadwick, F. (2003). *Internet Marketing: Strategy, Implementation and Practice*, 2nd edn. Financial Times–Prentice Hall.

DMIS (2002). DMIS in brief. Brief extracts from the Direct Mail Information Service, Winter.

ECCS (2001). Deutsche Bank finds value in its customer data. Case study on European Centre for Customer Strategies (D. Reed, ed.) (available online at www.uk.eccs.com).

Evans, M., Patterson, M. and O'Malley, L. (2000). Bridging the direct marketing–direct consumer gap: some solutions from qualitative research. In *Proceedings of the Academy of Marketing Conference*, University of Derby.

Godin, S. (1999). *Permission Marketing*. New York: Simon and Schuster.

Hughes, A. (1999). Web response – modern 1:1 marketing. Database Marketing Institute article (www.dbmarketing.com/articles/Art196.htm).

McKenna, R. (1991). *Relationship Marketing: Successful Strategies for the Age of the Customer*. Reading, MA: Addison Wesley.

O'Malley, L. and Tynan, C. (2001). Reframing relationship marketing for consumer markets. *Interactive Market.*, **2** (3), 240–6.

Peppers, D. and Rogers, M. (1993). *Building Business Relationships one Customer at a Time. The One-to-One Future*. London: Piatkus.

Peppers, D. and Rogers, M. (1998). *One-to-One Fieldbook*. New York: Doubleday.

Peppers, D., Rogers, M. and Dorf, B. (1999). Is your company ready for one-to-one marketing? *Harvard Bus. Rev.*, January–February, 3–12.

PricewaterhouseCoopers (2001). *Global Data Management Survey 2001*. New York: PricewaterhouseCoopers (available online at: www.pwcglobal.com).

Reicheld, F. (1996). *The Loyalty Effect*. Boston, MA: Harvard Business Press.

Reicheld, F. and Schefter, P. (2000). E-loyalty, your secret weapon. *Harvard Bus. Rev.*, July–August, 105–13.

Ross, V. (2001). Review of permission marketing. *Interactive Market.*, January–March, 292–4.

Smith, P. R. and Chaffey, D. (2002). *eMarketing eXcellence – The Heart of eBusiness*. Oxford: Butterworth-Heinemann.

WEB LINKS

Direct Marketing Information Service (www.dmis.co.uk)
European Centre for Customer Strategies (www.eccs.uk.com)
Marketing Law (www.marketinglaw.co.uk)
Olswang (www.olswang.com)

Chapter **3**

E-mail campaign planning

Overview

This chapter sets out a structured approach to planning e-mail campaigns. It also describes how an overall e-mail strategy can be developed.

Chapter objectives

By the end of this chapter you will be able to:

- develop a plan for how e-mail marketing integrates with other marketing
- identify the cost components of an e-mail campaign
- assess the main success factors in designing an e-mail campaign
- devise measurement and testing approaches to improve campaign performance.

Chapter structure

- Introduction
- Objective setting
- E-mail campaign budgeting
- Campaign design: targeting, offer, timing, creative
- Campaign integration
- The creative brief
- Measurement
- Continuous improvement of campaigns
- Testing
- Campaign management and resourcing

INTRODUCTION

The CRITICAL factors that influence the success of an e-mail marketing campaign were explored in Chapter 1. In this chapter we look in detail at how we can select the best options for these factors at the start of a campaign. This involves answering these types of question:

- What are we trying to achieve through our campaign(s)? What are the long- to medium-term e-marketing objectives and the campaign-specific objectives?
- What are our options for the type of incentives or offers in a campaign?
- How do we segment the list to target recipients with a relevant offer and creative?
- How can we integrate the e-mail campaign with other marketing campaigns through time?

- How do we measure the success of the campaign and how can the metrics collected be used to improve future campaigns?

OBJECTIVE SETTING

To develop objectives for an e-mail campaign, a good starting point is to look at how the campaign fits into your overall e-marketing plans across the next year. A key question when setting e-marketing objectives is the balance between e-marketing activities for customer acquisition, retention and brand building. Figure 3.1 shows how an acquisition-focused strategy will be aimed at increasing turnover through adding new customers. However, since the cost of acquisition is higher for new customers, this will result in a relatively low profitability in comparison with a retention strategy. A retention-focused strategy, achieving incremental sales, will have a lower cost of acquisition, so will be more profitable. These two strategies will usually be conducted simultaneously, but the balance of resources into each will need to be set by setting objectives for each. Examples of typical overall e-marketing objectives are:

- *customer acquisition*:

  - for an e-tailer: gain 10 000 new customers with an average spend of £80/year

  - for a business-to-business (B2B) service: gain 1000 new leads via the web site and convert to at least 50 new customers

  - for a business-to-consumer (B2C) financial service: migrate 5% of offline customers to online customers

- *customer retention*:

  - for an e-tailer: gain an average repeat purchases spend of £100 per year within the customer base

  - for a B2B service: reduce customer churn to less than 15%

  - for a B2C financial service: achieve purchase of additional products in 10% of the customer base

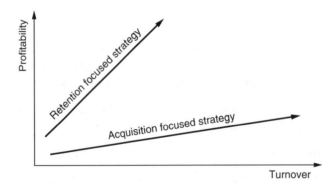

Figure 3.1   Focus for acquisition and retention strategies

- *brand building*: achieve brand interactions with 500 000 consumers through the web site and e-mail.

There may also be other aims that are not directly related to sales, such as gaining more insight into online customer behaviour, which is a research objective. Complete the Campaign checklist, Range of e-mail marketing applications, to think about your typical aims.

CAMPAIGN CHECKLIST

Range of e-mail marketing applications

The list below gives potential future e-mail marketing applications. Tick those that are relevant to you and assess their suitability on a scale of 1–3, where 1 = immediate, this year, 2 = next year, and 3 = possibly in the future.

For the priority 1 applications, write SMART objectives (SMART is: specific, measurable, achievable, relevant, time related).

- Generate leads from prospects (using a rented list) ☐
- Convert leads to customers (follow-up e-mails) ☐
- Sell more/additional products to existing customers (using a house list) ☐
- Deliver regular information to keep you at front-of-mind (e-newsletters) ☐
- Reduce churn: remind of renewals, e.g. subscription, contract expiry ☐
- Deliver customer service ☐
- Deliver loyalty programmes ☐
- Increase brand awareness and interactions with brand ☐
- Sales promotions ☐
- Announce new products, services, pricing and policies ☐
- Conduct market research by delivering surveys and focus groups ☐
- Conduct market research by pretesting response to different offers and creatives for TV or print ad campaigns ☐
- Alert customers to events in the marketplace ☐
- Invite customers to take part in online discussion, webinar or offline event ☐
- Drive visitors to web site to help achieve any of the above ☐

Note that many of these applications are achieved in conjunction with the web site and offline marketing.

To achieve the overall e-marketing goals referred to above, Chaffey et al. (2003) say that three main types of targets are needed:

(1) *Traffic building targets*. Use online and offline communications to drive or attract visitors' traffic to a web site.

Examples of SMART traffic building objectives:

- Generate awareness of web offering in 80% of existing customer base in one year.

- Achieve 10 000 new site visitors within one year.

- Convert 30% of existing customer base to regular site visitors.

Although traffic building objectives and measures of effectiveness are often referred to in terms of traffic *quantity*, such as the number of visitors or page impressions, it is the traffic *quality* that really indicates the success of interactive marketing communications (e.g. van Doren et al., 2000; Smith and Chaffey, 2002). The traffic quality is indicated by how many of the visitors are within your target market, and how many convert to action (see the section on conversion objectives below).

(2) *Web-site communications targets*. Use on-site communications to deliver an effective message to the visitor which helps to shape customer behaviour or achieve a required marketing outcome. The message delivered on site will be based on traditional marketing communications objectives for a company's products or services; for example, to create awareness of a product or brand, to inform potential customers about a product, to encourage trial, to persuade customer to purchase and to encourage further purchases.

Examples of SMART 'on-site' communications objectives:

- Generate 1000 new potential customers in Europe by converting new visitors to the web site to qualified leads.

- Capture e-mail addresses and profile information for 100 leads in the first 6 months.

- Convert 3% of visitors to a particular part of the site to buyers across the year.

- Achieve relationship building and deepen brand interaction by encouraging 10% participation of the customer base in online competitions and forums.

- Acquire 100 new contacts through viral referrals.

(3) *Mixed-mode buying targets*. This refers to sales achieved offline through follow-up of leads gained on the web site or via e-mail. This is dependent on successful integrated marketing communications.

Examples of mixed-mode buying objectives:

- Achieve 20% of sales made in the call centre as a result of web-site visits.

- Achieve 20% of online sales in response to offline adverts.

- Reduce contact-centre phone enquiries by 15% by providing online customer services.

These three different types of objective can be integrated by using conversion marketing objective setting, as described in the next section.

Conversion-based e-marketing objectives

Web marketing and e-mail marketing objectives can also be usefully stated in terms of conversion marketing. It is helpful to create separate objectives for the overall e-marketing plan and then to identify specific conversion objectives for each e-mail marketing campaign. The objectives for the overall e-marketing plan will typically be over a one-year period, with the e-mail marketing campaigns supporting the overall e-marketing plan. So, we can develop two types of objective:

- *Annual marketing communications objectives.* For example, objectives for achieving new site visitors or gaining qualified leads should be measured across an entire year since this will be a continuous activity based on visitor building through search engines and other campaigns. Annual budgets are set to help achieve these objectives.

- *Campaign specific communications objectives.* Internet marketing campaigns such as a direct e-mail campaign will help to fulfil the annual objectives. Specific objectives can be stated for each campaign in terms of gaining new visitors, converting visitors to customers and encouraging repeat purchases. Campaign objectives should build on traditional marketing objectives, have a specific target audience and have measurable outcomes that can be attributed to the specific campaign.

Overall e-marketing objective setting

Objective setting for gaining new customers using conversion marketing takes a bottom–up approach. You start with the number of new customers required to meet financial targets and then work backwards to see the different conversion rates needed to achieve this number of new customers.

Take, for example, the objectives of a campaign for a large, international B2B services company such as a consultancy company selling search engine optimisation. Here, the ultimate objective, across different geographical markets, is to achieve 5000 new clients using the web site in combination with telesales and sales representatives to convert leads to action. To achieve this level of new business, the marketer will need to make assumptions about the level of conversion that is needed at each stage of converting prospects to customers. Such a model can be built bottom–up for key segments and major markets. Let us assume that a 10% conversion rate occurs at each of the three stages shown in Figure 3.2.

There are three stages of converting a suspect to a client using an online approach:

- *Stage 1: Conversion of web browsers to visitors.* This is referred to as the attraction efficiency. The main source of visitors will be from search engines and related sites. As explained in a later section, this highlights the importance of search engine registration, optimisation and advertising using banner advertising and pay-per-click sponsorship. Offline promotion techniques such as direct mail and advertising can also be used to gain site visitors. We should divide site visitor objectives into those gained through online communications and those gained by offline communications.

- *Stage 2: Conversion of site visitors to registered site visitors.* This is referred to as the site conversion efficiency. It is dependent on a combination of the design of a site and the lead

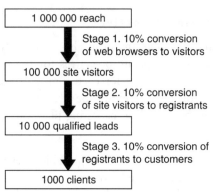

Figure 3.2 Conversion marketing approach to objective setting

generation offers. This is effectively how good you are at gaining the customers' permission to start a dialogue.

- *Stage 3: Conversion of leads generated from the site to customers.* This is referred to as the lead conversion efficiency. You have gained leads from the web site; what do you now do with these leads? One option will be to do e-mail promotion follow-ups to encourage the prospect to sign up to the service. However, for high-value products with a complex decision process, e-mail alone may not be sufficient to gain the customer. In this example of a B2B company the customer will be phoned in order to clinch the sale or to arrange further meetings.

How does this conversion-based approach relate to business-to-consumer sites? For a B2C business where the product is high value, high involvement and typically purchased offline, as with a car, the conversion process is similar to this B2B example. Here, stage 2 is a site visitor signing up for a brochure, or arranging a test drive. Stage 3 conversion will often occur in the car dealership.

For a lower value product that is commonly purchased online, such as books, CDs, software or travel services, the first two stages are similar. Building traffic or visitors is important in all cases. From here on, the exact conversion process will depend on the type of business model for a site. For a retail site, say selling software, where the purchase is online, stages 2 and 3 may overlap. Stage 2 registration will be part of stage 3 where purchase occurs. In this case, stage 2 conversion is typically where the customer becomes engaged with the site, perhaps by performing a product search and then clicking on a particular product and adding it to the shopping basket. E-tailers are concerned about the attrition rate, which is the proportion of customers who visit the site and then add products to their shopping baskets do not complete the sale.

Figure 3.3 shows how best case and worst case scenarios can be developed for objective setting. This spreadsheet model is available free at www.weboutcomes.com/total-email. The best case scenario here uses 10% conversion for simplicity. It can be seen that because conversion involves a three-stage process, reducing each of the three stages from 10% to 2% causes a large fall in the number of leads. This highlights the necessity of setting objectives for different conversion rates and then having good visibility of the status of conversion rates through the year. Knowing the drivers that affect the conversion rates and being able to control them is equally important.

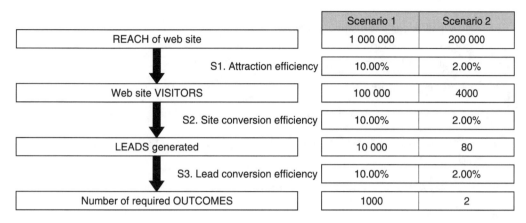

	Scenario 1	Scenario 2
REACH of web site	1 000 000	200 000
S1. Attraction efficiency	10.00%	2.00%
Web site VISITORS	100 000	4000
S2. Site conversion efficiency	10.00%	2.00%
LEADS generated	10 000	80
S3. Lead conversion efficiency	10.00%	2.00%
Number of required OUTCOMES	1000	2

Figure 3.3 Model of the best and worst case scenarios of the conversion objectives

Cost objectives

A further aspect of objective setting to be considered is the constraints on objectives placed by the cost of traffic building activities. A campaign will not be successful if it meets it objectives of acquiring site visitors and customers but the cost of acquisition is too high. This constraint is usually imposed simply by having an annual or a campaign-specific budget, a necessary component of all campaigns. However, it is also useful to have specific objectives for the cost of getting the visitor to the site, and the cost of achieving the outcomes during their visit. Typical cost measures include:

- cost of acquisition per visitor: the cost of gaining a new site visitor regardless of whether they register or purchase. It is dependent solely on the promotional method used

- cost of acquisition per lead or enquiry: this measure is of greater relevance since it measures a marketing outcome; however, it is dependent on both the promotional method and the effectiveness of the web-site design and communications in achieving an action

- cost of acquisition per sale (customer acquisition cost): the cost of gaining a sale or a new customer.

These cost measures for e-mail marketing will be compared against other traffic building techniques such as banner advertising or pay per click search engine advertising.

The next section, on budgeting, looks at how overall cost estimates are made. These are then divided by the relevant number of visitors, leads or sales to derive the three measures given above.

A summary of this section on objective setting is given in the campaign objective checklist.

CAMPAIGN CHECKLIST

Objective setting

General purpose of campaign

- Acquisition or retention balance?

   – new customer acquisition targets
   – migrating existing customers online target
   – customer retention targets

- Researching customers?

Target audience

- Segments targeted by geodemographics, lifestyle, customer value, psycho-graphics, etc.

Success measures (conversion e-marketing)

- Campaign reach

- Influence on awareness or perception of target audience

- Campaign conversion rate (response to action)

- Cost of acquisition (per visitor, lead or customer).

E-MAIL CAMPAIGN BUDGETING

This section looks at the main elements of an e-mail campaign budget, starting with the revenue estimate and then moving on to the variable costs and fixed costs. Figure 3.4 provides a typical example that you may want to refer to as we look at the individual components of budget.

Revenue estimate

The revenue estimate is calculated as follows:

$$\text{Total revenue} = \text{Number of e-mails sent} \times \text{Average value of response}$$

Starting with revenue, the simplest form of revenue calculation is on a revenue per response basis for a single campaign. The budget component is simply an average value per response.

This form of estimate is most suitable for a retailer where there is product sales directly tied into the e-mail campaign. Say, for simplicity, there was a single product available to a value of £10 for each response, then £10 would be the average value per response. If there is a range of products available from the e-mail we would have to make assumptions about the relative popularity of the different products to give an average price. There is also the likelihood that respondents to the campaign will purchase other products from the site that are not part of the e-mail offer.

Where products are not offered directly from the e-mail, it is more difficult to estimate the value per response. An idea of incremental revenue can be assessed on the probability that future purchases will be made. For a B2B company marketing a high-value product, it could be assumed that if 1 in 20 respondents is directly influenced to buy a product within the next 3 months as a result of the e-mail, the average value per response would be the value of the product divided by 20.

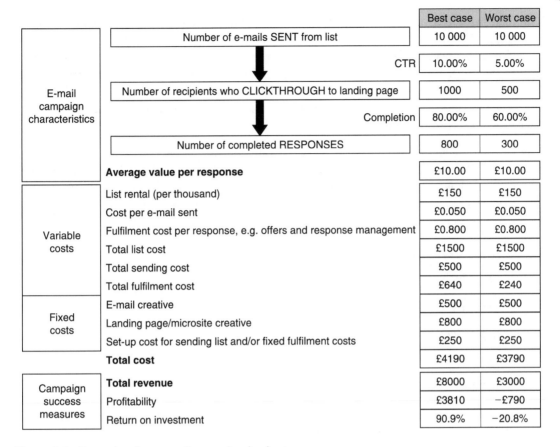

		Best case	Worst case
E-mail campaign characteristics	Number of e-mails SENT from list	10 000	10 000
	CTR	10.00%	5.00%
	Number of recipients who CLICKTHROUGH to landing page	1000	500
	Completion	80.00%	60.00%
	Number of completed RESPONSES	800	300
	Average value per response	£10.00	£10.00
Variable costs	List rental (per thousand)	£150	£150
	Cost per e-mail sent	£0.050	£0.050
	Fulfilment cost per response, e.g. offers and response management	£0.800	£0.800
	Total list cost	£1500	£1500
	Total sending cost	£500	£500
	Total fulfilment cost	£640	£240
Fixed costs	E-mail creative	£500	£500
	Landing page/microsite creative	£800	£800
	Set-up cost for sending list and/or fixed fulfilment costs	£250	£250
	Total cost	£4190	£3790
Campaign success measures	**Total revenue**	£8000	£3000
	Profitability	£3810	−£790
	Return on investment	90.9%	−20.8%

Figure 3.4 Example of an e-mail campaign budget

Variable costs estimate

Costs are divided into variable costs, which are dependent on the number of e-mails sent or responses received, and fixed costs, which are independent of the number of e-mails sent. Typical variable costs are:

$$\text{Total list cost} = (\text{Number of e-mails sent} \times \text{List rental price})/1000$$

(zero for house list)

$$\text{Total sending cost} = \text{Number of e-mails sent} \times \text{Cost per e-mail sent}$$

(zero if sent from in-house)

$$\text{Total fulfilment cost} = \text{Number of responses received} \times \text{Fulfilment cost per response}$$

The total list cost is a media cost which is only incurred if you are renting an opt-in list of prospects. This will be typically charged per thousand. The amount may range from £100 to £300 depending on the quality of the list, the degree to which it is possible to target prospects, and how many variables are used to select the members of the list. Buying lists is described in more detail in Chapter 4. If you are e-mailing to a house list set this cost to zero.

The total sending cost arises if you outsource the sending of messages using a company such as messageREACH, E-mail Vision or Mailtrack, which fulfils the broadcasting of your messages. The cost of broadcast per message varies widely according to the number sent (the larger the volume the smaller the cost), size of message, volume of graphics to be served and security arrangements. Typical costs are between 1 and 5 pence per message, but may be over 10 pence for small-volume, large-size messages. If you are mailing a house list from inside an organisation and this is part of your overall IT costs, you can also assign zero to this cost.

The total fulfilment cost is dependent on what your offer is. Parker Pens offered a free pen to businesses looking to subscribe to their service for customised business gifts. Clearly, the fulfilment cost here would be that of the pen plus postage. We are still reminded of the danger of providing an offer that costs too much to fulfil by the domestic appliance manufacturer who offered international flights costing in excess of the average value of the products that it was selling.

Fixed costs estimate

Variable costs include:

- e-mail creative costs
- landing page creative and database integration costs
- setup costs for sending
- fixed fulfilment costs, e.g. prize draw.

E-mail creative is the cost of designing and producing the e-mail layout and text and graphic content. These costs will clearly be higher for an HTML e-mail.

Landing page or microsite creative costs are for the design of the page(s) that will be reached following clickthrough. We have already emphasised the importance of these in the overall success of the campaign, since you need to maximise the number of clickthroughs who go through to complete the offer. A significant additional cost here is the programming and database integration used to capture the customer profile details. This will often be higher than the costs of designing and producing the page in HTML.

Some e-mail marketing bureaux charge a set-up cost for the first time their service is used. For others, this is included within the per-message broadcast fee.

There may also be fixed fulfilment costs depending on the offer. If, for example, you are offering a free computer or a fun-in-the-sun prize, this would be included here.

Other costs

These other costs are not shown in the budget model of Figure 3.4 for simplicity. You may want to identify these additional costs:

- list building costs for house list, i.e. revising the web site to capture new e-mail lists
- database management, i.e. upgrades to the database to store additional fields required for profiling

- testing: a separate spreadsheet model similar to Figure 3.4 could also be produced for each series of tests

- software purchase, e.g. for web page, or HTML e-mail design, e-mail broadcasting or tracking

- list cleaning and de-duplication: these are often outsourced. It is best if the costs are assigned to a particular campaign or series of campaigns

- measurement and reporting: some e-mail bureaux will charge separately for e-mail tracking or reports. Increasingly, these are included as part of the service.

Costs within the campaign can be compared for different sources of traffic, such as referrals from banner adverts on different sites. To be able to measure cost per action we need to track a customer from when they first arrive on the web site to when the action is taken.

CAMPAIGN DESIGN: TARGETING, OFFER, TIMING, CREATIVE

In Chapter 1, we looked at the CRITICAL variables under the control of the e-mail marketer that will govern the success of a campaign. Here, we will look at a simpler framework from Smith and Taylor (2002) which will help you to design an effective campaign. The four main variables are:

1. *Creative*: the design and layout of the mailshot

2. *Offer*: the proposition or the benefits of responding

3. *Timing*: the season, month or day when the offer or mailshot lands on a desk or in a house

4. *Targeting*: the segments we are targeting; the mailing list or section of a database.

Since no one has unlimited time and resources for designing the campaign, it is useful to think about the relative importance of these variables. Which would you say is most important? Rating these out of 4, where 1 is least important and 4 most important, the UK Institute of Direct Marketing suggests that these are the scores for a mailshot:

- Creative   1

- Offer   2

- Timing   2

- Targeting   4

The results for e-mail campaigns are likely to be similar, so do not neglect targeting in favour of creative!

We will now look at each of these four aspects of campaign design in rough order of importance. Since these variables are well-known from direct marketing, explanations will be brief and we will focus instead on specific issues in e-mail marketing.

Targeting

Targeting for e-mail marketing involves selecting a subset of the list for mailing, whether it is a bought-in list or a house list. There are many methods of breaking down the list. Imagine your list as a cube representing all the list members: what are all the different ways to slice and dice this cube to identify the special characteristics of the list members? Figure 3.5 gives an indication of the many different ways of targeting an e-mail list.

Let's run through 10 of the common options for targeting, highlighting their relevance to e-mail marketing.

1. *Demographics (age, gender, geography)*. These are generally the preserve of B2C markets. With the relatively low cost of creating and dispatching e-mail creative, a different style and tone of creative can be developed according to age and gender. A whisky brand developed different creative styles for younger and older drinkers, and also developed creative for female partners to encourage gift purchases. The Boots Dentalcare example, referred to earlier, used postcodes to target potential customers within a 20 minute drive-time of the branches.

2. *Lifestyle or psychographic*. The providers of lifestyle classifications such as MOSAIC or ACORN provide services to integrate this data with e-mail lists in order to target according to lifestyle.

3. *Business-to-business (company or individuals)*. For B2B organisations, the primary segmentation is usually according to company characteristics such as sector or size, proxied by the number of employees or turnover. Dell Computer uses a classification based on employee size as its primary segmentation. Different web-site and e-mail content is targeted at each of these segments. The individuals that make up the decision-making unit can also be targeted separately.

4. *Product (categories of purchase)*. This refers not to particular products, but to general categories. For example, an IT supplier may distinguish between customers who focused most on hardware or on software categories.

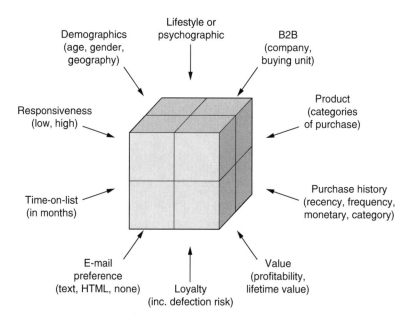

Figure 3.5 Options for targeting an e-mail list

5. *Purchase history*. This evaluates the characteristics of purchase through time using evaluation schemes such as recency, frequency and monetary value (RFM) analysis (see Chapter 2, pages 34–5 for an example). E-mail offers great potential for targeting according to history of purchase and category of interest. E-mail Vision has developed a rules-based personalisation approach for retailers which allows them to target by product and other characteristics in the following manner:

By spend (over last n months)
Customers who have spent £300+ get message A
Customers who have spent up to £300 get message B

By product
If profile says they buy books on-line get offer C
If profile says they buy CDs on-line get offer D

By interest
If they like golf give them message E
If they like tennis give them message F
If they like neither give them message G

The rules are devised such that the e-mail is created by combining these messages to form a unified e-mail.

E-MAIL MARKETING INSIGHT

Use automated rules-based personalisation for targeting groups of consumers with similar characteristics such as product interest or responsiveness.

6. *Customer value*. The simplest form of customer value calculation looks at the value to customer over a fixed period. For example, we could assess total spend across the past 3, 6 or 12 months, and customers could be placed in categories of spend such as the example above and given different offers. The future value of customers can also be calculated using lifetime value calculations. These include assumptions about the rate of churn, average spend per category and referrals to other members. Some companies such as Deutsche Bank use complex modelling of profitability for targeting purposes (see Nitsche, 2002, for a summary). Their approach is iterative, enabling the targeting capability to be refined through time.

7. *Customer loyalty*. Loyalty has been defined by Sargeant and West (2001) as 'the desire of the customer to continue to do business with a given supplier over time'. Customer loyalty is linked in with purchase history and customer value. Customer loyalty can be measured simply by the length of time a customer has been with the company, but more meaningfully by the frequency and value of purchase using RFM analysis. Understanding different levels of loyalty and developing campaigns to appeal to these different levels is part of retention planning, and we return to this topic in Chapter 5.

8. *E-mail preference*. This can simply refer to the format required for e-mails, whether text or graphical (HTML). Many companies are now also establishing a communication channel prefer-

ence, i.e. phone, e-mail or post. E-mail preferences may also state the type of content or offers that a list member has expressed an interest in receiving.

9. *Time on list (in months)*. This is arguably a more critical tool for targeting in e-mail marketing than in traditional direct marketing. With opt-in for e-mail communications we would expect that the susceptibility to response is highest immediately following opt-in. Response rates tend to be highest when the most recent list members are targeted.

10. *Responsiveness to e-mail campaigns*. This measure combines a number of targeting methods, such as purchase history, loyalty and time-on-list as part of the customer lifecycle. Jeremiah Budzik of DoubleClick, building on established models, suggests that customers should be segmented into different 'buckets' depending on their time on list, susceptibility and buying characteristics. Figure 3.6 shows how the new members on the list, referred to as 'Nellie News', have the greatest susceptibility or responsiveness to offers. Through time, however, responsiveness will fall and the aim is to target customers with good potential ('Peter Potential') to become high-value, loyal customers ('Betty Best'). Effectively, we are aiming to minimise the number of unresponsive customers who are ignoring their e-mail, but remain on the list ('Stella Stagnant'). Through targeting the high-potential new customer, as shown in Figure 3.7, it is possible to maximise the revenue of customers by converting more customers to higher value customers. Special offers and creative can also be developed to increase the value of 'Stella Stagnant'.

In databases used for e-mail marketing, particularly those that are currently separated from the main transactional or customer database, 'flags' should be included that indicate the type of customer, e.g. main product segment, frequent user. Five to 10 key characteristics should be identified that will determine the type of e-mail sent.

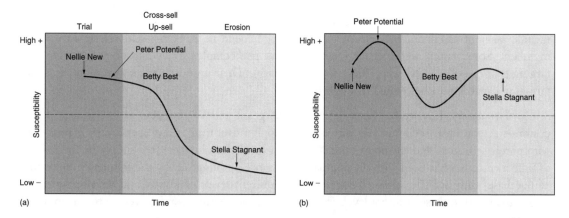

Figure 3.6 Customer lifecycle model of customer susceptibility to e-mail campaigns: (a) without incentivisation, (b) with incentivisation (Source: Jeremiah Budzik, Business and Technical Manager, EMEA Doubleclick, DARTmail, www.doubleclick.net)

		0 units	1–2 units	>3 units
	% of list	10%	4%	2%
	% of gross sales	0%	1.50%	1.50%
	Average £/list member	0	£25	£50
	Average units/list member	0	1.3	3.9
		0 units	**1–2 units**	**>3 units**
Mailings				
6–12	# of members	1500	650	300
	% of list	15%	6%	4%
	% of gross sales	0%	1.30%	2.20%
	Average £/list member	0	£33	£65
	Average units/list member	0	1.5	4.2

Nellie New
Betty Best

Stella Stagnant
Peter Potential
Betty Best

Example of customer buckets based on buying behaviour mapped to lifestyle curve

Figure 3.7 Enhancing customer value through e-mail targeting (Source: Jeremiah Budzik, Business and Technical Manager, EMEA Doubleclick DARTmail, www.doubleclick.net)

E-MAIL MARKETING EXCELLENCE

Enhancing customer value through e-mail campaigns

A summary is given of guidance from Jeremiah Budzik for maximising customer value through e-mail campaigns.

A small percentage of Nellies become Bettys; however, a majority need incentives to move to Peter status.

Treat your Bettys well and they will treat you well; they are your core customer base!

Some Peters will need an extra push to move to Betty status, or there is fear that they might end up in Stella's bucket.

When the population of Stellas increase, Bettys dwindle, and Peter makes no traction, it's time to refresh your house list and attract some Nellies.

Source: Jeremiah Budzik (Business and Technical Manager, EMEA Doubleclick DARTmail, www.doubleclick.net)

David Hughes of E-mail Vision suggests that targeting can be refined during campaigns or in follow-up campaigns according to the response to the initial e-mail. This is a response behaviour-based segmentation. We can again leverage the technology to automate this response process. E2Communications refers to this as 'response-based segmentation'. The categories of response to the e-mail we can identify are:

A. *Don't open*. If the recipient does not open the message this suggests that the list member is not responding to the subject line. This can be revised to have greater impact or refer to a different offer. The recipient may not be responding because of a lack of time, so another option is to send it out on a different day of the week, or at a different time. It is only possible to tell whether an e-mail is opened for an HTML e-mail.

B. *Open, don't click*. If the recipient does open the e-mail, but doesn't click on it, this shows that they are not responding to the creative or the offer. They have indicated a good level of susceptibility, however, so there could be a follow-up with a different creative and/or offer.

C. *Click, but don't act*. In this case the recipient has clicked through on one of the hyperlinks in the e-mail to the microsite or landing page. They have a very high propensity to act, but something has stopped them acting. A specific e-mail perhaps acknowledging their interest, but offering an improved incentive as an additional carrot to persuade them to act, may be effective here.

D. *Do act*. If the recipient does clickthrough and follows the instructions on the landing page, then the individual should be flagged in the database as having a high susceptibility. A follow-up with a complementary offer should be planned.

E-MAIL MARKETING INSIGHT

Use response-based segmentation to plan follow-up offers according to how recipients responded to e-mails.

A summary of the alternative responses and the related follow-up options are summarised in Figure 3.8. Further details on how to test for these actions are provided in the section on measurement later in this chapter.

We have considered a range of targeting options. Later in the chapter we will look at testing which can be applied to targeting. Remember that the more these different alternative ways of targeting are combined, the greater the targeting and the higher the response.

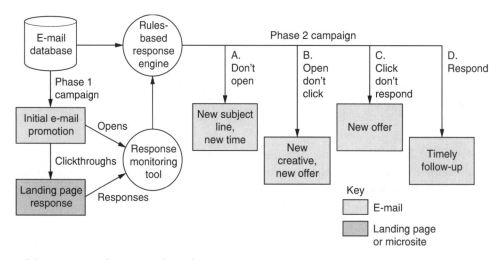

Figure 3.8 Automated response-based segmentation options

Offer

The offer is the next direct marketing variable that is critical to the response to the campaign. The offer is the incentive that we use to encourage action. In e-mail marketing incentives are used to encourage two distinct types of action. The first type of action is encouraging prospects and customers to provide e-mail address, profile information and permission to contact. This action can occur on the web site or offline media. This requires a lead generation offer. Figure 3.9 is an example of such a campaign, where the aim is to encourage e-mail recipients to enter the prize draw on a microsite in return for providing profile details and opting in to future communications. The second action is encouraging clickthrough from e-newsletters or e-mail promotions. This requires a sales generation or conversion offer.

As part of campaign planning suitable offers should be identified for each situation. However, we can make some general comments about offers that apply to both situations. First, the offer must always be relevant to the target audience, consistent with their needs, interests or aspirations. Clearly, we need the offer to appeal to the target audience, but there is a problem if the appeal is too broad. Imagine an offer for a B2B company that involves winning tickets to a Rugby World Cup game. This will appeal to consumers who may respond even though they have no interest in the company's products.

A decision should be taken as to whether these offers are available on the web only as a 'web exclusive'. In some cases it may be more cost-effective or practical to deliver offers using the web. It

Figure 3.9 Vodafone campaign (www.vodafone.com) (Source: David Mill, MediaCo, www.media.co.uk)

may also encourage an online dialogue. If, however, you want to give the customer the choice of which channel to use to deal with you, then the offer may also be made using traditional media. If a 'web exclusive' approach is taken, then this gives a great reason to visit the web site for offline communications rather than the bland 'visit our web site'.

Your options for types of offer can usefully be divided according to the type of value that they represent to your audience. Farris and Langendorf (1999) identify five different types of information value and we expand on these below. Different types of value include:

1. *Information value.* This can take a variety of forms. Most common for B2B is access to a report or white paper which can be downloaded as a Adobe Acrobat (.pdf) or Microsoft Word document. It may be that you already have this type of information available, so this can be a low-cost, effective option for B2B. What we are trying to do is to achieve one of the key success factors for internet marketing identified by Patricia Seybold (1999), which is to 'Help the customer do their job'. Such incentives are very effective, so it may be worthwhile creating some information specifically to achieve this. Examples include white papers about improving the efficiency of workflow in a particular job or information about the marketplace. Such information may not necessarily be in report form or delivered online. Registration that leads to further dialogue with the prospect at an online or real-world seminar is often most effective. The JD Edwards case study later in this chapter is an example of this. A research survey where the results are sent to a respondent is another form of dialogue. E-newsletters or industry alerts are yet another common form of information value, as are software tools or spreadsheet calculators. B2B car manufacturers in the fleet market often provide spreadsheets to help fleet managers manage the costs of running their fleet. Interactive calculators are also often provided for financial services for calculating loan repayments, for example. However, care must be taken that the offer does not act as a barrier to acquiring the customer. With the case of the prospective loan customer, the customer may go elsewhere rather than entering their details. A careful balance has to be struck between the power of the offer and the barrier that is represented by registration.

E-MAIL MARKETING INSIGHT

Assess carefully the balance between the strength of the incentive and the disincentive of providing information.

A final example of information value, and a favourite of mine, is to use the e-mail itself to deliver the value. Some companies offer a sequence of several e-mails over a period of several days or weeks to add to the customer's knowledge about a particular topic. The Dummies Books offer a tip of the day delivered by e-mail, which is perhaps too frequent. Meanwhile, Hitsnclicks (www.hitnsclicks.com) offers a series of seven mini-lessons on Internet marketing at a more manageable interval.

2. *Monetary value.* This is a straightforward discount or a buy-one-get-one free offer. E-tail e-commerce sites often offer a discount on the first order. Loyalty programmes that can be administered online are another way of offering monetary value. Finally, monetary value is also offered through prize draws or other contests. This is often the most cost-effective form of monetary value, since here monetary value is offered, but not all entrants receive it.

3. *Privilege value*. This is most likely to be privileged value to information. For example, media sites and information providers such as the industry analysts Forrester (www.forrester.com) and Gartner (www.gartner.com) have tiered levels of information access. A limited amount of information showcasing the service is available to all site visitors, more information is available to those who register and all information is available to paying subscribers. Here, the offer is fulfilled by providing a username and password to access an extranet. So, this offer relates back to information value, but it is an offer that is usually only open to particular segments. This can be a negative point for those who are not invited. Privileged value can also be provided by access to software downloads or trials.

4. *Service value*. Farris and Langendorf refer to offering a service that does something worthwhile for the customer, whether it is making their lives more convenient, keeping them informed or automating mundane tasks. Examples include online surveys or polls that offer learning and possibly entertainment, reminder services, personalised content such as that available at Silicon.com for IS managers and gift registries. Many of these examples of service value could be included in the other forms of offer described above; they are not mutually exclusive.

5. *Transactional value*. For e-commerce sites, the purchase process is clearly an opportunity to profile customers, but we do not want to increase attrition by asking too many questions in what may already be a lengthy process.

6. *Entertainment value*. This was not in Farris and Langendorf's original list, but is worth identifying separately. This is typically, but not exclusively a B2C offer. It could take the form of a game or quiz, screensaver or movie clip. Such offers are often tied in with viral campaigns. Here, the offer should be devised according to how well it can be passed on to a friend or colleague. Ways of communicating the offer to others apply to each of these different offer types.

So, offers will differ according to whether the audience is B2C or B2B. Time spent on devising an offer that your target customers will care about and act on is time well-spent. We have seen at the start of this section that typically the offer has a greater effect than the creative on response rates, but is as much time spent on the offer as on the creative? A detailed knowledge of your customer is needed to find the offer that will appeal to them. For example, for the B2B prospect, what are their real frustrations with the job and what information needs can help to reduce this frustration? For the B2C prospect, how will the offer affect their work–leisure balance? Why might they care?

Multiple offers are more effective than single offers, so it is useful to identify at least a primary offer and a secondary offer. The power of the two offers together will increase the pulling power of the campaign. The primary offer is used as the main appeal to the target audience to respond. The secondary offer is an additional tool to help to convert those who are inclined to respond, but need a further stimulus. The prospect's perception of the company and its web-site services can also be part of the secondary offer. The offer will not work if the company or web site does not have the credibility to deliver.

Another way of thinking about these offers is as 'free–win–save', and these keywords are often used to communicate the offer. Remember that 'save' can refer to saving time as well as saving money.

Finally, as we have mentioned before, the cost of the offer and fulfilling it must fit within the budget of the campaign. This must be modelled to ensure there is a satisfactory return on investment for the campaign.

Timing

Starting with the absolute timing, a frequently asked question is 'when is the best time to broadcast an e-mail promotion?' The flippant answer is that it will vary according to audience, but you should always test to find the best timing for your audience. If we assume that the e-mail will have the greatest impact if it arrives in the recipient's inbox while they are using the computer, then this would suggest that for consumer audiences, evenings or weekends might be the best time to dispatch. For business customers, we want the e-mail to arrive when they will give it the most of their attention, so we are looking for times in the week when business people are likely to be less busy. Industry wisdom dictates that the best day of the week for e-mail broadcasting is either Tuesday or Thursday. Presumably, on Monday people are recovering from the weekend and attending planning meetings, while on Friday they are winding down for the weekend or frantically trying to finish work scheduled for the week. Note that many e-mails are dispatched overnight when costs may be cheaper, or the workload on the computers is lower. A case could be made that the maximum impact will be during the day for the business user or during the evening for a consumer with an 'always on' broadband connection.

Relative time considers the timing of the e-mail campaign in comparison to other media. For example, does it precede or follow the offline launch of a cross-media campaign?

Another aspect of relative timing is frequency compared with the last e-mail. Is weekly, fortnightly or monthly best? How important is it that these messages are sent out on the same day of the week? Selecting the best frequency is covered in Chapter 5 in the sections on e-newsletters and promotional e-mails.

Creative

The creative of an e-mail campaign includes the message header (Subject line, From, To) and the design of body of the message, including the text structure, copy and graphics, if used. Creative also refers to the creative used for the web-site landing page. We cover options for designing the creative in depth in Chapter 6, so will not discuss them further here.

CAMPAIGN INTEGRATION

Many books and articles on e-mail marketing describe e-mail marketing in isolation from other media. However, an integrated campaign can increase the impact and response rate to the e-mail. Kotler et al. (2001) describe integrated marketing communications as:

> *the concept under which a company carefully integrates and co-ordinates its many communications channels to deliver a clear, consistent message about the organisation and its products.*

Integrated marketing communications will use a range of media such as TV, print advertising, direct mail and web site, in addition to e-mail. A range of promotional tools may also be used from advertising, direct or interactive marketing and PR. The different media and promotional tools that are used also need to be integrated through time such that the sequence of communications is most effective.

Clearly, there is a danger if e-mail marketing is managed by a different agency to the traditional DM agency and they are not briefed on the consistency of the message. A useful mnemonic referred to by Pickton and Broderick (2000) which highlights the characteristics of integrated communications are the four Cs of:

- *Coherence*: different communications are logically connected
- *Consistency*: multiple messages support and reinforce, and are not contradictory
- *Continuity*: communications are connected and consistent through time
- *Complementary*: communications are synergistic, or the whole is greater than the sum of the parts.

The JD Edwards case study illustrates these points well and uses a range of media, with promotional tools carefully integrated through time. In this case the different communications had a theme of retaining customers, but different metaphors were used in each to highlight the approach from the restrictive, rope and straitjacket, to blandishments such as chocolates and cheesecake. In this way the sequence of messages supported and reinforced the communication. Different media including telemarketing a direct marketing mailer and e-mail were also used in a synergistic way such that the whole was greater than the sum of the parts. Through the use of telemarketing and direct marketing, JD Edwards was at front-of-mind, so the e-mail was not unexpected and this contributed to the large number of responses.

E-MAIL MARKETING EXCELLENCE

JD Edwards launch CRM system using an integrated campaign

Campaign objectives

Software supplier JD Edwards wanted to launch its customer relationship management (CRM) programme in the UK. A 'Window into the World of CRM' event was organised for 21 March 2002 with a minimum of 30 attendees required from the direct marketing campaign.

Campaign tactics

An integrated campaign using four direct mail and three e-mail campaigns was produced (Figure 3.10). All messages were received by each list member. These were supported by a microsite to gather customer details (see Figure 2.10). Telemarketing was used throughout the campaign to gain prospects. Those contacted were offered the choice of hearing about a new product and hearing from independent experts on CRM. Those contacted included both JD Edwards' customers and prospects obtained from a bought-in list.

Creative

A series of high-impact direct mail pieces using key statements and imagery related to a Valentine's Day theme was used (Figure 3.11). The background of the e-mail was red to fit in with the theme and to achieve high impact. The following images and strap lines were used:

● Mailer 1/e-mail 1: man wrapped in rope: 'There are other ways of keeping your customers'

● Mailer 2: cheesecake: 'Keep them coming back for more'

● Mailer 3/e-mail 2: man in straitjacket: 'Once you've got them you'll want to keep them'

● Mailer 4/e-mail 3: heart-shaped chocolate box: 'Keep them sweet.'

Results

The target of 30 attendees was exceeded, with 80 registrations achieved via the microsite (see Figure 3.10). Over 200 prospects showing an active interest in the product were also gained. The e-mail was more effective than the direct mail at generating visits to the microsite, but not significantly so; for instance, mailer 1 generated 100 visits to the site, while e-mail 1 generated 120 visits.

Source: Philippa Edwards and Robert Perrin, Anderson Baillie Marketing (www.andersonbaillie.com)

The exact form of integration will vary in each case. However, we can draw out some general principles. Taking the example of the campaign to support the relaunch of a web site (Figure 3.12), we can make the following observations:

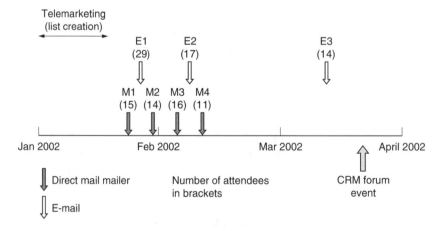

Figure 3.10 Campaign timing for JD Edwards CRM launch

Figure 3.11   JD Edwards creative: e-mail 3

1. *A combination of online and offline communications techniques is used.* The techniques to promote the launch include a range of communications media and promotion tools.

2. *Search engine registration must be planned well in advance.* This is important for all e-mail-related marketing where a web site is part of the offer. For example, when the UK's Chartered Institute of Marketing launched its 'What's New in Marketing' Newsletter, registering the site was not seen as a priority. Consequently, word-of-mouth recommendation of the newsletter which led to someone searching for a site they could not find would be wasted. In addition, there is a delay in each search engine indexing a site and then publishing it, even with paid-for express inclusion services.

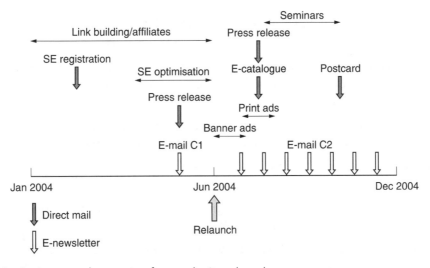

Figure 3.12   An integrated campaign for a web-site relaunch

3. *Online and offline PR can be useful in driving traffic to a newsletter site.* Online PR takes the form of online articles on related web sites, with links referring to the site. Offline PR can play a similar role. For example, briefing newspapers or magazines about the launch of a high-impact viral campaign in advance would assist in the success of the campaign.

4. *Developing an e-newsletter takes time.* While a one-off e-mail campaign can be produced in days, the same is not usually true for a newsletter. Newsletters stand or fail according to their content. Commissioning, editing and assembling content, even when sourced from within a company, will take weeks rather than days. To produce the first newsletter following the relaunch shown in Figure 3.12, work would typically need to start 2 months before the first issue. The first issue will also require a design template to be produced, as well as sourcing content.

THE CREATIVE BRIEF

The creative brief is a summary of the purpose of the campaign. It is used to communicate the aims of the campaign to the alternative agencies who may be conducting the work, or as a summary of intent if undertaken internally. The detail in the brief will depend on the experience of, and control required by the marketer directing the campaign. If they are relatively new to e-mail marketing, they may leave the details open and instruct the agencies who have been asked to submit a tender to provide their creative input.

The brief covers many of the topics referred to already in this chapter, so this section acts as a summary of the chapter to this point.

E-MAIL CAMPAIGN CHECKLIST

The creative brief

- *Aims*: lead generation, customer acquisition, retention: number required, level of sales anticipated. Changing awareness or perceptions about brand.

- *Target audience*: the demographics of consumers or characteristics of businesses or those in the decision-making unit. Pyschographic profiles of the type of person you are trying to reach.

- *Offer*: the nature of the offer: a general indication of information value, monetary value, saving or a more specific offer consistent with a brand.

- *Timing*: target date for completion of campaign. Relation to campaign in other media.

- *Integration*: how the e-mail campaign integrates with offline media campaigns such as advertising, direct mail or PR.

- *Creative*: the details will usually be left to the agency to devise, but a theme or tone may be suggested.

- *Microsite*: location of microsite: part of the sponsoring company's site, or a separate site. Notification pages required, e.g. successful completion, notification of error in form completion.

- *Information collection needs*: what fields should be used to profile the customer or research their views (including mandatory fields)? Specific form of wording required for opt-in. What validation will be used to check the data, e.g. valid postcode, e-mail address format? In what format is the data required, e.g. comma delimited ASCII text file, Access database?

- *Mandatory inclusions*: logo, link to privacy statement, terms and conditions, unsubscribe; is contact number required?

- *Budget*: an indication of maximum budget may be included.

MEASUREMENT

A valuable characteristic of e-mail marketing is that it enables detailed analysis of direct marketing campaigns. To date, we have simplified the measurement of campaigns to refer to four variables (number sent, number of clickthroughs, number who complete the form and number of recipients who become customers). For detailed analysis of a campaign, more metrics are available, and it is important to dissect these to identify the weaknesses in the campaign. Figure 3.13 summarises the metrics in diagrammatic form. Figure 3.14 illustrates one of the most widely used products used for presenting metrics.

One way to remember the different types of measure for e-mail marketing is the seven Rs. We will relate this back to Figure 3.13 and also to a traditional door-drop campaign. The seven Rs are: Receipt rate, Reader rate, clickthRough rate, conveRsion rate, Response rate, Rejects rate and Referrals rate.

1. *Receipt rate* (based on number of recipients):

$$\text{Receipt rate} = (\text{nSent} - \text{nBounced})/\text{nSent}$$

'Bounces' are returned e-mails that are not received by the intended recipient. There are two types of bounce:

- soft bounce: an e-mail returned because e-mail server not working (will resend later)

- hard bounce: an e-mail returned with address unknown.

The level of bounces corresponds to the level of 'gone-aways', people who no longer live or work at a particular address, of a conventional direct mail campaign. With e-mail we have the benefit that it is easier to see when someone has moved on and we do not have to waste funds by continuing to contact them.

Hard bounces are of greatest concern to e-mail marketers. A high bounce rate indicates an e-mail list with a high proportion of e-mail addresses with errors or that have become out of date. In the next section we look at what can be done to reduce the number of hard bounces to an acceptable level.

								Campaign 1	Campaign 2
Number of e-mails SENT from list								10 000	10 000
						Receipt rate		98%	90%
Number of e-mails RECEIVED from list								9800	9000
					Reader rate (open rate)			60%	40%
Number of e-mails READ or opened								5880	3600
				Response rate 1 (CTR of readers)				30%	10%
				Response rate 2 (CTR of recipients)				18.0%	4.0%
				Response rate 3 (CTR of number sent)				17.6%	3.6%
Number of CLICKTHROUGHS to landing page								1764	360
					Completion rate			80%	60%
				Response rate 4 (responses of number sent)				14.1%	2.2%
Number of FORMS COMPLETED (RESPONSES)								1411	216
						Referral rate		10%	2%
Number of REFERRALS								141	4

Figure 3.13 Detailed e-mail campaign diagnostics

2. *Reader rate* (more commonly referred to as the open rate, based on number of readers):

$$\text{Reader rate} = nReaders/nRecipients$$

For HTML e-mails, we can get an indication of the reader rate according to whether a marker graphic contained within the e-mail has been downloaded.

This rate corresponds to the proportion of people who evaluate the contents of the mailer and then open it in a traditional campaign. We have much better visibility about this process when using HTML e-mails. However, we do not know how many delete the e-mail immediately; the equivalent of throwing it in the bin.

3. *ClickthRough rate* (CTR):

$$\text{Clickthrough rate} = n\text{Click on Links}/nReaders \text{ or } nRecipients \text{ or } nSent$$

The CTR is a key measure as it indicates the quality of the creative and offer. If you achieve good clickthrough the campaign will be a success provided the landing page or microsite is of good

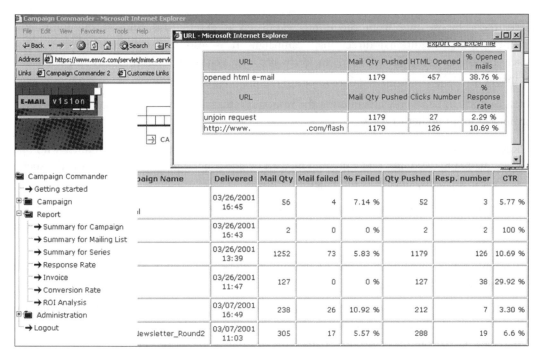

Figure 3.14 Campaign Commander e-mail reporting software (www.emailvision.com)

quality. The CTR can be reported in different ways, as shown in Figure 3.13. It is common to report it as a percentage of those who open the e-mail (nReaders), which is useful for assessing the effectiveness of the creative and the offer, but for overall campaign success it is better to use a percentage of those received or sent.

Remember that since you may have multiple hyperlinks in the e-mail, using total clicks for calculating clickthrough rates may be misleading since some recipients may click more than once. Some e-mail marketers use unique clicks, which determine clicks from unique visitors to the microsite. Alternatively, for newsletters in particular, which have many links, you will want to report CTRs for the different hyperlinks in the message.

4. *ConveRsion rate* of completing landing page form:

$$\text{Conversion rate} = \text{nComplete form}/\text{nClickthroughs}$$

This refers to the number of people that clickthrough and complete a form such as a registration page for a prize draw. Conversion rate can refer to converting to any outcome, whether it is completing the form, subscribing to a newsletter or catalogue or actually buying a catalogue. The response rate below refers to those who act on the initial registration.

The rate of reply form completion is not known for a traditional direct mail campaign.

5. *Response rate* (based on number of responses):

$$\text{Response rate} = \text{nAct}/\text{nRecipients}$$

Here, the response rate from the e-mail campaign is exactly the same as the information obtained from a traditional direct mail campaign. It is also useful to monitor the rate at which responses are received. The majority are received within 2 or 3 days of an e-mail campaign.

Great care has to be taken when quoting the response rate, since as shown in Figure 3.13, it can be formulated in a number of ways:

* Response rate 1: number of readers who clickthrough as a proportion of the number who open the e-mail. This response rate will often be used by agencies or managers to describe the success of their campaigns, since it is the biggest number!

* Response rate 2: number of readers who clickthrough as a proportion of those who received the e-mail (i.e. it excludes bounce). It is a better indication of the overall rate of success than response rate 1.

* Response rate 3: number of readers who clickthrough as a proportion of those who were sent the e-mail (number broadcast).

* Response rate 4: number of readers who complete an action as a proportion of those who were sent the e-mail. This action is usually responding to the form, but it could also include making a purchase, i.e. becoming a customer. This is the most meaningful indication of the overall success of the campaign, although, as discussed in the next section, each can be useful for understanding particular strengths and weaknesses of the campaign.

6. *Rejects rate* (more commonly referred to as unsubscribe rate):

$$\text{Opt-out rate} = nUnsubscribe/nRecipients$$

It is useful to monitor the unsubscribe rate of each campaign against the average unsubscribe rate. If the campaign unsubscribe rate is much higher it indicates a problem with the content or tone of the campaign.

7. *Referrals rate* (based on number of referrals of new prospects):

$$\text{Referral rate} = \text{Number of referrals/Number of respondents}$$

This refers to the viral element of an e-mail campaign, if used. If a campaign has involved generating additional leads through providing an offer to encourage disclosure of other e-mail addresses, then the referral rate can be measured as the number of referrals per respondent.

More detailed measures are also available, including number of clickthroughs per e-mail and which calls-to-action were responded to, for example, at the bottom, middle or top of the e-mail.

E-MAIL MARKETING EXCELLENCE

ABC Electronic defines auditing standards

ABC Electronic has an established service for auditing visitor traffic to web sites, principally for portals where authenticated traffic levels are the basis for selling advertising. In 2002, it started to provide independent auditing for e-mail campaigns. The agency Outrider was one of the first companies to use this service. Tom Peacock, Director of International at Outrider explained the reasons for setting up the service:

> *Email marketing is emerging as a popular and effective direct marketing channel that offers higher response rates, quicker turn-around times and more cost-effective implementation than the traditional 'letter-through-door' approach and therefore a key aspect of the work we do for our clients. Added to this it is far more accountable than traditional print methods and to prove this to our clients we have committed to audits as verification that we are operating a fully accountable and transparent service. We believe it is important for agencies to be accountable to their clients and to ensure the long-term health of the web as a marketing channel.*

Definitions of metrics devised by ABC Electronic include:

Distribution (net): 'the total number of emails successfully sent as part of a single campaign/distribution to all (SMTP) addresses on the distribution list. This number excludes EMAILS BOUNCED' (see below).

Distribution (gross): 'the total number of emails sent as part of a single campaign/distribution to all (SMTP) addresses on the distribution list.'

Duplication: 'the total number of identical SMTP addresses in the distribution list expressed as a percentage of the gross distribution, rounded down to the nearest whole number.'

Distribution ended: 'the date and time expressed in hours and minutes (GMT) when the last email in a campaign/distribution was sent to the last address on the distribution list.'

Distribution started: 'the date and time expressed in hours and minutes (GMT) when the first email in a campaign/distribution was sent to the first address on the distribution list.'

Emails bounced: 'the total number of emails in the gross distribution that generated an NDN (Non-Delivery-Notice) measured at least 24 hours after the time of the last email sent in that single campaign/distribution.'

Opt-in: 'a unique SMTP address that has been added to the distribution list as a result of a positive action by the address user.'

Percentage bounced: 'the total number of emails in the gross distribution that generated an NDN measured at least 24 hours after the time of the last email sent, expressed as a percentage of the gross distribution.'

Registered address: 'a contactable address (SMTP) in the distribution list that has requested the email service.' Note: this is not a measure of individual people or addressees, because individuals may have more than one registered email address.

Source: Press Release, ABC Electronic web site (www.abce.org.uk) 8 May 2002.

CONTINUOUS IMPROVEMENT OF CAMPAIGNS

In the section on targeting we saw how it is possible to target according to the past types of response to e-mails: whether they are opened or there is a clickthrough. In a similar way, it is also possible to take corrective action by reviewing the results of a campaign. This is particularly important in a multimessage campaign.

It is difficult to give industry averages of the value of metrics that may indicate a problem with the campaign, but estimates are given based on different campaigns known to the author.

Hard bounces > 5–10% (don't receive)

For good-quality lists, hard bounces should not exceed 2–5%. Levels above 5% suggest a problem that should be resolved. Possible alternative solutions to reduce the number of bounces involve exploring different reasons for the problem:

- If the list has aged (sometimes referred to as attrition) then cleaning the list is required. Indeed, the addresses with hard bounces should be removed from the list.

- A high level of hard bounces may indicate a problem with the verification of e-mail addresses when they were collected. Methods for verifying e-mail addresses include asking the customer to enter the e-mail address twice (entry confirmation), double opt-in, and a check that the e-mail is in a valid format such as a@b.com or a@b.co.uk. E-mail Vision uses 'Intelligent forms' which check for the existence of an SMTP mail server at the domain.

- Poor-quality control of manual data entry, e.g. e-mails captured at point of sale or by sales representatives. This can be improved through training which stresses the importance of valid e-mail addresses and shows how to check validity.

Soft bounces

These are usually in the range of 1–2%. No action required is required since most mail servers will keep trying until the message is successfully delivered.

Open rate < 5–20% (don't open)

The open rate will depend on how many users have a preview pane open (see Chapter 6, Figure 6.2). If a high proportion of users have the preview pane open, then this will increase the open rate. Despite many consumers using the preview pane, the open rate can fall to below 10%. This suggests a problem with the subject line, since the recipient will only click on the e-mail to open it if the subject line is relevant to them. So, the obvious action to improve the open rate is to consider alternative subject lines. Alternatives for improving the subject line are covered in Chapter 6; for example, personalising the subject line to refer to a particular product or person is likely to improve open rates. It may also be that the offer referred to in the subject line is not relevant or strong enough.

As well as problems in the subject line, other factors will affect the open rate. A From address that is unknown or confusing may decrease the open rate (see Chapter 6). For B2B mailings, the time of day may have been inappropriate (e.g. first thing on Monday morning). Consider testing and changing the time of day when the e-mail is sent.

Clickthrough < 5–10% (open, don't click)

If the clickthrough rate from e-mails that have been opened is below 5–10% then this suggests a problem with different aspects of the creative or offer. Improving these aspects of a campaign is referred to in Chapter 6. Remember that there may also be different hyperlinks for different call-to-action, so we will need to assess the success of each of these. In summary, different issues to review to improve the clickthrough rate are:

- *Position of the call-to-action hyperlink*: if it is at the bottom of long copy, then recipients may not scroll down to it; can the call-to-action be duplicated, higher in the e-mail?

- *Prominence of the call-to-action*: in text e-mails, the call-to-action hyperlink should be placed on a separate line for prominence. In HTML e-mails, the call-to-action can use specific copy, bold text or an image to increase its prominence.

- *Structure of the calls-to-action*: perhaps you have used multiple calls-to-action, but how are these structured? Are they crafted in a logical sequence or flow for the selling process? It may be helpful to think of traditional direct mail with a range of copy for each of details of offer/product, link to page, testimonials, additional offers and main call-to-action.

- *Length and size*: clickthrough may be decreased if the e-mail may be too long, if it is a rich media e-mail or if it contains graphics that have not been optimised for the web and takes a long time to download.

- *The offer*: if the e-mail is well-designed, and the above factors are unlikely to be causing the problem, then poor clickthrough is probably due to the offer. If the offer, or the way that it is described in the e-mail, is not sufficiently appealing to the target audience, then this needs improving.

Landing page form completion < 40–60% (click, don't act)

Once the recipient has clicked through, this shows a high level of interest in the offer: they have already committed time to reading and evaluating the e-mail. Given this investment in time, they are predisposed to complete the landing page provided it does not form too high a barrier. It should be possible to achieve over 40% of respondents who complete the form. If the proportion falls below this, then the main issues to look at are:

- Consider changing the number of questions asked or the number of screens required if the campaign involves an extensive research component.

- Perhaps the offer does not appeal as much as was thought from the subject line or body copy.

- Perhaps there is a problem with the privacy options. Does the landing page reassure the respondent that their details will not be shared with third parties, for instance?

- Perhaps the tone and design of the landing page is not consistent with the campaign or brand, which again will not help to reassure the respondent.

TESTING

The need for testing the different variables of an e-mail campaign would seem obvious, particularly since both agencies and clients are learning about this evolving medium. However, Andrew Petherick of Mailtrack says that 'amazingly little' testing is performed. He estimates that 80% do not test, and those that do test may not test a sufficient range of variables. He gives the example of a company that tested five different lists with the same creative. The response rates were from 3.5 to 3.8% and were felt to be disappointing, but the effect of changing other significant variables such as the subject line or offer was not tested. Reasons for the lack of testing are unclear. Some may see it as an extra cost, since responses rates are currently high. Others may see it as delaying a campaign that has to hit a deadline.

Testing for e-mail campaigns follows similar principles to that for traditional direct marketing. The key principle is that of only testing a single variable at a time. So, test e-mails can be sent out in batches of 1000 at a time, but with each batch containing a different offer, copy, day or time, etc. Testing is performed relative to a control group so the effect of changing the variables can be seen.

When testing, each test should be marked with key codes so that responses to it will be clear from studying the web server log. For example, these codes can be used to highlight the characteristics of each test:

- List = L1
- Segment targeted = S1
- Date/time broadcast = D1
- Offer = O1
- Subject line = SL1
- Content = C1
- Hyperlink = H1 (e.g. first hyperlink in message)
- Format = FT, FH
- Call-to-action = CA1.

These codes can then be combined into the hyperlink that is the call-to-action within the e-mail. A question mark '?' is used to separate the testing key codes from the landing page for the click-through. An example of what would appear in a text e-mail is:

http://www.company.com/promotion.htm?L1S1D1O1SL1C1H1FTCA1

or in an HTML e-mail:

<A HREF="http://www.company.com/promotion.htm?L1S1D1O1SL1C1H1FTCA1">Enter the prize draw </A>

Which appears as the altogether neater:

Enter the prize draw

The question mark (?) is used within the hypertext transfer protocol (HTTP) to denote that parameters or variables are going to be passed through to the page in what is known as a 'query string'. The code will then occur in the referrer's part of the web log in the same way that it shows which search engines and their keywords have been used to link through to a page. So, in the WebTrends analysis software the relevant place to look at is 'Top referring URLs by visits'. The benefit of this approach is that the same target page for each test can be used, thus obviating the need to create identical landing pages with different names.

The use of parameters means that the more usual form of the URL is:

http://www.company.com/promotion.htm?ref1="L1S1D1O1SL1C1FTCA1"&ref2="Code2"

Ampersands (&) are used to separate the different parameters.

E-MAIL MARKETING INSIGHT

Develop a standard set of key codes early on which can be used to test the response to different campaigns.

E-MAIL CAMPAIGN CHECKLIST

Typical testing variables for an e-mail campaign

These are given in approximate order of importance:

- List ☐
- Segment targeted ☐
- Offer ☐
- Subject line ☐
- Content: copy, style, tone, structure ☐
- Format (text or HTML) ☐
- Call-to-action copy and position of hyperlink(s) ☐
- Day of week ☐
- Time of day ☐
- 'From' address ☐
- Different forms of personalisation ☐
- Landing page (microsite) characteristics ☐

Consumers' suggestions on how to improve permission e-mail

eMarketer (2002) reported on a survey of 1250 US e-mail users and asked them for their opinions on how e-mail programmes could be improved. The results highlight the importance of the campaign planning variables that we have mentioned in these factors. From most to least important changes mentioned (two choices per respondent), the results were:

- Less frequent messages (42%)
- Better prices and offers (35%)
- More relevant, targeted messages (24%)
- More control over e-mail options (18%)
- Time savers and convenience (18%)
- Exclusive e-mail offers (17%)
- More self-personalised content (9%)
- More entertaining messages (6%)
- More timely messages (6%)
- More reminders (2%)
- More frequent messages (1%)

CAMPAIGN MANAGEMENT AND RESOURCING

Approaches to managing the whole campaign process in terms of which suppliers to use and the detailed suppliers to use are covered in Chapter 7.

REFERENCES

Chaffey, D., Mayer, R., Johnston, K. and Ellis-Chadwick, F. (2003). *Internet Marketing: Strategy, Implementation and Practice*, 2nd edn. Harlow: Financial Times/Prentice Hall.

van Doren, D., Flechner, D. and Green-Adelsberger, K. (2000). Promotional strategies on the world wide web. *J. Market. Commun.*, **6**, 21–35.

eMarketer (2002). Consumers want more from e-mail marketing. eStatNews from eMarketer, 20 May.

Farris, J. and Langendorf, L. (1999). Engaging customers in e-business, how to build sales, relationships and results with e-mail. Whitepaper (www.e2software.com).

Kotler, P., Armstrong, G., Saunders, J. and Wong, V. (2001) *Principles of Marketing*, 3rd edn. Harlow: Financial Times/Prentice Hall.

Nitsche, M. (2002). Developing a truly customer-centric CRM system: Part Two – Analysis and campaign management. *Interact. Market.*, **3** (4), 350–66.

Pickton, A. and Broderick, D. (2000). *Integrated Marketing Communications*. Harlow: Financial Times/Prentice Hall.

Sargeant, A. and West, D. (2001). *Direct and Interactive Marketing*. Oxford: Oxford University Press.

Seybold, P. (1999). *Customers.com*. London: Century Business Books/Random House.

Smith, P. R. and Chaffey, D. (2002). *eMarketing eXcellence – The Heart of eBusiness*. Oxford: Butterworth-Heinemann.

Smith, P. R. and Taylor, J. (2002). *Marketing Communications*, 3rd edn. London: Kogan Page.

WEB LINKS

Campaign Commander (www.emailvision.com)

Conversion marketing objectives spreadsheet (www.weboutcomes.com)

Chapter **4**

E-mail for customer acquisition

Overview

This chapter discusses how to use online marketing to acquire new customers and migrate existing offline customers online. Capture of e-mail addresses and profiling information is key to this, so a large part of this chapter is about building a house e-mail list. We will also explore how to use e-mail as part of online customer acquisition.

Chapter objectives

By the end of this chapter you will be able to:

- devise different approaches to building a house e-mail list
- evaluate the quality of rented e-mail lists
- assess the use of e-mail sponsorship or advertising
- use e-mail to convert leads to sales.

Chapter structure

- Introduction
- Building a house e-mail list
- Stage 1: Devising incentives
- Stage 2: Using online and offline communications to drive traffic to the web site
- Using a rented list of e-mails to acquire customers via e-mail
- Placing advertising in third-party e-mail newsletters
- Usenet
- Stage 3: Revising web-site design to emphasise offer
- Stage 4: Defining profiling needs and capture form
- Stage 5: Selecting permission levels: what does opt-in really mean?
- Stage 6: Drawing up a privacy statement
- Stage 7: Defining the opt-out
- Stage 8: Follow-up registration
- Other forms of customer acquisition
- Keeping e-mail addresses current
- Viral marketing
- Measuring acquisition effectiveness

INTRODUCTION

Customer acquisition means gaining new customers, right? Of course, but for success in e-marketing we need to look at separate strategies for gaining new *online* customers. This means strategies for acquiring prospects and converting these leads to customers, but also strategies for migrating existing customers to online customers. Figure 4.1 shows that the first stage is using different online and offline promotion campaigns to attract first-time visitors to the web site. We look at success factors for some of these techniques, such as search engine registration, e-mail to rented lists and advertising or direct mail using traditional media later in this chapter. All touchpoints between company employees and potential or new customers should also be used to encourage them to visit the web site and capture e-mail addresses. Such touchpoints include the salesperson, point of sale and support enquiry.

Once the first-time visitor is on the web site we ideally need to convert the visitor to action or, at least, to create a favourable impression. If we fail to achieve either of these, then the first-time visitor will never be seen again. For a new potential customer we want to start a dialogue by capturing an e-mail address and profile. For an existing customer, we also want to acquire an e-mail address, if we do not already have it. We may already have some profile information that could be linked to a customer reference or account number. We may also want to collect additional online-specific profile information such as preferences for HTML or text e-mail, or the type of newsletter in which they are interested. To convert as many of the first-time visitors to action, think about where your promotion directs them. If it directs them to the home page, then they will have to find the offers to acquire them; but if you direct them to a particular landing page or microsite, then the proposition will be clearer and there will be fewer distractions, so the conversion rate will be higher. If the first-time visitor arrives on the home page, then think about using different offers for the new customer and the existing customer. Many organisations use 'one-size (of offer) fits all'. Once we have converted our visitors to action, the final stage is to change the potential customers from leads to customers and the existing customers to online customers or repeat customers. E-mail can help to remind and inform the prospect and encourage them to go online. However, this final

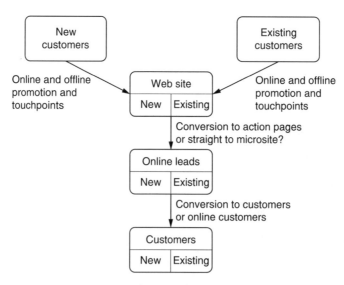

Figure 4.1 Two routes to customer e-mail acquisition

stage is not all achieved online. Phone calls, direct mail or visits from salespeople are often most important in helping to achieve this.

Since the two types of acquisition have much in common, we will look at a generic process for customer acquisition, but also consider different strategies for each type of acquisition. In this chapter, we will cover these stages:

1. Devising incentives

2. Using online and offline communications to emphasise offer and drive traffic to the web site

3. Revising web-site design to emphasise offer

4. Defining profiling needs and capture form

5. Selecting permission levels

6. Drawing up a privacy statement

7. Defining the opt-out

8. Follow-up.

Stage 2, using online and offline communications to drive traffic to the web site, is one of the most important aspects of this process, since if we can gain the visitors to the web site, we have an excellent chance to convert them to customers if the offer, design and privacy options on the site are also right. So, we will explore this in some detail. Different types of communication that we will describe include online communications techniques such as:

- search engine registration and optimisation

- using a rented list of e-mails to acquire customers via e-mail

- placing banner advertising on other web sites

- placing advertising in other e-mail newsletters.

Offline communications techniques that we will look at briefly include:

- direct mail promotions

- advertising

- PR.

BUILDING A HOUSE E-MAIL LIST

Maximising opportunities for capturing e-mail addresses from your current customers is key. A good starting point is your current figure for the proportion of current customers for which you have e-mail addresses. You can then set targets for this metric and devise techniques to increase this figure. When devising these techniques do not only think quantity, also think quality. What procedures can you use to maximise the number of valid e-mail addresses? E-mail addresses that have just one character wrong are no good to anyone since you cannot usually identify the miscreant character. A further aspect of quality is opt-in. As we describe the techniques below, also think about which are truly opt-in (see Chapter 2). Just because you have obtained an e-mail address from the customer does not necessarily mean that it is opt-in. It is only opt-in if the customer has proactively agreed, and expects to receive e-mail communications.

This section describes a range of offline and online techniques to increase e-mail address capture and to make sure that the accuracy is as high as possible.

E-MAIL MARKETING INSIGHT

When improving your coverage of E-mail addresses, think quality as well as quantity. Devise techniques to increase the accuracy of e-mail addresses collected.

Offline collection of e-mail addresses

Offline collection techniques of your e-mail addresses vary a lot according to the type of business. However, the constant is that you should use all touchpoints as an opportunity to collect e-mail addresses. For a grocery retailer, this could involve a campaign using an incentive at the point-of-sale to gain the e-mail addresses of loyalty card members. For the business-to-business (B2B) organisation, this could involve incentivising the sales representatives to capture e-mail addresses and to profile their key account customers. Using a prize draw promotion at a trade fair where customers are encouraged to drop their business cards into a box is another way of capturing e-mail addresses. Here, though, we have to be careful about opt-in. In the first case, the sales representative can be briefed that the customer should be informed that their address may be used to communicate with them in future, or may even gain their consent for this. This is opt-in. The second case, where business cards are dropped into a box, is not opt-in. The quality of the e-mail addresses is lower in this second case, and since they are not fully opted in, they could only ethically be used for a single campaign which would invite customers to double opt-in to further communications. Even then, some customers or prospects may consider this SPAM.

E-MAIL MARKETING INSIGHT

Use all customer touchpoints as an opportunity for gaining e-mail addresses.

Direct mail promotions also give opportunities for gaining e-mail addresses. In fact, whenever a prospect or customer has to fill in a form this is an opportunity. Collecting the e-mail address should be an inbuilt part of the sales process.

A further technique for high-value customers is to research the e-mail address. The example below shows how one B2B company employed research to gain e-mail addresses. The costs of acquisition are in low single figures.

E-MAIL MARKETING EXCELLENCE

Blue Solutions use phone research to build their house list

Blue Solutions Limited, a trading software distributor, wanted to increase the number of people who received their e-mail newsletter and replace fax broadcasting as their marketing method. Rather than employ a temporary staff member, they decided to enlist the help of data supplier Corpdata to research the e-mail addresses by phone to obtain an e-mail address which was then used for additional research using a questionnaire. Mark Charleton of Blue Solutions said:

A high percentage of all email questionnaires were received within a few days of the original contact. We received a 56% conversion rate from call to completion and, as a result, were able to capture an additional 788 email addresses to add to our database of 6500 records. The four day turnaround time was impressive especially when compared to the usual turnaround time of approximately three months.

Source: Caroline Piggins, Corpdata Press Release, 17 May 2002 (www.corpdata.co.uk).

In all of the offline cases we have looked at, the e-mail addresses are normally captured on paper and then keyed into the house-list database. Both of these stages introduce scope for error. Simple housekeeping procedures can help. Ask those writing down the e-mail addresses to write clearly and use capital letters. Explain the importance of getting the address right: what is the customer going to miss out on if the address is wrong? Where staff are with the prospect or customer, train them in what constitutes a valid e-mail address format and get them to check. Similarly, when the e-mail addresses are being keyed in, brief training can ensure that formats are understood. Software checks can also be built in to check formats.

Online collection

Online collection of e-mail addresses involves gathering e-mail addresses following incentivisation as part of permission marketing as described in Chapters 2 and 3. With online collection of e-mail addresses we can identify two tactics for collection. First, a routine visit to the site or normal 'footfall' on the site should be seen as an opportunity for the collection of an e-mail address. Secondly, specific e-mail acquisition campaigns should be used to drive traffic to a landing page or microsite to gather the e-mail address. As we will see, the full range of communications media and tools can be used to drive traffic to the site in this way. The Comet example in the box below gives an example of such a campaign.

The remainder of this chapter describes in detail how to go about collecting e-mails in this way.

E-MAIL MARKETING EXCELLENCE

Comet build house list

Campaign aims

Comet wanted to build its house list through targeting consumers with an interest in computers.

Offer

The offer to encourage registration was a prize draw to win one of three Intel Pentium 4 processor-based PCs.

Creative

The subject line was 'Comet has three brand new PCs to give away!' When the e-mail was opened the copy was simple, giving details about the prize on offer and the reason for offering it ('celebrating the launch of Pentium 4 processor'). The landing page was kept simple, with the respondents only asked for their e-mail address.

Results

Number mailed: 22 189
Clicked through: 4768 (21.5%)
Registered details: 4698 (98.5%)

Source: Andrew Petherick, MailTrack Head of Sales and marketing (www.mailtrack.co.uk).

STAGE 1: DEVISING INCENTIVES

The first step in acquisition is to devise incentives that will be used to encourage disclosure of the e-mail address and profile details when an existing or a potential customer visits the web site. For other contact points such as a point-of-sale different forms of offer may be needed. The alternative types of offers that can be used were covered in Chapter 3. As a reminder, these were:

- information value
- entertainment value
- monetary value
- transaction value
- privilege value.

We summarised the combination of offers as 'free, win, save'. Identifying different levels of offer will help conversion; for example, a primary offer and secondary offer to encourage the click-through or visit to the web site. Think about the combination of offers. Web sites that have creative, well thought through acquisition strategies have a combination of offers. The web site in Figure 4.2 has a wide range of offers available.

Finally, as we mentioned at the start of the chapter, it is also worth considering how different incentives will appeal to existing customers and potential customers visiting the web site.

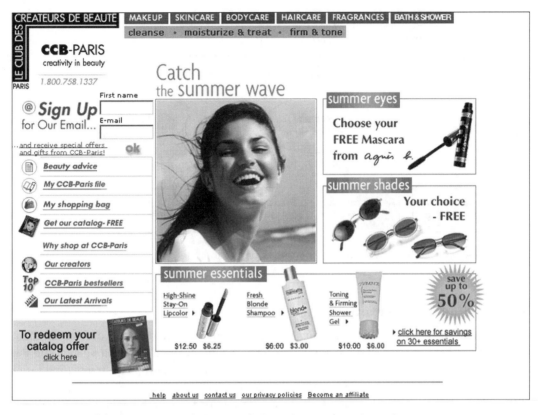

Figure 4.2   Le Club de Createurs de Beaute de Paris (www.ccb-paris.com)

STAGE 2: USING ONLINE AND OFFLINE COMMUNICATIONS TO DRIVE TRAFFIC TO THE WEB SITE

A range of communications can be used to drive traffic to a web site. These techniques will be well known to most e-marketers, so you may wish to skip this section which briefly summarises the options. Note though, that the best techniques change rapidly, so the techniques in which you invested last year may not be the best techniques this year. Figure 4.3 summarises the range of online and offline techniques that are available and that will be considered in this section, starting with the online techniques.

Search engine promotion

With all Internet users actively using search engines, and for many sites, with search engines being the main source of traffic, using search engines effectively is vital. In an e-mail marketing context, search engine promotion is most relevant for driving information seekers to the site, whom we then seek to acquire through relevant offers. However, search engine promotion is also important for other forms of e-mail marketing such as campaign microsites, viral marketing and e-newsletters. If your campaign gains word of mouth and others are seeking it on the Internet, they are likely to use search engines to find it.

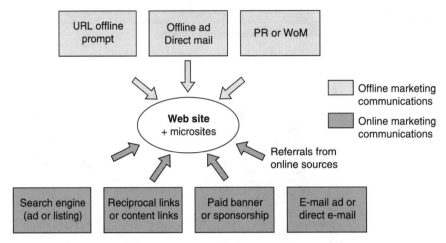

Figure 4.3 Alternative options for online and offline promotion

Search engine representation

The first thing to consider when evaluating your search engine promotion is your search engine representation. Forget about who you think you are registered with or who your agency said they registered with, and look at the facts. Some of the search engines will drop registrants for a variety of reasons. The best way is to refer to your site statistics package or application service provider (ASP) and check the referrers' section (called top referrers or top search engines in WebTrends, which is still the most widely used package). You need to be registered with the top 10 or so search engines that account for the majority of the traffic. To find out the top 10 search engines, look at a compilation such as Danny Sullivan's search engine watch. In many cases, the big three of Yahoo!, Google and MSN will account for over three-quarters of your search engine traffic.

In the 'good old days' registration with search engines was free. With some notable exceptions such as for Google (www.google.com), this is no longer the case. For others such as the Microsoft Network (www.msn.co.uk), it is worthwhile paying to be registered using fast or express inclusion.

Search engine optimisation

After registration, the next thing to consider is how to get the highest listing you can on search engines. The position in which you are listed depends on a complex range of factors that differ from one search engine to the next. These factors are determined according to the process shown in Figure 4.4. Search engine listings are dependent on the match between keywords typed in by users and an index of similar words that have been rated for relevance. The relevance is assessed by information collected from a software agent, referred to as a spider or a robot, when it visits sites that have been registered. The spider will collect information such as where the word appears on the page, whether it occurs in titles or section headers, and so on. This information will be processed by an algorithm which will determine a relevance score for a page. The higher the relevance score, the higher the search engine listing will be. A summary of the factors is included in the checklist in this section.

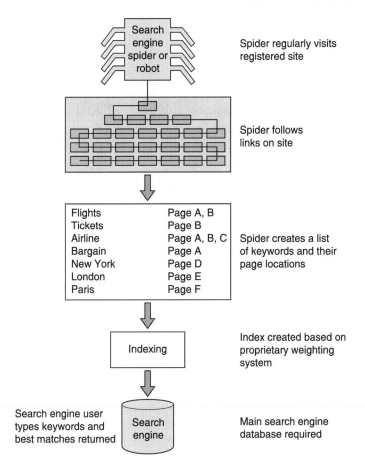

Figure 4.4 Search engine indexing process

It is generally agreed that if you are not in the top 10 or so of site details or 'hits' returned by search engines, then you will be missing out on getting your name in front of search engine users. Of course, to be in the top three or four is preferable. How easy it is to get in the first 10 is largely dependent on the keywords you are using. If you use a generic keyword such as 'insurance' it will be very difficult owing to intense competition. If you are offering a niche product that may be sought with keywords such as 'women car insurance old cars' it is easier to get a higher listing. Many of the companies that offer 'guaranteed top 10' listings will achieve this through combinations of specialised keywords.

So, once registered, the objective is to get your site into the top 10 of site listings by search engines for your category. The process is widely known as *search engine optimisation*. How is this optimisation achieved? Well, the answer is somewhere between an art and a science, and techniques that work are constantly changing. For this reason, many e-marketers turn to specialist agencies who need to keep up to date and keep delivering results to stay in business. For those who cannot afford these agencies or who like to keep up with the latest techniques, two of the best guides are by Danny Sullivan: Searchenginewatch (www.searchenginewatch.com) and the Clickz weekly columns at www.clickz.com. It is very difficult to summarise the complex art of search engine optimisation, but I have attempted to highlight some of the key aspects to watch out for in the checklist below.

E-MAIL CAMPAIGN CHECKLIST

How well is your site or microsite registered with search engines?

1. *Is it a regular process?* Search engine algorithms change, search engine popularity changes and so does your competitors' activity. Depending on the importance of search engine-derived traffic to your business, you need to regard search engine promotion as a regular activity, whether it is monthly, 6 monthly or yearly.

2. *Revise body copy.* You should use tools such as Keywordcount to examine the frequency of keywords and then increase keyword density, particularly at top of the page.

3. *Review title tags for each page.* These are indicated to the search engines by the <TITLE> HTML tag which instructs the browser to make them appear at the top of the page. Do your <TITLE> tags vary by page, do they just include the company name, or do they include a product or service name which will help boost your search engine position?

4. *Review meta tags.* These are HTML tags in the header of the document that are not visible to the reader of the page, but act as summaries for the search engines. View them by choosing View, Source in Internet Explorer. Examples of the two most important meta tags from my site Marketing Online (www.-marketing-online.co.uk) are:

< meta NAME="keywords" CONTENT="Internet marketing training, Internet, marketing, Internet marketing, links, e-marketing training, e-commerce, electronic commerce, e-business, on-line, online, marketing, electronic commerce, strategy, strategic, marketing communications, marketing planning, consultancy, audits, design, talks, briefings, workshops, seminars, UK, British, Britain, International, European, Europe, information" >

< meta NAME="description" CONTENT="Marketing Online is a knowledge source about Internet marketing and e-marketing for marketing professionals and students. Internet Marketing training courses available." >

The keywords meta tag example above shows that you should include a range of alternative keywords for your particular service and narrow down scope geographically. Note, though, that you can have too many keywords: most search engines work on keyword density, so it may be more effective to simplify to 10 keywords than 30. Note also that meta tags are not the only criteria used by search engines, indeed Google is thought to ignore them completely.

5. *Review keywords in headings <H1> and links.* Some search engines also increase relevance if your keywords are used in the section headers. Many sites will use graphics for headings, so may miss out on this. Links to particular sites that include the keywords may also boost relevancy.

6. *Check Image ALT tags.* To display a graphic to a browser the following HTML instruction is used:

   < IMG SRC="logo.gif" ALT="Company name, service name" >

   Many designers do not use the ALT tag, since they do not know its relevance, but it can help to boost keyword relevance.

7. *Think doorway pages.* Although at number 7 in this list, doorway pages are very important. They use the techniques described above, but optimised for particular keywords and specific search engines. They have links to the home page (or relevant content page), but not in the reverse direction, so they are submitted separately to the index page.

8. *Use Keywordcount and Wordtracker.* These are tools to identify alternative keywords. Use Keywordcount (www.keywordcount.com) to assess current keywords used by your site and competitors. Use Word Tracker (www.wordtracker.com) to identify suitable keywords from its database of keywords used by the search engine.

9. *Run a link-building campaign.* Remember that Google page rank uses the number of links into your site, with weightings for the most popular sites, as a criterion. This is often neglected by search engine optimisation companies. You should develop a campaign to maximise the number of links in to your site.

10. *Subscribe to Searchenginewatch.com or hire a professional.* The techniques that work change subtly and continuously. Take steps to follow the changes.

Search engine advertising

Serving a relevant banner advertisement when a particular keyword is entered has been established practice since the mid-1990s, when the original search engines such as Altavista and the Yahoo! Directory used this technique. While this approach is still available, the decline in clickthrough rates from banner adverts has seen new techniques become more popular. Placing a text advert with a link next to it is now available in a variety of search engines, and for now offers a popular way to advertise due to higher reported response rates than banner adverts and because campaign cost is based not on the number of adverts served (e.g. £20 per 1000, CPM), but on the number of clickthroughs achieved. As a result, this is often referred to as pay per click (PPC) advertising.

Brokers are typically used to place these text adverts on different search engines. The two most important are Overture (www.overture.com) and Espotting (www.espotting.com). In addition,

Google (https://adwords.google.com) has its own Adwords Select programme which is cost per click (CPC) and an Adwords programme which is cost per thousand (CPM). An indication of the service provided by Espotting is shown in Figure 4.5. Bid management software Such as GoToast (www.gotoast.com) can be used across a range of services to optimise the costs of search engine advertising. Amounts are capped such that advertisers do not pay more than the maximum they have deposited.

The position of adverts in the search engine is usually above the returned results, where they are highlighted as 'sponsored' or 'featured' links. Google Adwords selected links are to the right of the results in Figure 4.6. Within this list, companies bid to be featured near the top; often, only the top three are displayed.

Clearly, advertisers will consider the advertising costs carefully in relation to the initial purchase value or lifetime value that they feel they will achieve from the average customer. Table 4.1 shows how costs differ between different keywords from generic to specific. The initial purchase cost can be calculated as follows:

$$\text{Initial purchase cost} = (100/\text{Conversion rate}) * \text{Cost Per Click}$$

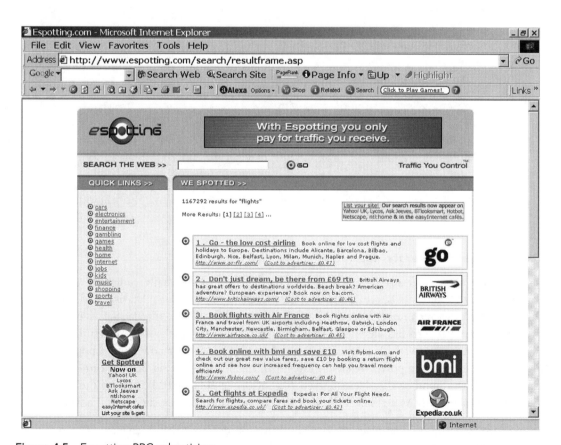

Figure 4.5 Espotting PPC advertising

Figure 4.6 Google advertising displayed for 'Internet marketing training'

Table 4.1 Representative costs from Espotting

Keyword or keyphrase	Cost per click	Initial purchase cost at 10% conversion rate	At 1% conversion rate
Insurance	£1.61	£16.10	£161.00
Car insurance	£1.18	£11.80	£118.00
Women's car insurance	£0.30	£3.00	£30.00
Old car insurance	£0.05	£0.50	£5.00

Given the range in costs, two types of strategy can be pursued in PPC search engine advertising. If budget permits, a premium strategy can be followed to compete with the major competitors who are bidding the highest amounts. Such a strategy is based on being able to achieve an acceptable conversion rate once the customers are driven through to the web site. This is not a form of advertising to use unless the effectiveness of the web site in converting visitors to buyers is known. Using specific landing pages from these adverts can also be used. A lower cost strategy involves bidding on more specific phrases, such as old car insurance. These will generate less traffic, so it will be necessary to devise a lot of these phrases to match the traffic from premium keywords.

USING A RENTED LIST OF E-MAILS TO ACQUIRE CUSTOMERS VIA E-MAIL

Rental of a list provides a more rapid method of gaining customers than gradually building a house list. Here, a list of e-mail addresses is purchased and then sent to potential customers with an offer that is again intended to obtain permission to contact a prospect in future. Subsets of lists are usually purchased according to different criteria such as age, gender or income. These subsets are chosen by applying 'selects' against the database. This term derives from the Structured Query Language (SQL) query that is performed, for example:

SELECT * FROM list WHERE Sex="MALE" AND Income>50000

The Virgin Atlantic Fly Free for Life campaign referred to in Chapter 1 used these lists, selects and numbers:

TheMutual.net	HTML & Text	10 000	30+, £40k+, have clicked on travel offers
DoubleClick	HTML & Text	15 000	Economy, professional
Claritas	HTML & Text	15 000	Economy travellers, non-European destinations
Guardian newsletter	Text	5 × 35 000	Long-haul travellers
Virgin Wines database	HTML & Text	90 000	

Of the 190 523 e-mails delivered there was a clickthrough rate of around 30%, resulting in over 50 000 visits to the microsite. So, buying good-quality lists with the right selects to produce a targeted audience, combined with the right offer and creative buying lists, can be a very effective method of building the house list.

Remember that with e-mail lists, you often pay for a single contact with the customer: you do not actually own the list or have a physical copy. The e-mail list is carefully controlled by the list owner so that unsubscribes can be managed and it remains opt-in, and the list is not used to contact customers too frequently with similar offers. It is important that the steps above are followed to maximise collection of e-mail addresses when the customers visit the microsite intended to capture their details.

Of course, the list that is purchased must be opt-in, otherwise it is nothing less than SPAM. So, when looking to purchase a list from a broker or the list owner, the first question should always be 'is it an opt-in list'? Unfortunately, the answer will usually be 'yes', whether this is the case or not, so a follow-up question should always ascertain the exact opt-in mechanism. In spring 2002, the E-Mail Marketing Association (EMMA), castigated list owners for selling lists that purported to be opt-in, but were in fact opt-out. In a later section in this chapter (see Figure 4.13), we see that a true opt-in form involves a positive action on behalf of the subscriber by checking a box. Many lists have used an opt-out approach.

Even if a consumer has agreed to receive e-mails by opting in, there is a risk, particularly if time has elapsed, that they did not recall doing this. This presents a danger since, if the consumer receives an e-mail as part of this list, they may perceive it as SPAM, particularly if the name of the sender is different to the party that originally collected the data. For this reason it is vital to use a statement of origination in the body of the e-mail when dispatching e-mails. The statement of origination highlights the list owner (who collected the data) and who the list was sent on behalf of. A typical statement of origination is:

> *This e-mail is sent to you using opt-in contact information that you supplied to <list owner>. It is sent on behalf of <company name renting list>. For more information please visit <www.listowner.com>.*

Such a statement of origination should appear at either the top or bottom of the e-mail. Many prefer the top to avoid the perception of SPAM and encourage the reader to read on. Figure 4.7 gives an example of this approach. It can be argued that such a statement of origination should be included in all e-mail, even if it is to a house list, since a prospect or customer may have forgotten that they opted in to receiving the e-mail.

Is a landing page necessary?

Standard practice when mailing to an opt-in list is to use the call-to-action hyperlink to direct the recipient to a landing page. A form on this page is then used to capture e-mail addresses and profile the respondent. With the increase in ability to receive HTML e-mail, an alternative is to include the form within the e-mail. This could arguably reduce the attrition of clicking through. However, a strong argument against using this approach for B2B campaigns is that the JavaScript used to validate forms may not be allowed through company firewalls. Alternatively, as we will see in Chapter 7, the HTML may be stripped completely by some firewalls, or not displayed correctly in corporate groupware packages such as Lotus Notes or Novell Groupwise.

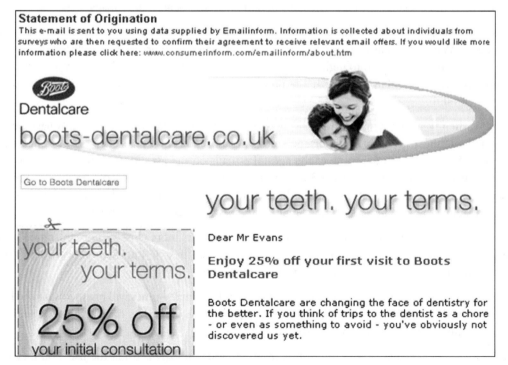

Figure 4.7 Opt-in e-mail campaign to a rented list from Claritas (www.claritasinteractive.co.uk)

List management

You should also check who manages opting out from the list. Opt-outs can only realistically be managed by a single party. This means that the e-mail addresses on an opt-in list will not typically be provided to you when you rent or purchase. Typically, when you rent an opt-in e-mail list it will be for a broadcast, or series of broadcasts controlled by the list owner, who will manage all of the opt-outs or unsubscribes. Managing unsubscribes would be difficult to impossible if the list were rented or provided to different purchasers for a period.

E-MAIL MARKETING INSIGHT

When sending e-mails to an opt-out list, a statement of origination should always be used to highlight the list owner (who collected the data) and who the list was sent on behalf of.

More questions to ask when purchasing an opt-in list

When purchasing an opt-in list, many of the questions to ask a list vendor or list broker will be similar to those for a traditional list. Typical questions and issues are:

- *Is the list opt-in and what form of opt-in was used?* (This has been covered above.)

- *Location of e-mail capture*: which particular site was used to collect e-mails and profile information? Was it an independent site set up for this purpose (see section on acquisition centres, below) or is it associated with a particular content site such as an online magazine?

- *Invalid e-mail addresses*: how often is the list cleaned of duplicates and out-of-date e-mail addresses? What mechanism is used for this? Check whether there is a straightforward opt-out mechanism that will lead to higher responses. Also ask what the typical bounce rate is on past campaigns (as explained in Chapter 3, a bounce occurs when the e-mail is returned because it is no longer valid).

- *Recency*: when were the e-mails on the list added? You need to ask how long e-mails have been collected on the list. This is important since the more recent the e-mails, the higher the response. So, ask about the profile of the ages of e-mails on the list. For instance, what proportion are less than 1 year, 6 months or 3 months old? Is it possible to select according to the age of e-mails on the list? Some list owners send out a probe e-mail to detect which e-mail addresses are still valid. An example of such an e-mail from emarketer.com is shown below.

- *Targeting options*: what selects can be used to target consumers more closely? For consumer lists, age, gender and postcode would be expected, but is further lifestyle information available? The box below shows the options available on the Claritas list.

- *Exclusivity*: a key concern is the previous use of the list. How many times will prospects on the list have received e-mails? A particular concern is competitor use of the list: have there been similar offers, or offers from competitors? If so, when was this?

- *Responsiveness*: you can ask about the results from previous campaigns using the list. You may be met with a 'how long is a piece of string?' answer, saying that it will depend on the quality of the creative, offer, timing and targeting, as reviewed in the last chapter. However, what about the best campaigns using the list: what response did these achieve?

Testing lists

Purchasing an unknown or unproven list can result in disappointing quality, in terms of both bounces from the list and response rate, so always test if the list is unproven. As well as testing the quality of the list, the effectiveness of different selects can be evaluated. Typically, 1000 addresses may be used for a test and, if successful, this will be scaled up. Testing can also be performed for the subject, creative and offer. However, if you do the full range of tests with 1000 addresses you could soon use up all of the targeted members on the list you are considering. Another method is to test aspects such as the offer and creative with other online forms such as banner advertising.

Cost-related questions

It will be apparent that the questions above relate mainly to the quality of the list. Once you are happy that the list is of suitable quality, you can turn to the question of cost. The main issue is the CPM. The rate card costs can be expected to vary between £100 and £300 per thousand. Some vendors will charge according to the number of selects, so closer targeting, using more selects, may add a cost of £50 per additional selects.

Other cost questions concern how much is charged for additional services. These costs will depend on how the cost is split among the list owner, the broker and those broadcasting the e-mail. Assuming that you are talking to a single supplier, check whether the following will cost extra:

* *testing*: can you sample the list by sending one e-mail to 1000 list members?

* *transmission*: is there an additional cost for transmission? The typical cost is between 1 and 5 pence per thousand.

* *tracking*: is there an additional cost for measuring and reporting? Some vendors charge for this separately, but it is an inclusive cost for most.

A description of all the costs of an e-mail campaign was included in the budgeting section of Chapter 3.

Customer acquisition centres

The Internet has proved a paradise for 'compers', consumers who love to enter competitions and prize draws. Thanks to the hyperlink, such consumers can now visit a single site which links to a range of competitions and can enter more competitions than ever before. For example, Loquax (www.loquax.co.uk) offers a directory of the latest links. Demand for such sites has provided the impetus for many companies to build very large lists of consumer e-mails. They have created portals that offer 'compers' and other Internet users the chance to sign up to competitions and other offers, but only on an opt-in basis.

Some of these companies, such as Claritas with E-mail inform (www.emailinform.co.uk) and Consodata with Yoptin (www.yoptin.com), are established database marketing organisations. Others, such as Offer Me More (www.offermemore.com) from Context Partners (Figure 4.8) and OK-Mail (www.ok-mail.co.uk) from IPT Ltd, are newer entrants. What they share is the size of the lists, which have been created in a very short time, which range from hundreds of thousands to over a million. ProMail, which manages such acquisition centres for several companies, now has over 8 million subscribers, of which some may be multiple registrants. Many of these acquisition centres have partnered with major portals to help to build subscribers. Offer Me More, for example, is available to Lycos users.

For business-to-consumer (B2C) organisations these acquisition centres offer tremendous potential for customer acquisition. Why focus all your efforts on trying to drive traffic to your own site when you can partner with other sites with established traffic levels? Companies that offer promotions such as a prize draw on one of these sites can then add all entrants to its house list for future use in campaigns which aim to convert these prospects into customers.

Figure 4.8   Offer Me More

E-MAIL MARKETING EXCELLENCE

The Gardeners Club recruits members through OK-mail permission list

The Gardeners Club (www.gardenersclub.co.uk) is just like any other club for people interested in the garden, but online. We need to recruit members to The Gardeners

Club and feel that using e-marketing through permission-based email campaigns could prove a most productive communications channel. There are a number of operators offering various e-marketing email services and we have recently tested a number including OK-mail.

What we wanted to achieve

We wanted to compare the cost of membership recruitment with other marketing activities that we have used (e.g. above and below the line advertising and other direct marketing initiatives). We set an objective through the OK-mail campaign to recruit a new member at a cost of £2.50 or less.

How many sent out

Our target audience is broad; all those with a declared interest in the garden, gardening, garden products and services and related areas. A test sample base of 22 000 was selected.

Extra incentives

For comparative purposes, no additional inducement was provided: membership to The Gardeners Club is free.

Results

From our own tracking analysis we found that approximately 10% of the sample 'clicked-through' from the email to The Gardeners Club web site. The Gardeners Club operates a closed site (visitors must become members to access the whole club site) apart from the introductory pages. Pleasingly, conversion of a visitor to member was comparable to previous findings in that 60%+ of new visitors from the OK-mail campaign registered as members. Overall, a conversion of around 6% membership was achieved from the sample at the maximum target cost.

Source: Martin Kiersnowski IPT (www.ipt-ltd.co.uk). Article by David White, Sales and Marketing Director, The Gardeners Club.

E-mail appending

E-mail appending works by a service bureau comparing your customer file against a compiled file of opted-in e-mail addresses. All matched people receive an e-mail explaining that, as customers of the company, they will receive e-mails from your company unless they opt out.

As Dwek (2002) points out, e-mail appending sounds like a great solution since you pay only per e-mail match. However, he says that he knows of half a dozen companies that tested appending, not one of which rolled out or even retested. Part of the reason for this is that if e-mails are added in this way, customers have not proactively signed up, so are less likely to be responsive than opt-in companies. A further problem is accuracy. What if the e-mail addresses on the list are out of date, or are secondary e-mail addresses? Many Internet users have multiple e-mail accounts. Dwek (2002) reports that studies indicate that 3% of all e-mail addresses change each month, so if you are matching against a list where the average name is a year old, up to 36% of the e-mail addresses you match are likely to be out of date! For these reasons Dwek suggestions caution in using appending services, but suggests that there are two situations where they may help. First, when you have collected a substantial proportion of customer e-mail addresses, you could use the technique for those you have not been able to collect actively. Secondly, you could use the technique to contact inactive customers with a view to reactivating them.

An additional form of appending for B2B companies is to check known formats of e-mail addresses for different companies to compare with customer names. So, a customer, Daniella Kelly West, who works for company Plastech with a web address of Plastech.com, is likely to have an e-mail address of:

daniella.west@plastech.com
dwest@plastech.com
d.west@plastech.com or
westd@plastech.com

Other combinations using middle names or initials such as d.k.west@plastech.com are more diffi-cult to ascertain unless middle names are known. An e-mail can be sent to each of these addresses and the one that does not bounce is known to be a valid address.

Banner advertising, including advertising in third-party e-mails

We will look at two forms of banner advertising that can be used for driving traffic to a web site. First, traditional banner advertising on another web site, then advertising in e-mail newsletters. Since this is a book on e-mail marketing we will spend more time on the second option, although it is used less widely.

Placing banner advertising on third-party sites

The decline in popularity of banner adverts has been well-documented as clickthrough rates fell from single digit to ever-decreasing percentages. The effectiveness of banner adverts in creating a response seems to have declined as Internet users have become familiar with banner adverts and their novelty, and have subconsciously filtered them out. However, banner advertising is not dead. The portals on which the majority of adverts are served have not taken the decline in one of their main revenue streams lying down. New larger advertisement formats such as skyscrapers and large block adverts have increased the impact of banners, and revised costs per thousand have helped to attract advertisers. There has also been a realisation that with the new formats, the role of banners is not just the immediate response. Brand awareness is enhanced and many tracking studies have shown that with awareness, action often follows at a later stage. Taken together, these factors have meant that banner advertising is far from dead, and in most countries advertising revenue is growing, often as traditional media advertising is declining.

Figure 4.9 shows a simple model of banner advertising. The portal visitor who clicks on a banner advert at an advertising site is then referred through to the site of the company who paid for the banner advert (destination site, Figure 4.9). This provides landing page content tailored to the campaign that appears immediately on clickthrough without the distractions of a link to the standard site. At this point an offer is often used to encourage e-mail disclosure. Alternatively, the link can take the prospect through to a landing page on a microsite.

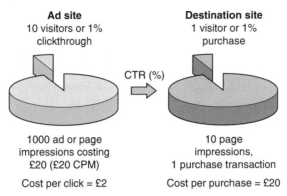

Ad site
10 visitors or 1%
clickthrough

Destination site
1 visitor or 1%
purchase

CTR (%)

1000 ad or page
impressions costing
£20 (£20 CPM)

Cost per click = £2

10 page
impressions,
1 purchase transaction

Cost per purchase = £20

Figure 4.9   A simple banner advertising model

Although banner advertising is usually thought of simply as a traffic building technique, there are several alternative objectives which were first summarised by Cartellieri et al. (1997):

- *deliver content*: information on-site can help to communicate a company's offering.

- *enable transaction*: an e-tailer may use banner adverts to increase sales.

- *shape attitudes*: an advert that is consistent with a company brand can help to build brand awareness.

- *solicit response*: an advert may be intended to identify new leads or as a start for two-way communication.

- *encourage retention*: an advert may be placed to remind prospects about the company and its service.

Creative options for banner adverts are generally limited in size to the CASIE standards, although the advertising industry is still experimenting with new formats which have greater impact. The full banner advert is the most important. Banner adverts are based on .GIF graphic files that are usually hosted on a separate server. To the user, these appear as part of the web page. 'Interstitial' adverts can either be adverts incorporated within text on the page or intermediate adverts before another page appears. Superstitials are pop-up adverts that require interaction by the user to close them down. Banners can also be static, not changing over time, or more commonly animated, typically with a rotation of three to five different images. More sophisticated varieties are interactive, where the user can type in an e-mail address to register for information, or rich media, using a combination of animation, video and even sound.

As for traditional advertising, testing creative is important, but banner adverts have the benefit that they can be updated during the campaign in line with the clickthrough response. The creative of many of the adverts encourages the user to clickthrough with devices such as 'Click here'.

Banner advertising is purchased for a specific period. It may be purchased for the advert to be served:

- on the run-of-site (the entire site)

- on a relevant section of the site

- according to keywords entered on a search engine.

Payment is typically according to the number of customers who view the page as a CPM advert or page impressions. Typical CPM is in the range of £10–50. Other options that benefit the advertiser if they can be agreed are: per clickthrough, e.g. Valueclick (www.valueclick.co.uk), or per action, such as a purchase on the destination site.

Banners can be targeted through:

- purchasing on a site (or part of site) with a particular visitor profile

- purchasing at a particular time of day or week

- banner advert networks: companies such as DoubleClick provide the facility to advertise on a range of their properties and target in a range of ways as shown, in the E-marketing excellence box below.

E-MAIL MARKETING EXCELLENCE

DoubleClick

DoubleClick offers advertisers the ability to dynamically target advertisements on the Web through its 'DART' targeting technology. There are four basic categories of targeting criteria:

1. *Content targeting.* Allows placement of advertising message on a particular interest site or within an entire interest category such as Automotive, Business and Finance or Entertainment.

2. *Behavioural targeting.* An audience can be targeted according to how they use the Web. For example, advertisers can select business users by delivering advertisements on Monday–Friday between 9 a.m. and 5 p.m., or leisure users by targeting messages in the evening hours.

3. *User targeting.* This enables advertisements to be placed according to specific traits of the audience including their geographic location (based on country or Zip code), domain type (for example, educational users with addresses ending in .edu or .ac.uk can be targeted), business size or type according to SIC code or even by the company for which they work, based on the company domain name.

4. *Tech targeting.* This is based on user hardware, software and Internet access provider. For example, engineers tend to use UNIX operating systems and graphic designers tend to use Macintosh systems.

PLACING ADVERTISING IN THIRD-PARTY E-MAIL NEWSLETTERS

Placing advertising in a third-party e-mail newsletter may be a more favourable option than traditional banner advertising. If the content of the newsletter is well-targeted to the audience, then engagement will be high, and it is arguably less easy to avoid an advert in an e-mail newsletter. Combined with the right creative and offer, the clickthrough should be significantly better than with traditional banner advertising, which is in single digits.

Banner adverts will vary in format according to the newsletter format. Adverts in text e-mails are generally less easy to ignore than those in HTML e-mails, where the adverts are more consistent with traditional banner adverts. This, however, depends on the impact of the banner advert, which is determined by its size, animation and colour contrast with the remainder of the e-mail. E-mail newsletters with informative content are also often printed for reference, so consider the impact of the advert in the printed version. Other factors that will affect the impact will be the number of advertisers, your position in the newsletter and the ratio of copy to adverts. If there are more than three advertisers in a newsletter you are bound to have less impact than if you are the only one in a newsletter.

To consider your options for positioning and costs of advertising, view the media kit for one of the main opt-in list suppliers. For example, at the time of writing, for ListUniverse (list-universe.com/media-kit/) the following options are available to the site hosting the content:

- *Feature Advert Position (Skyscraper Vertical Web Banner)*: advert placed to the left or right of a range of content; $2500 per week.

- *HeadsUp*: for List-Universe, each advert includes a headline, six lines of text, URL and logo or image. Options are top, middle and bottom, with rate card rates from $500 to $75 per week.

- *Banner adverts*: these are $15 CPM for the top and $10 CPM for the bottom.

- *Advertorial*: a 200–300 word article by the editorial staff relevant to the list reader, often a case study featuring the company's services; $750 per week.

- *E-mail text adverts*: these are for reaching the audience when they are scanning through text e-mail newsletters, before they have clicked through on the links to receive the richer content and adverts described above. These are seven times 60 characters including the URL, and cost $20 CPM for premium position.

When considering which newsletter to advertise in, there will typically be a choice of high-reach newsletters that will be more expensive and less expensive options with a smaller reach. From your budget you may only be able to afford one placement in a newsletter if it is to an audience of say 50 000. For a list to a smaller, niche audience of say 5000, it may be possible to afford a placement each month throughout the year. Repeated exposure should lead to greater recall of the advert and the overall number of leads may be higher. You can also experiment with different offers and creative. However, if you have a great offer and you get the creative right first time, the high-reach newsletter may be the best option.

As for traditional banner advertising, you will have a choice of CPM, CPC or cost per customer acquisition. Since the number on the list is known, there is usually a single fee for an advert, relating to its position in the e-mail. If possible, you should negotiate a CPC deal.

Finding the best lists in which to advertise is difficult in the sense that there are millions of them. However, the marketer is likely to know the best lists, since they may already be subscribing to them; if they do not, search engines will turn up the best-quality newsletters. For the B2B marketer, e-mail newsletters from trade associations, trade magazines, conference organisers, and independent analysts and portals all offer options. The B2C marketer should try the resources of lists such as List central (www.listcentral.com) or Listz (www.listz.com).

USENET

There are over tens of thousands of specialist Usenet newsgroups, to which millions of messages are posted each day. Usenet provides discussion forums or electronic bulletin boards used by communities of interest. For example, I may read uk.rec.climbing, which has questions posted about rock climbing. Questions or statements are posted by one person who is looking for further information and others will reply, and lists of related questions will be held together in what is known as a 'thread'. Usenet is mainly used by special-interest groups such as people discussing their favourite pastime. They are not used much by businesses, unless it is as a means of studying consumer behaviour. There are some newsgroups for announcing the introduction of new products or staff vacancies. Newsgroups tend not to be used extensively by business people or consumers, since they have to be aware of them and have the technical know-how to set them up. Setup can be difficult because a special piece of software known as a newsreader used to be required to read and contribute to newsgroups. When web browsers were developed, additional newsreaders were developed as extra modules; however, it was less clear how to access these in comparison with a web browser. Today, it is much easier to access newsgroups, since specialist web sites and search engines such as Google (www.google.com) enable users to access newsgroups without the need for special software.

The marketing applications of newsgroups usually involve obtaining ad hoc marketing research in the form of feedback from customers. For example, a company manufacturing cat food may find comments in the rec.pets.cats newsgroups. These may be positive or negative comments about a brand, but each will be useful. Another example might be a pharmaceutical company that monitors sci.med.pharmacy for news about new drugs that are being introduced by its competitors, or perhaps unofficial information from clinical trials. By posting to such groups and other forums awareness about a company can be raised and some clickthroughs may be achieved through the e-mail signatures.

Newsgroups are named in a particular format, broken down into several parts, the first part usually indicating the type of information or country to which it refers and the last part the specific topic:

- alt: alternative, e.g. alt.comedy.british or alt.music.kylie-minogue

- rec: recreation, includes the largest number of groups, e.g. rec.climbing or uk.rec.climbing

- talk: discussions, e.g. talk.politics.tibet

- biz: business, a surprisingly small number of these, e.g. biz.marketplace.investors is used to offer new investment products

- comp: computer queries solved, e.g. comp.virus

- sci: range of scientific discussions and opinions, e.g. sci.med.cardiology, or documents

- soc: social issues, e.g. soc.geneaology.misc

Offline traffic building

Since most of us spend more time in the real world than the virtual world and established communications tools and media work, the role of offline communications techniques should not be underestimated. Often, in large organisations, however, the e-marketers do not have control of the advertising budget, so the opportunity may be missed.

Advertising

Much offline advertising of a company's online presence is incidental rather than specific. By incidental I mean that the web address is added as an afterthought to the print, outdoor or TV advertisement. This is often deliberate. If we are advertising insurance, for example, we would prefer viewers to phone up rather than using the Internet, where they may easily be diverted from our offer. It is not surprising that much direct response advertising still uses the phone to generate leads: it works best. There may be some circumstances, however, where the web can be used to manage direct response. For example, a Mastercard prize draw to win tickets to the 2002 World Cup used TV advertising to drive site traffic as means of gathering e-mail addresses. Alternatively, if we are serious about using offline media to drive traffic we can use more than a web address to appeal. Print advertising can readily feature an Internet value proposition as part of a strap line related to the web address. Regardless of the form of advertising, if its aim is to capture e-mail addresses, do try to use a URL that helps you to track the campaign and avoids the need for the customer to try to find the relevant offer on the home page. It is still common to see adverts with the URL:

> *www.company.com*

For user convenience, a better choice would be:

> *www.company1.com/<insert campaign name here>*

But best for tracking advert effectiveness is:

> *www.company1.com/<insert campaign name here> + referrer digit (e.g. 1)*

PR

PR is a powerful and relatively low-cost form of offline communication. There is still demand among the general and specialist media for stories about e-everything, provided it is fresh news. PR can leverage events such as site launches and relaunches with new services, particularly when they are first in a sector. Press releases can be issued through normal channels, but using e-mail linked to the full story on the web site to send information to the journalists more rapidly. Options for getting mentions on the new online-only news sources and listings should also be explored.

The WhatsNextOnline e-newsletter (Whatsnextonline E-newsletter 2002) reported in a survey of 277 journalists that the journalists thought that a one-screen, tightly targeted e-mail pitch rather than a mass mailing through a wire service was the way to reach them. The newsletter reported their biggest complaints with PR pitches was that they were not newsworthy, not relevant to their area and full of hype. They want the pitch 'fluff-free in the body of an e-mail, not as an attachment'.

Direct mail

Physical reminders about web-site offers are important since, as we said before, most of our customers spend more time in the real world than in the virtual world. What is in our customers' hands and on their desktop will act as a prompt to visit your site and overcome the weakness of the web as a pull medium. Examples include brochures, catalogues, business cards, point of sale material, trade shows, direct mail sales promotions, postcards (in magazines), inserts (in magazines) and password reminders (for extranets).

STAGE 3: REVISING WEB-SITE DESIGN TO EMPHASISE OFFER

When your web site was first designed, how important a criterion would you say was the visual prominence of offers to acquire customers? Judging by many current sites, the answer is that it was low priority. Yet one of the main aims of a web site has to be converting visitors to customers. This will not happen unless it is a design objective. In the Big Red Fez, Seth Godin presents many examples of where visitors are not encouraged to action. He says:

> *I imagine the web as a series of offer pages, all competing for us to click. And if those sites make it really clear and obvious where the monkey's banana is, then the time-starved, not very bright consumer (that's you and me folks!) will go for it.*
>
> *Some people might object to the characterisation of web surfers as monkeys. After all, they say, we are smarter than that. No actually, we're not ... we're busy or distracted, or we have never been to a particular site before and we're not mind readers.*

E-MAIL MARKETING INSIGHT

Maximise lead generation from your web site through evaluating site design and offers.

The example below gives an example of how CommonTime has revised its site design to improve acquisition. We can also make these general points about how to increase conversion rate:

1. Try to increase the prominence of calls-to-action, by:
   (a) improving position on screen: are calls-to-action above the fold, or do visitors have to scroll down to reach them?
   (b) size: how prominent are they? Can you see the acquisition wood from the brochureware trees? Use of graphical banners can assist.
   (c) colour: is a distinctive colour (in keeping with the design of the site) used to highlight the call-to-action?
   (d) animation: can movement be used to draw attention to the call-to-action?
2. Increase the range of calls-to-action on the home page as shown in the example in Figure 4.2.
3. Don't neglect text-based calls-to-action. If your graphical calls-to-action look too much like banner adverts, then some site visitors may naturally filter them out. Try different forms of words for the calls-to-action or the heading.

4. Look at consumer concerns. Think about the barriers that may stop them giving their details. Is your privacy statement prominent enough? Is it clear or impenetrable? Have you explained why you are asking them to provide their details?

5. Don't forget the big picture. If the design, style and content of the site do not suggest credibility of your organisation to deliver, then it does not matter how prominent the calls-to-action are. The visitor will be more to likely hit the back button.

Finally, experiment with these variables. One of the benefits of web-based marketing is that you can 'suck it and see'. Try changing headings and offers, and count the leads and use the site statistics to monitor the traffic patterns. One approach is to use different URL parameters from different forms of wording to monitor their effectiveness. For example, we could have three links from graphical or text hyperlinks each linking the landing page *register.htm* as follows:

> *http://www.company.com/register.htm?l1*
>
> *http://www.company.com/register.htm?l2*
>
> *http://www.company.com/register.htm?l3*

The number of visitors who have clicked on these three types of links is then highlighted in the referring URLs report of WebTrends or similar packages.

E-MAIL MARKETING EXCELLENCE

CommonTime enhances site design for customer acquisition

Figures 4.10 and 4.11 give an example of how a company has moved from an original, technically led home page design to a marketing-led, conversion-orientated home page design.

STAGE 4: DEFINING PROFILING NEEDS AND CAPTURE FORM

In a similar way to that described in the last section, we can monitor the effectiveness of the landing page in converting those who have expressed an interest to action. You can compare how many leads you receive, compared with how many click on the links and go through to the page. A number of steps can be taken to maximise the response rates.

1. *Information requested on forms should be kept to a minimum.* Make it short. Early practice on information collection through online forms seemed to be to collect as much information as possible to build up profiles of customers. There was a backlash against this, with users refusing to fill in too much information. Some companies then went to the other extreme and captured the minimum information, usually just an e-mail address. Each company should decide on a realistic minimum for its purposes. Remember that you can gain more information on the customer as the relationship develops. We suggest the following minimum information for B2C organisations:

- e-mail address
- first and last name

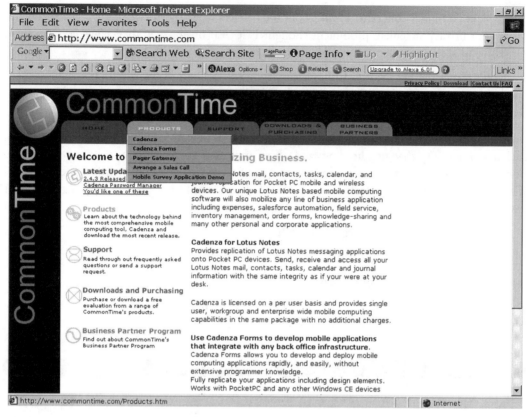

Figure 4.10 Original CommonTime site

- age
- gender
- geographical location
- product interest
- preferred means of communication (opt-in and whether HTML, with pictures for simplicity, or text)

and for B2B:

- e-mail address
- first and last name
- company name
- company size (employees or turnover)
- company sector/product if applicable
- role of individual in buying decision (job title is usually a proxy for this)

Figure 4.11 Enhanced CommonTime site

- number of staff responsible for
- preferred means of communication.

Also remember that we need to record time on list, so another field can automatically be added to the database for date when first added. Yesmail research shows that someone who has opted in within 30 days is more likely to respond than someone who has opted in within the last 90 days.

E-MAIL MARKETING INSIGHT

Minimise attrition from profiling questions by asking the minimum number of questions.

Through an e-mail it will be possible to keep in contact with the customer and work back to other information such as company name and position.

2. *Explain the reason why information is being collected.* A customer will more readily give up personal information and spend time filling in a form if they know the reason why it is being collected. Explain how it will benefit them by the proposition of the communications such as a newsletter.

3. *Explain clearly the use to which data will be put.* This is required by law in a privacy statement, but if the data will not be shared with third parties this should be highlighted since it may encourage opt-in.

4. *Make it easy.* Use the features of HTML to ease data entry. For example, use drop-down lists where appropriate. These improve data quality by giving consistent data in the database. However, don't you hate those lists of 137 countries with Afghanistan at the top? Surely prospects can enter their own country?

5. *Indicate mandatory fields.* Extra information can be collected from customers if they have time by marking essential fields in a suitable way (perhaps with an asterisk or by highlighting in bold).

6. *Validate.* Checks should be performed after the form is filled in to check that the user has filled in all mandatory fields. Fields should also be checked for validity: has the customer entered a valid e-mail address with the '@' symbol, is the postcode or zip code valid? The user should be clearly prompted with what information is wrong and why. Such validation can be performed using scripts such as Javascript.

7. *Provide 'opt-in'.* Check-boxes should be made available that the user can select if they do not want to receive further information through e-mail or communications through other media.

8. *Provide prompt confirmation.* After a user has filled in a form, a company should respond to acknowledge confirmation of receipt as soon as possible and describe what the follow-up actions will be. For example, if a customer has ordered a product, the confirmation note should thank the customer for shopping with the company and state clearly when they can expect to receive the product by courier.

Figure 4.12 shows an example of well laid out forms used to collect customer information from the RS Components company referred to in the case study in Chapter 6. Note that mandatory fields are

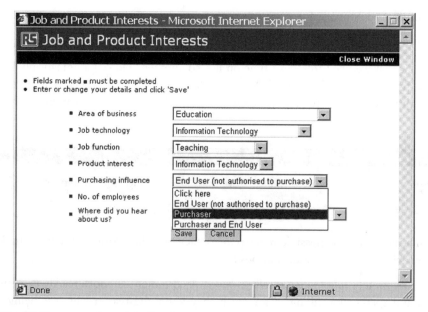

Figure 4.12 RS Components registration form

marked with a square symbol and the company is informing customers about its obligations under the Data Protection Act. In this form, the company is collecting information about the needs of the customer, so that site content and promotions can be matched with the customer's interests.

STAGE 5: SELECTING PERMISSION LEVELS: WHAT DOES OPT-IN REALLY MEAN?

This is important. We covered the merits of opt-in and opt-out as part of the introduction to permission marketing in Chapter 2, but what does opt-in mean in practice, at the level of boxes on forms and associated wording? In making these decisions, what we have to achieve is a balance between obtaining quality profiles and legal and ethical constraints. Many e-mail marketing gurus and legal advisers say that e-mail *must* be opt-in, and this is the received wisdom. But when faced with the reality of designing a form for collecting prospects, the reality is not this simple. Despite the opt-in mantra, many companies are not practising true opt-in: it all depends on how the forms are designed.

True opt-in requires the potential customer to *agree proactively* that they are prepared to receive future communications by selecting the option using a tick-box or ratio-button. Opt-out is where the person completing the form has to *decline proactively* the offer of receiving further communications. Consider the alternatives in Figure 4.13. Which is opt-in? Figure 4.13(a) is clearly an opt-in

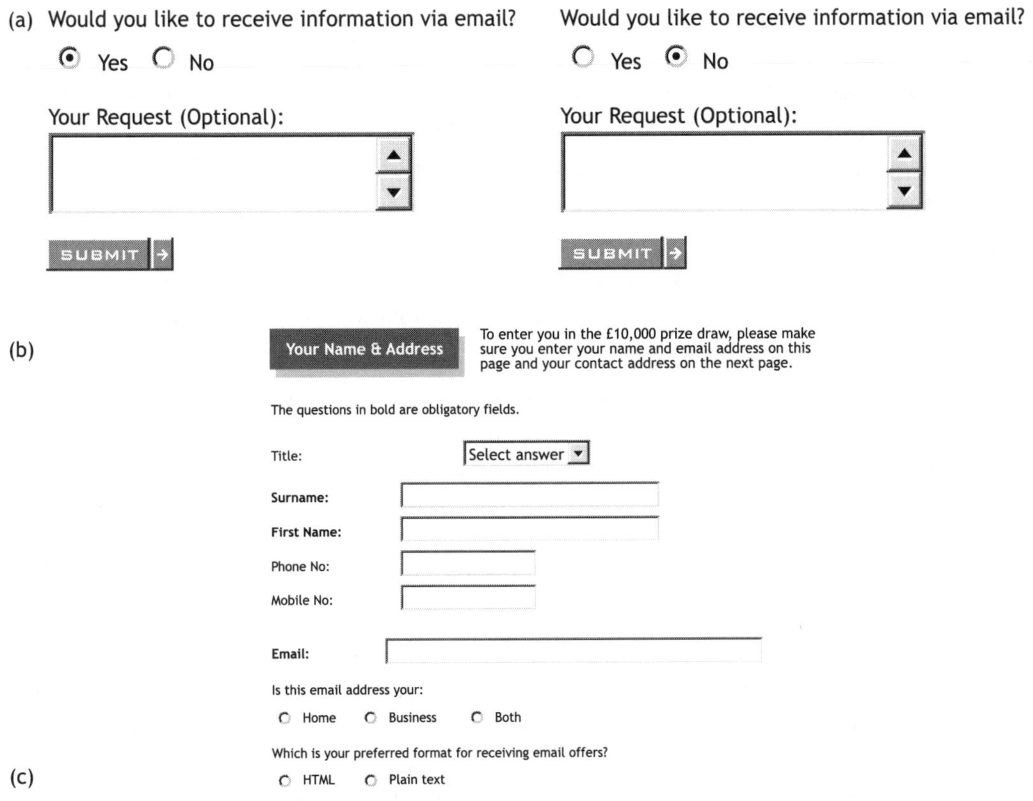

Figure 4.13   Options for obtaining opt-in

form, whereas Figure 4.13(b) is an opt-out design, but what about Figure 4.13(c)? This is less clear: it uses an opt-out approach, but it is more subtle. The implication is, from the way in which the question is phrased, that it is agreed that future information can be received.

Permission marketing is a matter of degree and in the same way SPAM is a matter of degree. So, how can you make the decision as to whether to offer opt-in or opt-out? Several factors are involved, but the most important are the number of responses and brand perception. Proponents of opt-out argue that more targets can be added to the database using this approach since some people filling in the form will not notice or care about this option. However, such members of the list are likely to be less likely to respond to any offers in subsequent e-mails than those who consciously decided not to opt-out, whereas there will be some targets who do. As a result, a greater number of responses will be achieved, although the overall response rate will be lower. Proponents of opt-in argue that if the action is not proactive, then recipients of e-mail will not recall agreeing to receive information. They also argue that the future of legislation is not known and with many proposing a strict opt-in regime, it is safest to collect only opt-in addresses now, as part of planning for the future. Some may view the e-mails received as SPAM and the perception of the brand will be damaged. However, if a statement of origination is included this damage may be ameliorated. An example of a statement of origination is as follows:

'This e-mail is sent to you by/using data supplied by <Company X>

It has been said that 'SPAM is in the eye of the beholder', so to minimise damage, e-mail marketers should view e-mails as a spectrum from pure opt-in to pure SPAM. This is an example of how a business person reacted when they received an unrecognised e-mail:

> *No request was made to me nor permission given to use my personal data and it is therefore an offence under UK and European data protection legislation.*
>
> *I am copying this correspondence to the Information Commissioner with a request to initiate action against you.*

In this case, the prospect had received an e-mail from a rented list, but had no recollection of receiving it. It indicates the need for careful checking with the list provider about the form of opt-in, signing an agreement with them that the data is legal following data protection law, and that they are using a clear statement of origination.

An example of what can happen when a company contacts customers who believe they have opted out is provided by Boots The Chemist. Boots gave applicants for their loyalty card the option to opt out of further (paper-based) mailings. According to a report at Marketing Law (www.market-inglaw.co.uk) over half a million customers did this. When Boots contacted them after some time to explain new promotions there were 28 complaints to the Advertising Standards Authority. In this case, sending out the mailing to those who had opted out was a breach of the data protection law and the complaints were upheld.

Delving a bit deeper, there are two further options available which are both variants of opt-in. Double opt-in is where a confirmation e-mail is sent to the recipient after completion of the initial form. The recipient has to reply to confirm that they wish to receive information. This approach is often required by e-mail list servers (Chapter 7) since, historically, this is the way in which they operate. While this technique has the benefit of making doubly sure that the sender wants to receive the information, there is a nuisance factor involved. Notified opt-in is a more common approach, which involves sending a standard autoresponse e-mail explaining that the subscription has been received, and giving details on how to unsubscribe if the e-mail has been sent in error. Both of these forms of message can also be used for marketing purposes.

One final approach for opt-in is to differentiate between whether communications are desired between the organisation hosting the web site and third-party companies. If there is no intention of generating revenue from selling the e-mail list to third parties it is worth stressing that 'your details will not be passed to third-party companies'. Receiving unexpected e-mails is a common complaint and fear among consumers, so explicitly excluding the possibility of undesired third-party e-mails can help in increasing the number of customers who opt in.

So, which approach to collecting e-mail addresses on online forms is best? We can say that opt-out is best for size of list, but worst for responses and because it will annoy those who cannot recall agreeing to receive information. We can also say that opt-in is best for quality, since it will have higher response rates and is less likely to damage the brand. What is less easy to say is which is best for overall number of responses. Opt-out is likely to give more responses, since some who did not notice that they had the choice of opt-out are likely to respond.

As a summary to this section, see the box 'EMMA definitions of opt-in'.

E-MAIL MARKETING EXCELLENCE

EMMA definitions of opt-in

The E-mail Marketing Association (EMMA, www.emmacharter.org) uses these definitions related to opt-in:

Opt-in means an approach in which a user who desires to be added to a list must request, actively, such as by checking a box on a web page, to be added to the list. Any personal data collected without a positive action from the individual will be deemed to have been collected on an opt-out basis. Without a positive action from the individual, they will be deemed to have opted out of having their personal data being used for direct marketing purposes.

Double opt-in means an approach in which after a subscription has been received and entered, a confirmation E-mail reply containing (i) the source of the subscription request and (ii) instructions to confirm subscription to the list is required.

Notified opt-in means an approach in which after a subscription has been received and entered, a confirmation E-mail reply containing (i) the source of the subscription request, (ii) instructions for how to unsubscribe from the list, and (iii) instructions for how to report that the subscription request was in error is sent to the user.

Opt-out means that a user who is about to be added to a list, at the point of personal data collection, can actively indicate that permission is not granted.

Source: from Charter, E-mail Marketing Association (www.emmacharter.org).

STAGE 6: DRAWING UP A PRIVACY STATEMENT

Many companies have a privacy statement on their web site, but does it cover the right areas? EMMA (www.emmacharter.org) has developed the following guidelines for privacy statements as part of its charter for best practice by its members. This is an abbreviated version of what it suggests should be present in the privacy statement:

1. *Identity of list owner*: the company name and address of the list owner for data that has been collected.

2. *Uses of data*: the uses to which the personal data will be put and the choices the user has regarding the use of the personal data.

3. *Third-party use of data*: the categories of third parties to whom the personal data may be disclosed, including, but not limited to, any list manager, service bureau or database manager.

4. *Nature of data*: the nature of the personal data collected.

5. *Data collection methods*: this refers to collection by techniques that will not be immediately evident to the user. Such techniques include cookies, which are necessary to identify repeat visitors and to reconcile a site visitor to information held about them in a database. Clear-gifs are also referred to. These can be used to record site visits. It is recommended that the privacy policy should explain that the data collected by such techniques does not constitute personal data and is only used for the purposes of analysing the effectiveness of e-mail marketing material. There should also be links to the opt-out sections in relation to the use of such techniques.

6. *Combined data sources*: the possibility that the list owner may acquire information about the user from other sources and add such information to its house files. For example, lifestyle data or credit references could be obtained from another source.

7. *Opt-in policies*: whether the requested personal data is necessary to the transaction between user and list owner, or is voluntary. The consequences of failing to provide the requested information should also be explained.

8. *Security of personal data*: the steps taken by the list owner to ensure the technical and organisational measures taken to protect the security of the personal data.

9. *Opt-out procedures*: explaining how the opt-out process will work.

10. *Access to data*: this describes the processes for the user to be provided with a copy of their personal data, and to contest and correct inaccuracies, or request that their personal data be deleted.

You may also want to consult the latest data protection legislation in your country. For the UK, the legislation is at www.dataprotection.gov.uk/dpdoc.nsf.

STAGE 7: DEFINING THE OPT-OUT

The opt-out should be a prominent notice, usually at the end of the e-mail, which allows user to unsubscribe by e-mail (typically with the word 'UNSUBSCRIBE' in the subject line) or by clicking through to a web page. As we have mentioned, defining the procedure for opt-out is part of the privacy statement. You may know from personal experience that opting out in practice is often difficult. In fact, Spammers use the opt-out reply as a means of checking that yours is a valid e-mail; you are then likely to receive yet more spam. Many opt-out procedures simply do not work. Whether this is deliberate or due to a problem with implementation is unclear.

The opt-out should not necessarily be viewed as a bad thing: it is part and parcel of permission marketing, it will save you expense in targeting someone who is not predisposed to your service, it will even help to increase your response rates. As we said in Chapter 3, the level of opt-outs or unsubscribes should be monitored through time, since a rapid increase in opt-out highlights a problem with a campaign. The opt-out can even be viewed as an opportunity. Perhaps the customer may prefer information about other services that they were unaware of: so offer them alternatives. Perhaps you can use it to research problems with different aspects of the marketing mix or the e-mail marketing itself. Prompt with a short questionnaire or a free-form field to obtain feedback. The BBC Alert site (www.bbc.co.uk/alert) is a good example of best practice in this area.

E-MAIL MARKETING BEST PRACTICE

Perform the opt-out on the web site and use it as an opportunity to communicate.

STAGE 8: FOLLOW-UP REGISTRATION

Many organisations seem to plan their acquisition only up to stage 7. In this way they are losing potential from the follow-up. By carefully executed follow-ups, a company can encourage conversion, show that it is responsive and educate the customer more about its services.

The nature of follow-up will vary according to the type of offer. For some applications a simple automated response may be sufficient. For example, on subscribing to a newsletter it is conventional to receive a notification message, 'thank you for subscribing, you will receive the next newsletter shortly'. To me, this is a lost opportunity. At the very least, there should be a link back to the archive or web site. But better still, why not add content to the e-mail notification about current promotions on the site or topics from the last newsletter?

Following a lead generation offer, there should be a hard-hitting e-mail to reinforce the benefits of the service and the next stages. Giving a personal touch and combining the e-mail with a phone call is a great benefit here. Figure 4.14 gives a great example of a follow-up that links through to more detailed information on the web site.

E-MAIL MARKETING INSIGHT

Do not neglect the opportunity provided by the follow-up to registration.

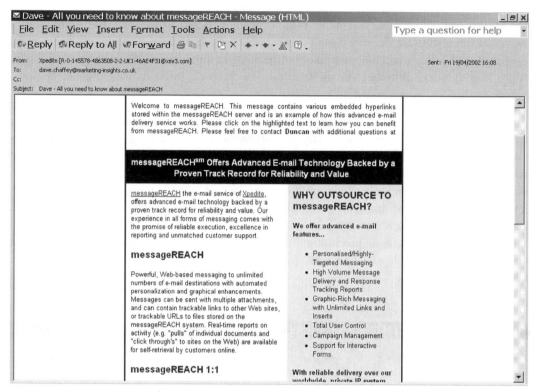

Figure 4.14 Follow-up to a lead generation registration from messageREACH (www.messagereach.co.uk)

Leveraging the registration follow-up

Example 1. E-mail from House (www.house.co.uk)

Thank you for registering with House, the new online home of British Gas and Scottish Gas. You can now take advantage of the range of services that are only offered to House members, services like:

– managing your British Gas and Scottish Gas energy and telephone accounts online in one place

– a personalised energy efficiency audit of your home

– a secure messaging service for messages to and from House to ensure your details remain private

– a comprehensive home movers service in partnership with great names such as Rightmove, Charcolonline and the Post Office

– free neighbourhood reports from Experian

– dedicated customer services teams waiting to help you

You can access your account by clicking the log in button on the top right hand side of any page of the House site. Don't forget to bookmark us.

If you need help please visit *http://www.house.co.uk* and click on any questions? or get in touch with the House Customer Contact Centre by clicking contact us.

Thank you for joining House, we look forward to your next visit.

Kind regards,

Lindsay Grieve
General Manager, house.co.uk

Example 2. E-newsletter from Cranfield School of Management

Thank you for registering to receive the next issue of Cranfield On-line. In the meantime, please feel free to view our current articles via the link below: You have selected the following areas of interest: Corporate Strategy Creativity and Innovation Information Systems Marketing Project Management

View current archive articles –
http://www.cranfieldsom.info/apollo/welcome/?uid=91916

Update your details/areas of interest –
http://www.cranfieldsom.info/apollo/login.asp?uid=91916

Multistep messages

Multistep or multistage e-mails are a more sophisticated form of follow-up. Here, a sequence of e-mails follows initial registration. The beauty of this approach is that the conversion process can be automated, as shown in the example below.

E-MAIL MARKETING EXCELLENCE

MAD use multiple e-mails to encourage subscription

Marketing publications from MAD (www.mad.co.uk) are available on a trial 30 day basis. MAD makes use of automated multistep or sequenced messages to encourage subscription. Figure 4.15 shows the sequence of messages. Note how the offer is escalated through the month, with additional carrots dangled to encourage registration. Such a sequence of messages is also used to encourage subscription renewal.

Multistep messaging can be applied to many events in the sales cycle. For example, if an annual insurance renewal is due, e-mail can be used, in combination with other media, to encourage the

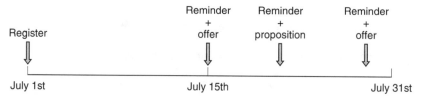

Figure 4.15 Automated multistage messages to encourage magazine subscription at MAD

customer to renew. If there is a major seminar event, or major product launch, a series of e-mails can be sent leading up to the event.

OTHER FORMS OF CUSTOMER ACQUISITION

The process for customer acquisition described in this chapter is appropriate for many situations, but it is not the only process. We do not have to use the web site to gain customers. The box below shows how customer acquisition for a retail service may involve driving customers to the retail location. Couponing may be used by manufacturers in a similar way.

E-MAIL MARKETING EXCELLENCE

Boots use e-mail to drive footfall

Boots Dentalcare were opening a range of new practices around the UK. For an initial test campaign, Claritas Interactive selected 105 000 individuals living within 30 minutes drive time of each of the selected 26 practices' postcodes. To maximise the response to the campaign, Claritas ensured that each name had been double opted in, and had not been e-mailed in the last three weeks.

E-mail proved to be an effective element of the communications mix (see Figure 4.7), outpulling radio and local print advertising. According to Caroline Addison at Boots Dentalcare, 'The campaign was so successful that the phone did not stop ringing according to many of the branches involved.' The immediacy of e-mail was also highlighted by the volume of calls received by Boots Dentalcare practices within four hours of sending out the e-mails.

Redwood New Media, which developed the campaign for Boots, ensured that it had high production values. Each e-mail was 'individualised' by using name personalisation and providing information on their nearest practice details including address, opening hours and telephone number. As attention span to e-mails can be short, copy was succinct and highlighted Boots' fresh approach to dentistry, and the value and benefits it offers.

As an additional response maximiser, the e-mail was designed to be self sufficient, giving recipients all the information they need to register as a patient, but also linking them into the Boots Dentalcare website, www.boots-dentalcare.co.uk, to find out more about the overall service offered. To incentivise people to register, they were also sent a printable voucher worth 25% off their initial consultation.

Source: Matthew Kelleher, General Manager, Claritas Interactive (www.claritasinteractive. co.uk).

KEEPING E-MAIL ADDRESSES CURRENT

When, eventually, you have reached the magical figure of having 90–100% e-mail coverage for your customers, it does not end there. This is when the really difficult task of keeping your e-mails current begins. An effective process for this, as with gathering e-mail addresses, should use all touchpoints to give the opportunity for the contact to update their e-mail addresses. Options for changing e-mail addresses should be available on the web site (and are required by the data protection laws in some countries). These options are rarely seen outside e-tail e-commerce sites. You could even include a 'change e-mail address' in your e-mail communications, since this may catch some customers who are about to change address through a planned move.

ECOA

Electronic/e-mail change of address (ECOA) services are being used increasingly. An ECOA service such as FreshAddress.com (Figure 4.16) provides a central location where an address book is maintained. When an address is changed, all those in the address book are notified. Other services, which are mainly US based, include Experian Exactis, Return Path and Veripost. In an interview with Clint Symons (Symons, 2002), William Kaplan, the CEO of FreshAddress.com, explained the value of the service as follows:

(1) We recover customers for clients at an average cost of less than $.50 per email address as compared with a typical customer acquisition cost for companies of $10–$11 per customer. This amounts to a saving of approximately $10 per customer acquisition, or roughly 1/20th of their average cost.

(2) The annual opportunity costs (i.e. lost revenue) of losing a customer range from $2 per customer to $100 or more.

(3) Bouncing email addresses cost on average a couple of cents to send each time, utilise significant tech time, bandwidth, and server space to handle, and often result in clogging a company's feedback pipeline, resulting in slower response times to customer inquiries. I would estimate this cost to be on the order of $.25 to $1.00+ per bouncing address over the course of a year.

However, the article also notes that the proposition for the service may not be clear for many users: if they are changing their address, they simply e-mail to their address list before making the transfer.

FreshAddress offers additional cleaning services based on corrections for syntax, typographical, formatting, top level and 'dead' domain errors. These services can be useful to correct addresses where the e-mail address was inaccurate when collected or entered.

Figure 4.16 FreshAddress.com Source: ECOA service (Source: Bill Kaplan, www.freshaddress.com)

VIRAL MARKETING

Viral marketing harnesses the network effect of the Internet and can be incredibly successful in reaching a large number of people rapidly, in the same way as a computer virus can infect many machines in minutes. Viral marketing is word-of-mouth delivered and enhanced on line. For rapid transmission, the e-mail has to have a 'WOW' factor: it has to have a big entertainment impact on the recipient, which usually means not news, but rather sex, humour or even violence. Rapid transmission happens since, if we have the WOW factor, it is easy to pass on the e-mail to friends or colleagues by typing their name into the box on the form which is conveniently provided on all viral campaigns. So transmission can happen by:

- *Word-of-web*: the viral content is passed on by typing into a web-based form, which is converted into an e-mail that is sent to recipients and contains a link to the web site containing the viral web site.

- *Word-of-e-mail*: some viral content such as jokes or amazing sexual exploits are transmitted by e-mail only. It is easy to forward to other like-minded individuals in your address book. Often, word-of-e-mail works in combination with word-of-web. Pepsi used e-mail to deliver e-mails containing links to video footage of punditry from players and managers which linked through to a web site. Having large videoclips as attachments to e-mails is impractical.

- *Word-of-mouth*: traditional word of mouth is also important: if the WOW factor is large, people will speak about the campaign and seek it out via the search engines. So, again, your campaign should be registered on the search engines.

Types of viral

It is common for marketers to ask an agency to do a viral campaign or add a viral element, but there are different types of viral, and some are more viral than others. These are common types of viral:

- *Pass-along viral*: towards the end of an e-mail it does no harm to prompt the recipient to pass the e-mail along to interested friends or colleagues. Even if only one in 100 responds to this prompt, it is still worth it.

- *E-mail a friend viral*: this is the tried and tested viral technique, the five minute viral referred to in more detail below. It is another form of pass-along viral which is achieved on the web site by having a form to forward information about a particular page. Many of these fail in the implementation: they are annoying for the recipient since they only pass along a link: I know that the marketers are trying to get me to clickthrough to the site, but a bit more information such as an introduction to the article gives me the chance to decide whether it is worth it.

- *Incentivised viral*: this is what we need to make viral really take-off. It is what most people mean when they talk about 'making it viral'. By offering some reward for providing someone else's address we can dramatically increase referrals. Remember the Virgin Atlantic case from Chapter 1; more responses were received from the viral element than from those initially sent, and this is not uncommon.

A common offer is to gain an additional entry for entry into a prize draw. This was the approach used by Virgin Atlantic. The marketer must decide how many names they can get away with, given the offer. So, the respondent may need to provide one, two, three, four or even five friends to get that additional entry. As well as limiting the offer according to the number of referrals, think about limiting it by action. This is encouraging the person transmitting the virus (the sneezer) to encourage the friend to take part, perhaps by phoning. For instance, there could be an extra entry for each friend who actually takes part in the prize draw, rather than just providing their address. In this case we may be able to gain some permission from the referred person. Other ways of encouraging action are to provide the extra entry only if the friend registers for a site or newsletter, orders a catalogue or even makes a purchase.

Shocking viral marketing

A well-known example of viral marketing was launched by MTV in 2001. The 'Headrush' campaign was to showcase a new programme. The creative involved a streaming videoclip that simulated a man's head exploding as he inflated a rubber boat which was bounced on by a boisterous child. This clip was seen by millions of people: a staggering number, since it would be thought that the clip would be disturbing to and unwanted by most people. Judge for yourself at Punchbaby (www.punchbaby.com), which has a variety of commercial and uncommercial clips for the not easily shocked. The line between what is commercial and uncommercial is blurred: portal Lycos has advertised its viral top 10 list in the broadsheet media to gain traffic!

The above example shows both the best and worst of viral marketing. It can reach a large number of people rapidly, yet since it often involves shock tactics it could be damaging to a brand, unless it is in keeping with an iconoclastic brand. Shocking virals do reach large numbers, but whom do they reach? Male 18–35 in all likelihood; if they are forwarded outside this category they could damage the brand. However, viral marketing does not have to shock; games can successfully help to build awareness and gain prospects for a company. For example, bank First Direct invited Internet users to 'Stuff the Cat' with varying sums of money. Success results in the cat exploding. E-mail addresses, but no other profile information, were collected as part of the campaign. Another example is 'Wax the Wimp' from Vauxhall cars, which is targeted at a young female audience. It invites players to strip chest-hair off a model, accompanied by squeals. A banner advert is displayed while the game is operational.

Incentivised viral marketing

One form of viral marketing that does not rely on standout content for transmission is the use of incentives to achieve referral. We have all received e-mails that offer us a free mobile phone of our choice if we send the e-mail to 10 others. Of course, this type of viral marketing is in all likelihood a scam, but it has a legal and effective relative. An incentive is used to encourage the recipient to forward an offer to friends. For example, an e-tailer could offer a 10% discount on future purchases if the e-mail is forwarded to five friends. The mechanism for viral referral is usually a landing page rather than manual forwarding as is the case with the scam. Using the landing page for referral enables the e-mail marketer to send a tailored message to the referees. It also enables capture of the referred addresses and monitoring of the campaign.

A viral campaign is most effective when the offer not only requires provision of the friend's name, but is also dependent on their taking some action. Brewer (2001) gives the example of a campaign where not only did five names have to be provided, but three of them had to actually subscribe to a catalogue or e-mail. Better still, the offer is true 'member get member', and one of the friends has to become a customer. Brewer (2001) warns of the problem of not capping viral incentives such as a $5 credit for every five friends referred. He says this can end up causing a marketer customer service, financial and privacy-related problems.

Godin (2001) writes about the importance of what he terms 'the Ideavirus' as a marketing tool. He describes it as 'digitally augmented word-of-mouth'. The ideavirus differs from word-of-mouth in that transmission is more rapid, it tends to reach a larger audience and it can be persistent: reference to a product on a service such as Epinions (www.epinions.com) remains online on a web site and can be read at a later time. Godin emphasises the importance of starting small by seeding a niche audience, which he describes as a 'hive', and then using advocates in spreading the virus: he refers to them as 'sneezers'. Traditionally, marketers would refer to such grouping as customer advocates or brand loyalists.

The viral campaign is started by sending an e-mail to a targeted group that is likely to propagate the virus.

The speed of transmission and impact of the message must be balanced by naturally negative perceptions of viruses. A simple, yet elegant method of customer acquisition is the 'e-mail a friend' facility, where a form is placed on an article that enables a customer to forward the page to a colleague. Other techniques include forwarding particular information such as a screensaver or an online postcard.

Five-minute viral marketing

A rapid, cheap, but effective form of viral marketing is simply to include an 'e-mail a friend' or 'e-mail a colleague' form on a page. This works for B2C, where product information can be sent to members of a family (e.g. 'this is what I am looking for, for Christmas please'). This also works well for B2B, where product information or information about events such as seminars can be shared between different members of the buying unit.

Technically and in terms of page design, this is straightforward. All that needs to be added to the page is:

- an 'e-mail a friend caption' and box to highlight the option
- a box for the contact's e-mail
- a box for the sender's e-mail and name (so that the recipient knows where the e-mail is from)
- an explanation of the privacy implications (usually in a pop-up window or separate page, so as to not confuse the matter)
- a freeform text field to add an optional short message (this is sometimes omitted, but is crucial)
- HTML code to post the form to a script which will forward the e-mail and message and also populate the house list with these e-mails.

OK, so maybe not a five-minute job, but a day should do it. Once it is set up for one page, however, it will only take five minutes to add it to other pages since it is generic code and design. Think of the locations in which you could use this code:

- as part of a viral campaign
- in an e-mail newsletter or subscription page
- in product catalogue pages
- in sales promotion web pages
- for events such as seminar registration.

In terms of return on investment this has to be the most cost-effective e-marketing possible. Once set up, the form needs no maintenance and even if it is not used frequently it is still helping acquisition, conversion and retention.

Creating successful viral campaigns

Designing creative with the WOW factor is 99% of a successful viral campaign, but there are blunders that can be made that will kill even the campaign with the best creative. For the virus to propagate it needs to be seeded to the right people, the influencers that are connected to the target market. For viruses with a fantastic general appeal, it may be sufficient just to seed to employees and encourage them to send to friends and colleagues. Generally, more specific targeting may be used. B2B store location consultancy Geo-business introduced an up-to-the-minute e-mail circular of store openings, closures and relocations, which was first sent to managers among their clients. In this specialist field, the information proved of such value that it quickly spread round several hundred of the specialists in this area: excellent PR for the company. This virus was sustainable since those interested could register to a newsletter form of the virus.

Seeding may also occur to a house list. The band Oxide & Neutrino ran a campaign where an 'eFlyer' containing video and sound clips was sent to the house list and referrals were encouraged using entry into competitions.

The viral effect of a campaign can be augmented by PR. If it is a dramatic campaign, media mentions, whether on the web, TV or radio, or in print, can help to drive the campaign. A viral campaign based on Christmas cracker cards found that the largest single source of traffic to the site was a mention on a radio show with millions of listeners.

Barriers that may kill the viral effect include:

- *Size*: if the viral content is a videoclip or streaming video it may be too large, e.g. over a megabyte; this will reduce referrals, particularly for those who have to download it across a modem.

- *Media format:* using a non-standard format for the viral content if it is rich media can kill viral. The majority of users will have Windows Media Player to play .AVI files, but may not have the facility for the latest Shockwave animation. However, for a young audience this is less of a problem, since their street cred is low if they are not up to date.

- *Attachments*: if the viral content is in the form of an attachment such as a videoclip or Flash animation, then this may reduce transmission since some company firewall software will not allow such large attachments to penetrate.

- *Cumbersome referral mechanism*: most virals are not seen as profiling and data collection exercises, since that would kill the impulse of forwarding to a friend. As a result, most virals just require your e-mail address and those of friends. Fields to make it easy to forward to several friends should be included. With games, the referral mechanism is best immediately after the game has been played, and is not mandatory but an option before further plays.

Further examples of rich media are given in Chapter 8.

Legal issues in viral marketing

E-mail marketing always involves careful assessment of the legal consequences as described in Chapter 2, but nowhere is this more true than for viral marketing. Viral marketing typically involves collecting two main pieces of information, first, the e-mail address of the recommender or referrer and, secondly, the e-mail address of the recipient. The difficulty is that there is not usually sufficient opportunity to offer opt-in or even opt-out. We cannot say, 'please opt in before playing this great game', because this kills the immediacy. The recipients of the e-mail likewise have no option to opt in or opt out.

Typically, the way in which the e-mail addresses collected in such a way are used is as the basis for a single future campaign to convert the initial interest into a more permanent dialogue. A campaign with an additional offer can then be used to target both referrers and recipients.

Data protection legislation is not that clear on this area, although it is generally agreed that an e-mail address on its own does constitute personal data, so it is subject to these regulations. EMMA (www.emmacharter.org) has a special guideline on viral marketing and recommends a single follow-up e-mail only. Its guidelines say:

> *If a member [of EMMA] is provided with an individual's e-mail address through the referral of another user, that member is permitted to send the referred individual one e-mail which should:*
>
> *(i) include the e-mail address of the person who provided the individual's e-mail address to the member*
>
> *(ii) invite the individual to subscribe to a specified list or lists and*
>
> *(iii) clearly inform the individual that their personal data will be removed from the file unless the individual opts-in to receiving further e-mails.*
>
> *The list owner should ensure that each referred person is only sent one such e-mail though they may have been referred by a number of different people.*

Further examples of viral campaigns can be found at the Viral Bank (www.viralbank.com).

MEASURING ACQUISITION EFFECTIVENESS

To finish this chapter as it started, how should companies monitor the success of their acquisition campaigns? The metrics discussed at the start of the chapter were the percentage coverage of all customer e-mails in the database, together with an indication of quality: how many are valid, current e-mail addresses?

To control e-mail acquisition on a monthly basis, reporting should also be in place to measure:

- the number of new e-mail addresses captured each month
- the percentage of site visitors who contribute e-mail addresses
- conversion rates from qualified leads captured to customers.

For a fuller picture of the success of acquisition, these measures should be recorded for visitors referred from different sources. Successful referrers with a relatively low cost of acquisition and a high conversion rate can then be built on in future site promotion.

REFERENCES

Brewer (2001). Tips for optimising viral marketing campaigns. *Clickz Newslett.*, 22 February (www.clickz.com).

Cartellerieri, C., Parsons, A., Rao, V. and Zeisser, M. (1997). The real impact of Internet advertising. *Mckinsey Q.*, **3**, 44–63.

Dwek, D. (2002). Is appending too good to be true? *DM News*, 26 June (www.dmnews.com).

Godin, S. (2001). *Unleashing the ideavirus* (available online at www.ideavirus.com).

Symons, C. (2002). How useful are ECOA? *Opt-in News*, 27 June (www.optinnews.com).

Whatsnextonline E-newsletter (2002). What's Next Online #52/Internet PR Tools. 9th January 2002. Published by B.L. Ochman at www.whatsnextonline.co.uk.

WEB LINKS

E-zine Tips (ezine-tips.com)
List Central (now List Universe) (www.list-universe.com)
Liszt (now Topica) (http://www.liszt.com)
Whatsnextonline (www.whatsnextonline.co.uk)

5

Using e-mail for customer retention

Overview

This chapter describes using e-mail for the retention of customers and visitors to a site who have subscribed to a newsletter.

Chapter objectives

By the end of this chapter you will be able to:

- decide on an approach to develop an integrated e-mail retention campaign
- take the key decisions to develop an effective e-newsletter.

Chapter structure

- Introduction
- Planning retention
- E-newsletters
- Virtual communities and discussion lists

INTRODUCTION

Much that is written about e-mail marketing focuses on acquisition. However, much of the actual marketing activity and expenditure is focused on retention. Forrester research has forecast that spending on e-mail marketing services and technology will reach €1 billion in Europe by 2004. Of this expenditure, they estimate that well over 80% will be on retention campaigns. Why is this the case? One reason is fear: owing to concerns about customer privacy, many businesses are not prepared to purchase opt-in lists. Rather, they would prefer to build their own house list using the approach described in Chapter 5. Another reason is the return on investment. We have seen in earlier chapters that the costs of customer acquisition are usually measured in tens or even hundreds of pounds. However, the cost of getting an existing customer to purchase again is much lower. The cost per order for an e-mail campaign can be in single figures. However, it is not only the removal of acquisition costs that makes retention strategies favourable: the cost of sales will be lower, particularly for business-to-business (B2B), we will not incur switching costs when customers leave, and loyal customers will be more responsive to cross-selling and up-selling and can help to generate more referrals. For all these reasons it is well-known that a small increase in customer retention can generate large increases in profitability. Reicheld and Sasser (1990), in a cross-industry study, estimated that by reducing customer defections by just 5%, profitability could be increased from 25% to 85%.

So, once we have acquired the customer's e-mail address and converted to our first sale, how can we use e-mail to develop the relationship, to build loyalty, to encourage further sales? This chapter answers these questions. We start by looking at developing a retention plan. This encourages a long-term rather than a short-term view of retention campaigns. This chapter then focuses on two key methods of retention: regular e-newsletters and sales promotions. Newsletters are covered by looking at the different types of decision, such as how to gain subscribers, what content should be included, and what the best frequency is. Finally, we look at some examples of sales promotions.

Remember that retention can have different meanings according to the context. For most companies it begins at the point of the first sale; when a prospect becomes a customer. Online, though, we may have prospects who are visiting the web site which we want to convert to customers. But to achieve this, we have to retain them as visitors and prospects for long enough through ongoing communications such as e-newsletters. This distinction is important, since when designing e-newsletters, for example, the intended audience is not solely existing customers, but also prospects. For some media sites such as portals or online newspapers, we will also have site visitors who return to the site and use it as a free service. The media owner may be looking to convert them to a paid-for subscription, but in the meantime, they are still a source of revenue since their eyeballs help to bring advertising to the site.

PLANNING RETENTION

Producing a plan for retention encourages a long-term view of the aims for our campaigns and enables them to reinforce each other, rather than their being isolated. To build a retention plan, work towards building a campaign timeline for the next 6, 12 or 18 months, such as that shown in Figure 5.1. This helps to form a picture which shows the different forms of communication and their frequency. These issues are considered in the next section.

Understanding loyalty

Loyalty has been defined by Sargeant and West (2001) as 'the desire of the customer to continue to do business with a given supplier over time'. Customer loyalty can be measured simply by the length of time a customer has been with the company, but more meaningfully by the frequency and value of purchase using recency, frequency, monetary value (RFM) analysis. Understanding different levels of loyalty and developing campaigns to appeal to these different levels are important parts

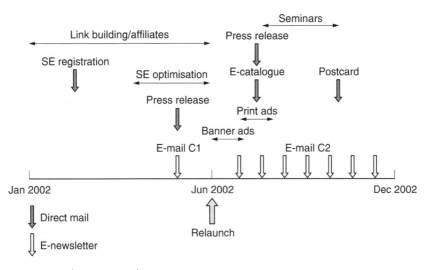

Figure 5.1 Retention planning timeline

of retention planning. Sargeant and West (2001) identify four different levels of loyalty. These may exist in any market, or within any customer base, but different levels may be more prevalent in particular markets. The four levels of loyalty are:

- *No loyalty*: customers move between one supplier and another at will. This particularly occurs when their perception is that products from different suppliers are similar, with few differentiating features. Sales promotions involving discounts are often used in such markets to encourage repeat purchases.

- *Spurious loyalty*: products or services are still perceived as similar, but consumers tend to favour one brand owing to inertia. This may be because there are switching costs involving time and effort. For example, bank customers rarely switch, in contrast to users of an ISP, because of the effort in changing their account details.

- *Latent loyalty*: consumers have a preference for a particular product or service, but do not exclusively buy from one source. Other situational factors, such as accessibility to the product or availability of money, may stop them always purchasing this product.

- *True loyalty*: there is a clear preference for a particular brand among competitors and purchase patterns will reflect this.

If loyalty can be identified from buying patterns, then different types of retention offer can be used for different customers. It may be that we only want to encourage a relationship with those customers who exhibit latent or true loyalty, since we will achieve the highest returns in this way. Lifetime value calculations can be used to identify these customers.

Lifetime value calculations

Lifetime value is the total net benefit that a customer or group of customers will provide a company over their total relationship with a company. Modelling is based on estimating the income and costs associated with each customer over a period of time and then calculating the net present value in current monetary terms using a discount rate value applied over the period.

Customers can then be segmented according to lifetime value, and different promotions strategies developed for the most profitable and least profitable customers. Strategies usually involve preferentially targeting the most profitable customers and minimising communications with the least profitable customers.

FRAC analysis is also used to assess the value of customers to an organisation. It is based on the premise that the most valuable customers and those that are most responsive to campaigns are those who purchase most frequently, have purchased most recently and have the largest transactions. The elements of the FRAC framework are:

- *frequency:* the average time between purchases (or the average number of purchases in a specific period, such as a year)

- *recency:* the length of time since the last purchase

- *amount:* the average value of customer purchases

- *category:* the type of product purchased.

In FRAC analysis, points are assigned to each customer according to each of the elements; for example, 1 point for an average purchase frequency of 12 months through to 5 points for a purchase frequency of 2 months or less. The analysis is readily automated and then customers with higher FRAC values can be preferentially targeted.

Understanding loyalty drivers

To plan retention, we must know what encourages loyalty. We need to be clear about the factors that matter for our customers. Reicheld and Schefter (2000) suggest that what is key for organisations to understand is what determines not only service quality and customer satisfaction, but also loyalty or repeat purchases. From their research, they suggest five primary determinants of loyalty online:

- quality customer support
- on-time delivery
- compelling product presentations
- convenient and reasonably priced shipping and handling
- clear trustworthy privacy policies.

The importance of these factors is also suggested by a J.P. Morgan report, e-tailing 2000. This suggests that the factors of greatest concern are fulfilment and support, rather than pricing (Figure 5.2).

So, to achieve loyalty, e-mail campaigns alone will clearly not be enough. This is not to say that price-based promotions will not be persuasive or will not work, but for greatest effect, the creative for e-mail campaigns and e-newsletters must build on and reinforce the factors that determine loyal behaviour. For example, the creative for an e-tailer will contain references to customer satisfaction or support quality ratings. This also indicates the importance of support e-mails, which we will look at in Chapter 7.

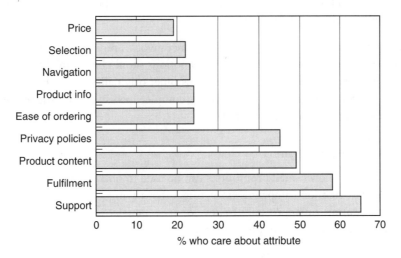

Figure 5.2 Loyalty drivers for e-commerce (Source: Wyman, 1999)

The precise nature of these loyalty drivers will differ between companies. Reicheld and Schefter (2000) reported that Dell Computer has created a customer experience council that has researched key loyalty drivers, identified measures to track these and put in place an action plan to improve loyalty. The loyalty drivers and their summary metrics were:

- Driver: *Order fulfilment*; metrics: ship to target (% that ship on time exactly as the customer specified)

- Driver: *Product performance*; metrics: initial field incident rate (the frequency of problems experienced by customers)

- Driver: *Post sale service and support*; metrics: on-time, first-time fix (the percentage of problems fixed on the first visit by a service representative who arrives at the time promised).

Rigby et al. (2000) assessed repeat purchase drivers in grocery, clothing and consumer electronics e-tail. It was found that key loyalty drivers were similar to those identified by Dell, including correct delivery of order, but other factors such as price, ease of use and customer support were more important.

Form of communications

Once we have identified our customers' loyalty drivers, a good starting point for planning retention campaigns is to think about your options for the range of e-mail and traditional communications that you plan to use. Such options include:

- regular newsletter e-mail to keep customers informed about industry, company or product news

- e-mail discussion lists, perhaps related to customer support or a user group

- e-mail promotions: special offers, competitions and discounts to encourage repeat visits to the company web site and then convert the visit to a sale. These are explored in the next section

- viral e-mails, for example, customers on the house list are encouraged to enter the e-mail of a friend or colleague to forward information or entertainment to them (this is combined retention and acquisition, covered in Chapter 4)

- promotions to encourage renewal: where the product involves renewing a contract, as is the case for insurance or mobile phones, for example, promotions should be planned to achieve this. The timing of these will vary according to when the customer originally signed the contract, so this is an automated approach and may involve several reminder messages (multistage messaging) and different media (telesales may also be used).

E-mail promotion campaigns

In this section we look at how e-mail promotions can be used to obtain repeat sales. Since the main principles of effective retention campaigns (targeting–offer–timing) were covered in Chapter 3, in this chapter we concentrate on approaches to developing e-newsletters. Figure 5.3 shows an example of a text promotion targeted at those who have expressed a preference for an IT-related newsletter.

Offers

The types of offer that we can use in retention campaigns were reviewed in Chapter 3. We summarised the main types of offers as 'free–win–save'. The type of offer used with sales promotions will also vary according to the type of site. Promotion campaign options include:

- for retail sites: loyalty schemes, discounts, buy one get one free, free shipping or free gift

- for B2C sites: bricks and clicks sites, prize draws, competitions

- for B2B sites: competitions, seminars (webinars) about new products, new content or new services.

Web response

When planning e-mail campaigns, always consider how they can best be combined with offline promotions such as direct mail or advertising. The same landing pages or microsite can be used for an e-mail component and a direct mail component of a campaign. This approach was called the web response model by Hughes (1999). The web site is used as the direct response mechanism where the customers express their interest in the offer, hence 'web response'. Web response can be taken further by developing different offers for different segments. For example, a Netherlands-based bank devised a campaign targeting six different segments based on age and income. The e-mail or initial letter contained a personal identification number (PIN) that had to be typed in when the customer visited the site. The PIN had the dual benefit that it could be used to track responses to the campaign while, at the same time, personalising the message to the consumer. When the PIN

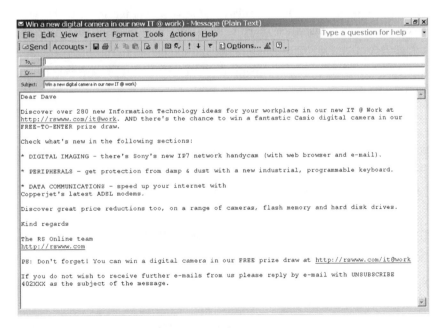

Figure 5.3   RS Components text newsletter promotion

was typed in, a 'personal page' was delivered for the customer with an offer that was appropriate to their particular circumstances.

Frequency

A key question in planning retention campaigns is getting the frequency of campaigns right. We are looking to achieve the right balance between overexposure and underexposure. With overexposure, the recipient receives e-mail from the same supplier so frequently that they do not have the time to read it. Underexposure is where opportunities are lost since the customer does not receive e-mails sufficiently frequently, perhaps owing to problems in resourcing the campaign. In terms of metrics, we are looking to maximise clickthrough and minimise unsubscribes, so these metrics should be monitored, as for newsletters, to get the frequency right. Some companies have regular monthly competitions, but these will tend to have less impact than irregular promotions. Such irregular promotions include event-based tie-ins.

E-MAIL MARKETING INSIGHT

Graph the response rate and unsubscribe rate of your e-marketing campaigns over time. Try to maximise clickthrough and minimise unsubscribe rates.

If messages are received too frequently from an organisation, their effectiveness will fall. Frequency options include:

- *regular newsletter type*: for example, daily, weekly, monthly. Let customers choose the frequency
- *event-related*: these tend to be less regular, but give a higher impact. They are sent out perhaps every 3 or 6 months when there is news of a new product launch or an exceptional offer
- *multistage messaging*: e-mails are automatically sent out before a renewal, to encourage re-subscription.

Frequency options are discussed further with respect to newsletters in section on e-newsletters, below.

Targeting

The section on targeting in Chapter 3 reviewed a wide range of choices for targeting. These may be summarised as:

- demographics (age, gender, geography, B2C characteristics)
- lifestyle or psychographic (B2C characteristics)
- company or individual role in decision-making unit (B2B characteristics)
- product (categories of purchase)
- purchase history (RFM analysis; see Chapter 2, pages 34–5 for an example)
- customer value

- customer loyalty

- e-mail preference

- time on list (in months)

- responsiveness to e-mail campaigns.

Enhancing customer knowledge

Retention strategy involves not only cross-selling and up-selling, but also learning more about the customer. There should be a plan gradually to understand more about the customer in terms of their characteristics. Figure 5.4 shows a plan for increasing knowledge about the customer over time. While it is good to have such a plan for data collection, the methods for storing and integrating this data are not straightforward. For example, information on customer preferences, e-mail response behaviour and buying behaviour may all be held on different systems. So, retention planning also involves an approach for integrating data from all these different sources. It also needs to consider methods of keeping customer information fresh, encouraging customers to update their e-mail address if it changes and changing preferences. This should be built in to retention campaigns. All such campaigns and newsletters should have the option to update the customer preferences or profile. Indeed, periodically, this should be one of the main aims of a campaign, to learn more about customers and keep their information up to date.

Customer surveys

Campaigns intended to develop customer satisfaction surveys should also be incorporated within the retention plan. These show that the company is not just exploiting the relationship, but looking to find ways to improve its services. A good resource on best practice for developing online surveys is Pete Comley's Virtual Surveys (www.virtualsurveys.com).

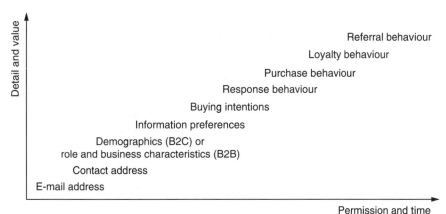

Figure 5.4 Plan for increasing detail of customers over time

E-MAIL MARKETING INSIGHT

Give customers access to their profile (via web site and e-mail) to enable them to update it.

E-NEWSLETTERS

Many web sites now have a prominently placed 'Sign up to our newsletter' box. But is this enough? Our site visitors will visit scores of sites offering e-newsletters. Even if we can persuade the visitor to subscribe, can we keep them? They will receive scores of e-mails each day and the unsubscribe is only one click away. As Martin Lindstrom puts it:

> *Did I mention I received a newsletter yesterday? No probably not, because I received 18 newsletters. I get about 65 newsletters a week. If I were to dedicate just 5 minutes to each one, I'd spend 6½ hours a week reading them all.*

When devising an e-newsletter, a host of decisions needs to be made for it to be effective. Use these lists of decisions to plan an e-newsletter or improve on your current e-newsletter. This section is about the decisions that you make as you plan the launch of an e-newsletter. These decisions are directed towards how to gain subscribers and how to keep them.

Decision 1: What is the newsletter's purpose?

All design decisions should be controlled by the primary purpose of the e-newsletter. For example, the structure, content and frequency of a newsletter to gain repeat purchases for a consumer site will be quite different from a newsletter intended to increase the value of a business brand through providing relevant information. If the aim is to generate revenue through advertising, then the decision will be different again.

Decision 2: How should we gain subscribers?

There are two aspects to gaining subscribers; first, there are various sources where e-mail addresses can be collected. Secondly, you must sell the benefits of the newsletter so that potential subscribers are happy to give up their e-mail addresses. Approaches to gaining customers' e-mail addresses were covered in more detail in Chapter 4. We start with gaining subscribers.

1. *Existing e-mail addresses*: if you have existing e-mail addresses collected from the web site, by sales representatives or from responses to direct mail, these can be used to encourage subscription. Since these potential subscribers will not have specifically agreed to opt in to this newsletter, a typical approach is to send them a promotional e-mail inviting them to receive the newsletter. It is also standard practice to send a single reminder to those who do not subscribe.

Subscription can be through replying to the e-mail or preferably a clickthrough to a registration page for the newsletter. This could also be used to collect customers' preferences for the newsletter, such as HTML or text format, or for further profiling of the customer and their interests.

2. *Researching e-mail addresses*: if you have names and contact phone numbers for existing customers or prospects then you can pay for a third party to research these by phone. This is a relatively low-

cost approach, amounting to single-figure pounds or dollars, since the researcher only has to ask for the e-mail address. This gives the benefits of a low cost of site visitor acquisition and it is an opt-in approach. In this case, the e-mail address can be added manually to the list of those receiving the newsletter or a further e-mail can be sent, as in case 1, to give a double opt-in. This has the benefit that the newsletter is not considered to be SPAM.

3. *Bought-in lists*: a list purchased from a list vendor can be used for the purpose of gaining subscriptions to newsletters. Here, e-newsletters are being used for customer acquisition rather than customer retention.

4. *Driving traffic to the subscription page*: this uses a range of online and offline techniques such as are used to attract visitors to any site. Of the online promotion methods, search engine registration will work well if previous newsletters are kept in an archive which is indexed by search engine spiders. For offline promotion methods, a specific advert mentioning the newsletter is not likely to be cost-effective, but the e-newsletter could be mentioned as a reason for visiting the web site; for example, rather than 'Visit our website', use 'Visit the website and subscribe to a newsletter keeping you up to date on our industry'. Direct communications combined with other incentives may be cost-effective. Finally, referrals from friends or colleagues are a low-cost method of driving traffic to the subscription page. What's New in Marketing (www.wnim.com) ran a prize draw offering a free DVD and videos if the e-mail addresses of three colleagues were mentioned. In 2002, in the UK, Dell Computer ran a campaign to encourage prospects to sign up to a newsletter. The primary offer was to Win A Notebook. (www.dell.com/uk/winanotebook). On typing in this URL, entry was only possible if the prospect agreed to subscribe to the e-newsletter (the secondary offer).

Decision 3: What is our proposition and what do we call it?

The other key aspect in gaining subscribers is developing a compelling proposition that encourages subscription, and that overcomes the barriers to giving up an e-mail address. Imagine that your potential subscriber already has ten monthly newsletters, five weekly newsletters and four daily newsletters. What differentiating feature is going to make yours the 20th newsletter they subscribe to and keep subscribing to? Many web sites have a field on the home page with the instruction 'Sign up for our newsletter', but far fewer sites explain why. Explaining the proposition is now a key to success.

Another issue with the proposition is whether you see the newsletter primarily as a value-adding, information-providing tool or as a sales tool. In a B2B context, the newsletter will often be more effective if it is the former. For a B2C retailer the newsletter is often effectively a catalogue update and consumers expect to see the latest products and offers. Nevertheless, all companies could usefully consider the balance between information and sales in their e-newsletters.

Figure 5.5 is an example of a newsletter that clearly expresses its proposition and value. Its audience is medical students and their lecturers.

The name should summarise the proposition and be a clear differentiator. What's New in Marketing and AvantMarketer are good examples. There are many newsletters called Newsletter, eNews or eAlerts, but not so many called fleshandbones. However, if the newsletter is branded consistently with the organisation distributing it, this is not a great problem since the organisation name will prefix the newsletter and it can be located as part of the main web site at

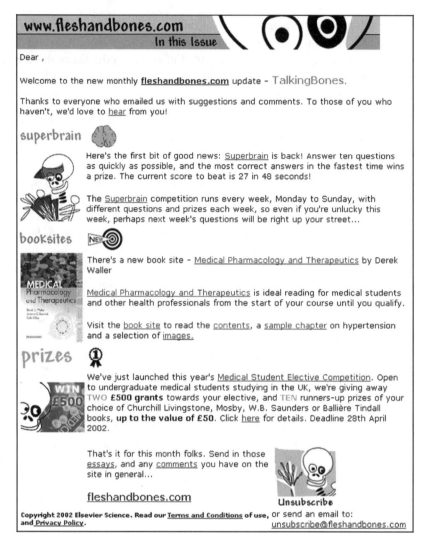

Figure 5.5 Fleshandbones.com (Source: Rhian Whitehead, Elsevier Science)

www.<company_name>.com/<newsletter>. Since some subscribers to a popular newsletter will be informed by word-of-mouth, it is often helpful to have a separate domain name registered to help people to find it.

Decision 4: How will the subscription process operate?

This should be as seamless as possible. Many sites have a single text-box on the home page for simplicity. As we have just mentioned, sufficient space should be given around the box to explain the proposition of the newsletter, with options for finding out more, or clicking on a sample newsletter. A separate subscription form will be necessary if you want to profile the recipient. Remember that many newsletter subscribers will not expect detailed profiling for a newsletter, but if an additional offer is available this may be acceptable, and forms will be necessary for this profile information. Once they have subscribed on the site, it should not be necessary for subscribers to fathom out a machine-generated subscription confirmation. Unfortunately, some list servers use such an approach. There is a great opportunity after subscription to communicate further with the subscriber. After they have filled in the subscription form and pressed submit, a confirmation page is usually served which can give further information about the newsletter or other offers. Similarly, the autoresponse e-mail sent after subscription can be used, as shown in the example below.

E-MAIL MARKETING EXCELLENCE

Subscription confirmation

Many e-mail newsletters provide the opportunity to review previous newsletters or update options on subscription. This one does.

Thank you for registering to receive the next issue of Cranfield On-line. In the meantime, please feel free to view our current articles via the link below: You have selected the following areas of interest: Corporate Strategy Creativity and Innovation Information Systems Marketing Project Management

View current archive articles –
http://www.cranfieldsom.info/apollo/welcome/?uid=91916

Update your details/areas of interest –
http://www.cranfieldsom.info/apollo/login.asp?uid=91916

Decision 5: Who is our audience?

This decision links straight into the next one on content. Different newsletters or sections of the newsletter may be needed for different customer segments or audiences. This can be achieved through customer selection of the product interest or by automatic categorisation dependent on purchase history.

Remember that many newsletters need to appeal to both customers and non-customers (prospects). Think about how well your newsletter achieves this. For B2B newsletters, also think about different information needs for different types of subscribers according to their role in the buying unit.

Decision 6: What is our content?

The e-newsletter will live or die according to its content, as for any periodical publication. Think carefully about the type of content that will lead to regular reading by subscribers and that will prevent unsubscription. What special offers or nuggets of information can be provided that are indispensable? The content needs of the audience should be researched before the launch. Many organisations will have existing communications that have content suitable for a newsletter. Content research should also occur after the launch: What's New in Marketing (www.wnim.com) conducted a survey 6 months after launch to enquire about what which content was good, bad or missing. Remember that for many newsletters readers may be prospects or customers, so develop content to appeal to both.

Achieving the correct balance between using the newsletters as a sales tool and as a value-adding, information-supply tool is key. Remember the structure too: the most enticing content needs to be above the fold when the e-mail is opened. Start with what you feel are the strongest articles for your audience. Have regular columns plus new topical articles separate from these columns in each issue.

Finally, there is the opt-out or unsubscribe option. This should be simple and it should work.

The content is also important in influencing the structure and design of e-mails. This is covered at the end of Chapter 7.

Decision 7: What length should we use?

One of the benefits of e-newsletters compared with paper-based communications is their ability to deliver a large amount of valuable information at a low cost. Of course, this is a double-edged sword. Too much information will make the e-newsletter unwieldy and your message will not get across or the recipient will not be able to locate the information relevant to them. When we want to convey a lot of information, as is the case with many newsletters, we have to decide on the split of content between the e-mail newsletter itself and the site where more detailed content may be hosted. Figure 5.6 shows five options for selecting the correct balance between content in the e-mail and on the web site. To simplify the example, let's say this newsletter contains just three different content areas, or three different articles. The options are:

(a) *Minimise content in e-mail, full content on web site in multiple pages*: here, the e-newsletter contains the links and a very short summary of the article, linking through to the full article on the web site. An example of this approach is shown in Figure 5.7. This has the benefit that the newsletter can be scanned very rapidly by the recipient for articles of interest. However, there is no indication of the quality or relevance of the content, which is possible with approaches (c) to (e). It also less easy for the other articles to be read, compared with the next option (b).

(b) *Minimise content in e-mail, full content on web site in a single page*: as in the previous case, the e-mail has limited information, but on clicking through to the web site, a single page newsletter is presented containing all of the articles. This has the benefit that the interested reader can rapidly find the information in all of the articles. This approach is used by e-Consultancy (www.e-consultancy.co.uk). It will not work so well for very long articles, such as those in Figure 5.7.

(c) *Some content in e-mail, full content on web site (multiple pages)*: this is similar to the approach in (a), but here the e-mail newsletter is longer since it contains a short extract from each article. Typically, a more >> option link will be available to take the user through to the web site. This makes it easier for the reader to decide whether the content is relevant to them. This approach is used by Nua.com (www.nua.com/surveys).

(d) *Some content in e-mail, full-content on web site (single pages)*: this is similar to (b), but again has the advantage that an idea of the relevance of the content is given in the e-mail and it is easier to find other content from the same newsletter on the web site.

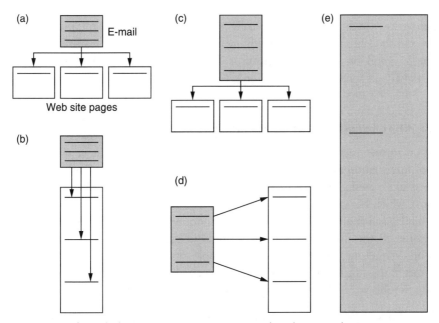

Figure 5.6 Options for split between content in an e-mail and on a web site

(e) *All content in e-mail*: this approach was used by Searchenginewatch.com (www.searchengine-watch.com) at the time of writing. A lot of detailed content about web searching is provided in two detailed text e-mails, sent each month. Here a clickthrough is not required to the site at all (although some longer articles may require this). This approach is arguably the best method of communicating information to the recipient. However, for the marketer calls-to-action encouraging further participation are more difficult to achieve from the newsletter than from the web site.

This decision is difficult since the preference on length varies according to the individual. For many, including this author, part of the power of e-mail newsletters is to be able to get a rapid briefing on developments about a particular topic. If you have to clickthrough to a web site and then understand the structure of the web site, as is the case with the What's New in Marketing web site (www.wnim.com), this slows down the experience.

Decision 8: Should we archive?

For a B2B newsletter the question is not should we archive, but how? Archiving a B2B newsletter, as long as it has quality content, provides an excellent resource for your customers. They will return to the resource as they face particular issues. As mentioned above, this can also assist in generating new subscribers since specialist articles indexed by search engines will gain new visitors who may look to tap into your expertise. For a B2C newsletter the issue is less clear-cut. If the e-newsletter is providing news or interesting content then similar arguments apply: it is a resource that will encourage repeat visits and can also, via search engines, act as an acquisitions tool. For B2C newsletters from an e-tail site, it is inappropriate to archive the content since product information and offers will quickly date.

When an archive is content rich, as is typically the case with a media or news site, the utility for the user can be improved by developing a 'Related articles' feature. ClickZ (www.-clickz.com) has a good related articles feature. This lists items related to the current article according to which category they fall into, or according to similarity in keywords in the title or body.

Decision 9: What format (text or HTML) should we use?

The decision on format relates closely to the decision on length since it is arguably difficult to present a lot of information as text in a long newsletter. However, the text-based approach is used by some successful e-newsletters. For example, the Searchenginewatch newsletter (www.searchen-ginewatch.com), which has over 100 000 subscribers, uses this approach and splits the newsletters across two e-mails each month. Alternatively, the Iconocast e-marketing newsletter (www.icono-cast.com) presents all the information about a single in-depth article in an HTML newsletter. What's New in Marketing (Figure 5.7) is an example of a relatively brief HTML newsletter. You can tell that this is an HTML newsletter, since the hyperlinks are not prefixed by 'http://' and do include the full path of the web page for the articles.

For the customer, this issue again comes down to personal preference. Remember that, tradition-ally, e-newsletters have been text based and this is consistent with most personal communications conducted between colleagues and friends. It can be argued that a text-based e-mail newsletter will be perceived by the customer as adding value rather than the hard-sell.

(a)

Figure 5.7 What's New in Marketing (www.wnim.com): (a) e-mail content and (b) web site

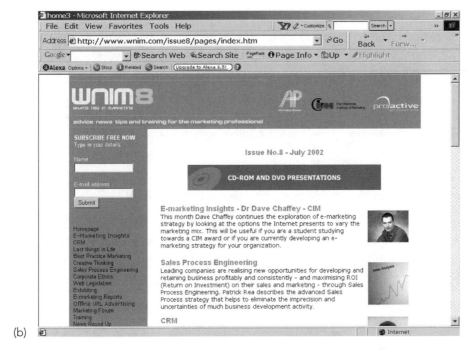

(b)

Figure 5.7   *Continued*

For the business, if the objective is to achieve action to repeat sales through promotions the HTML format can be used to present the offers with greater impact. If the objective is to add value through providing information to assist the customer, the text format has greater utility.

Some rules of thumb, which you are welcome to disagree with:

- HTML, relatively brief, works best for B2C
- text, relatively long, works best for B2B
- give a choice of text or HTML (with pictures or graphics)
- HTML e-mails cost more to create and dispatch.

Design issues for structuring HTML and text e-mails are presented in Chapter 7.

E-MARKETING EXCELLENCE

What's New in Marketing Newsletter (www.wnim.com)

The target audience for this audience is marketing professionals and students. When it was first launched in autumn 2001 it was e-mailed to Chartered Institute of Marketing Members (www.cim.co.uk), plus the Proactive list of marketing professionals and AP list of subscribers to the Marketing Managers Yearbook (around 15 000 in total).

The execution involved a first mailing to the full list. A reminder was e-mailed a fortnight later to those who had not subscribed. Subscription occurs on the site, as shown by the graphic.

The newsletter was delivered via the web site; a brief e-mail giving each month's topics directed the audience to the site. Archives were recorded on the web site. Additional traffic was driven by search engine registration.

Each recipient of the newsletter was encouraged to forward it on to three colleagues by being entered into a prize draw run by Proactive Productions. The prize was a DVD player and 10 DVDs. A 'chatroom' component was also added.

The initial mailing resulted in 3000 subscribers in October 2001, and the reminder mailing increased this total to 4704. By December there were 6600 subscribers with only 33 unsubscribers. By mid-2002 the number of subscribers had increased to 14 000.

Some learning points:

- The web site hosting the newsletter had some Flash components, so it could not be read by some recipients.

- Explanation in the initial mailing that subscription on the web site was necessary was not sufficiently clear.

- It was not initially registered with search engines: this would have prevented access by those subscribers who had heard of it by word-of-mouth.

- Additional subscription details were too limited for follow-up. In December three new profiling fields were added to the subscription form: job title, industry and location.

Decision 10: Which frequency and time of dispatch should we choose?

Before deciding on frequency we need to decide whether the newsletter will be episodic or periodic. Think of most newsletters that you receive: they are probably weekly or monthly. Why is this? Are we still in the print mentality of dailies, weeklies and monthlies? This may be one reason. Another reason is that a newsletter may become part of the recipient's routine. At the moment I receive the DM Newsletter on Tuesdays. Fewer others arrive on that day, so I expect it and I usually have time to check it out. If you receive a satirical newsletter on a particular day, you may even look forward to it. However, how many organisations actually achieve this regularity? More often it is Tuesday one month, Thursday the next.

But viewed differently, if an e-mail newsletter is regularly arriving on exactly the same time each week or month, then it becomes part of the landscape or 'daily grind', and you may start to ignore it; however, you are not ignoring it completely, the provider is still at front-of-mind. To avoid becoming part of the landscape one approach is to theme the newsletter, or have a distinctive offer each month which is prominent in the subject line.

E-MAIL MARKETING INSIGHT

Ensure that your newsletter does not use the same subject line every month.

So, it is very difficult to have an impact with a regular newsletter after a few months. You can partly get round this by using a different theme each month, highlighting the theme and a special offer in the subject line. In other words, it is a regular, monthly campaign.

Resourcing is a further issue. Consider the case of a publisher, issuing 20 different newsletters monthly for different groups of titles. The product managers will have to prepare them, which will take 1–2 days/per month. This may not be worth it if the subscriber numbers are poor. An alternative approach is to use a 2–3 month cycle of e-mails to their audience, based on launches of significant books. This is likely to have a higher impact and require fewer resources. Where resourcing is a problem, which will make it difficult to publish the newsletter on the first Monday of each month, for example, using a quarterly approach, where the newsletter is published at any time in the quarter, may be best.

Since there are no simple rules about frequency, giving a choice is the best option if you can resource the different options. See the Land's End (www.landsend.com) site for an example where there is a choice of weekly or monthly. The trick is to find the frequency that has the optimal readership and action rate. Anyone who has subscribed to a daily newsletter has probably unsubscribed as soon as possible, unless they have a specific need to be briefed about a particular industry through e-mail alerts or a newswire service. For example, iMarketingNews (www.imarketingnews.com) provides a choice of weekly or daily e-mails according to how up to date its readers need to be. The BBC e-mail alert service (www.bbc.co.uk/alert) is also a source for good practice. The method of unsubscribing is useful where it offers to change your frequency. Likewise, I do not read weekly newsletters; to state the obvious, there would be 52 e-mails per year to read from one organisation. I find 12 manageable. A quarterly frequency may be appropriate for many B2B organisations, and these would attract the greatest open rates and lowest cost per action.

To test frequencies, you can plot the number of opens, number of clickthroughs and number of unsubscribes for different frequencies. Andrew Petherick of Mailtrack suggests that if the number of unsubscribes increases above 1 or 2% then this is cause for concern. Of course, a 1% unsubscribe for a monthly newsletter is less of a concern than a 1% unsubscribe for a daily newsletter.

A related issue is the exact time of dispatch. An issue at a consistent time each month or week may be best, since the customer expects to receive the e-mail. As the number of e-newsletters increases perhaps the first day of the month or Monday morning is not the best choice since there will be greater competition for the subscribers' attention.

Decision 11: Which mechanism should we use for broadcast?

Internal options include a standard e-mail platform or specialist mailing software. For example, small volumes of messages can be managed from the distribution lists feature of Microsoft Outlook. Mailing software such as Gammadyne Mailer can be purchased.

External options include a broadcaster or ASP service such as MessageREACH. This is the most expensive, since the cost is per e-mail. However, there is a wide range in cost, with some services costing several cents per e-mail while others such as WangoMail (www.wangomail.com) offer 10 000 e-mails for $75 per month which is less than one cent per e-mail. Specific software options are described in more detail in Chapter 7.

Decision 12: How should we measure the success of our newsletter?

Measurement for e-mail newsletters is similar to other campaigns. As mentioned above, the following metrics will assess the effectiveness of the newsletters over a set period:

- clickthroughs to more detailed content or promotions
- number of unsubscribes
- number of new subscribers.

E-MAIL MARKETING EXCELLENCE

Orient Express Trains, Hotels and Cruises

Figure 5.8 shows an example of a monthly newsletter from Orient Express. In addition to newsletters, this company uses sophisticated targeting to send out offers to different types of customer depending on the type and location of service used (e.g. hotel or cruise), type of hotel visited, frequency of use and trigger dates (such as anniversary of visits). Lifestyle- and age-based campaigns are planned for the future.

The typical results for this newsletter are: 60% open rate, 20% clickthrough, 1.5% unsubscribe, i.e. industry average. The company and its agency look carefully at how to engage those 40% who open but do not clickthrough by varying the offer, structure and tone of the newsletter.

E-mail marketing excellence

Usability guru Jakob Nielsen (2000) suggests these methods for gaining and keeping e-newsletter subscribers:

- Use double opt-in to ensure that users expect to receive the e-newsletter.
- Don't just talk about 'valuable offers', but provide explicit information about what types of information and offers the mailing list will contain; how frequently it is published (people are more likely to subscribe if the frequency matches their needs: consider offering different publication frequencies to serve different market segments); how to see a sample newsletter before subscribing: people are more likely to sign up if they know what they will get.

Figure 5.8 Orient Express newsletter (Source: David Hughes, E-mailVision (www.emailvision.com)

- Provide an easy unsubscribe in the foot of every e-mail message. When users unsubscribe they should get an acknowledgement message that confirms that they have been removed from the list.

- Provide an archive for news features that remain relevant. Nielsen notes that at the time, his AlertBox newsletter about usability received 28 000 subscribers, but those accessing the archive exceeded 200 000. So, 86% of readers prefer to check out the columns 'as and when'. He notes that when he changed from a free command-based interface to a more usable web-based subscription process, the number of subscribers increased from around 200 to 500 per week.

VIRTUAL COMMUNITIES AND DISCUSSION LISTS

Since the publication of the article by Armstrong and Hagel in 1996, entitled 'The real value of online communities', and John Hagel's subsequent book (Hagel, 1997) there has been much discussion about the merits of using the web for virtual communities. The potential of virtual communities, according to Hagel (1997), is that they exhibit a number of positive feedback loops (or 'virtuous circles'). Focused content attracts new members, who in turn contribute to the quantity and quality of the community's pooled knowledge. Member loyalty grows as the community grows and evolves.

Behind the hype, what virtual communities offer at a basic level is group conversations about topics of interest to members of the group. Contributions or postings are added using an e-mail package or through fields on a web-based interface. These conversations are mediated by servers that distribute messages either through e-mail or as listings on a web page. One of the leading discussion groups for discussing the latest in Internet marketing is UK Netmarketing (www.chinwag.com). This uses e-mail as the main communications mode. Contributions are posted by e-mail and received by e-mail, either as one message per post, or as a daily digest. An archive of posted messages is available on the site and can be searched using Google. Other groups include the forums of E-consultancy (www.e-consultancy.com) and The Wall of Revolution magazine (www.revolutionmagazine.com). These both use a web-based interface for posting and reading messages. E-mail-based discussion groups seem to be more popular since most of us spend more time in our e-mail package than our web browser and we do not need to remember to visit the site to make a post.

If you are considering using discussion groups as part of your retention strategy, the main choice is between hosting the discussion group on your web site and forming or partnering with an independent site. For example, Boots The Chemist has created Handbag.com as a community for its female customers, rather than using the main Boots sites. Another, less costly alternative is to promote your products through sponsorship or cobranding on an independent community site or portal, or to become involved in the community discussions. If not, you may be better off contributing to independent communities. When posting to groups, it is important to contribute by adding insights that will help group members. Posting messages that are thinly veiled product plugs will cause offence and anger. Simply restrict your comments to insights and add your web address and proposition in a short signature to your e-mail. If it sounds as if you know what you are talking about, potential customers will check out your site.

Since many successful communities thrive on their independence from suppliers and vendors, this makes it difficult for a B2B supplier to get their own community to reach critical mass. However, if you already have an active user group for your products and the products are complex in terms of installation and usage, then support-related interest may sustain a discussion group.

Depending on market sector, an organisation has a choice of developing different types of community for B2C, communities of purpose, position, interest and communities of profession for B2B.

1. *Purpose*: for people who are going through the same process or trying to achieve a particular objective. Examples include those researching cars, e.g. at Autotrader (www.autotrader.co.uk) or stocks online, e.g. at Motley Fool (www.motleyfool.co.uk). Price or product comparison services such as MySimon, Shopsmart and Kelkoo serve this community. At sites such as Bizrate (www.bizrate.com), The Egg Free Zone (www.eggfreezone.com) or Alexa (www.alexa.com) companies can share their comments on companies and their products.

2. *Position*: for people who are in a certain situation, such as a those with a health disorder or at a certain stage of life, such as communities set up specifically for young people and old people. Examples are teenage chat site Dobedo (www.dobedo.co.uk), Cennet, http://www.cennet. co.uk/'New horizons for the over 50s' www.babycenter.com and www.parentcentre.com for parents and The Pet Channel (http://www.thepetchannel.com/).

3. *Interest*: for people who share an interest or a passion such as sport (www.football365.com), music (www.pepsi.com), leisure (www.walkingworld.com) or any other interest (www.deja. com).

4. *Profession*: for companies promoting B2B services. For example, Vertical Net has set up over 50 different communities to appeal to professionals in specific industries such as paints and coatings, the chemical industry or electronics. These B2B vertical portals can be thought of as 'trade papers on steroids'. In fact, in many cases they have been created by publishers of trade papers, for example, EMAP Business Communications has created Construction Plus for the construction industry. Each has industry and company news and jobs as expected, but also offers online storefronts and auctions for buyers and sellers, and community features such as discussion topics. The trade papers, such as Emap's *Construction Weekly*, are responding by creating their own portals.

What tactics can organisations use to foster community? Despite the hype and potential, many communities fail to generate activity, and a silent community is not a community. Parker (2000) suggests eight questions that organisations should ask when considering how to create a customer community:

1. What interests, needs or passions do many of your customers have in common?

2. What topics or concerns might your customers like to share with each other?

3. What information is likely to appeal to your customer's friends or colleagues?

4. What other types of business in your area appeal to buyers of your products and services?

5. How can you create packages or offers based on combining offers from two or more affinity partners?

6. What price, delivery, financing, or incentives can you afford to offer to friends (or colleagues) which your current customers recommend?

7. What types of incentives or rewards can you afford to provide customers who recommend friends (or colleagues) who make a purchase?

8. How can you best track purchases resulting from word of mouth recommendations from friends?

A good approach to avoiding these problems is to think about the problems that you may have with your community building efforts. Typical problems are:

1. *Empty communities*: a community without any people is not a community. The traffic-building techniques mentioned in an earlier section need to be used to communicate the proposition of the community.

2. *Silent communities*: a community may have many registered members, but a community is not a community if the conversation flags. This is a tricky problem. You can encourage people to join the community, but how do you get them to participate? Here are some ideas:

   Seed the community. Use a moderator to ask questions or have a weekly or monthly question written by the moderator or sourced from customers. Have a resident independent expert to answer questions. Visit the communities on Monster (www.monster.co.uk) to see these approaches in action and think about what distinguishes the quiet communities from the noisy ones.

3. *Make it select*: limit it to key account customers or set it up as an extranet service that is only offered to valued customers as a value-add. Members may be more likely to become involved.

4. *Critical communities*: many communities on manufacturer or retailer sites can be critical of the brand. Think about whether this is a bad thing. It could highlight weaknesses in your service offer to customers and competitors, but enlightened companies use community as a means to understand their customers' needs and failings with their services. Community is a key market research tool. In addition, it may be better to control and contain these critical comments on your site rather than their being voiced elsewhere in newsgroups, where you may not notice them and can less easily counter them. The computer-orientated newsgroup on Monster shows how the moderator lets criticisms go so far and then counters them or closes them off. Particular criticisms can be removed.

Finally, remember the *lurkers*, those who read the messages but do not actively contribute. There may be 10 lurkers for every active participant. The community can also positively influence these people and build brand.

REFERENCES

Armstrong, A. and Hagel, J. (1996). The real value of online communities, *Harvard Business Review*, May–June, 134–41.

Hagel, J. (1997). *Net Gain: Expanding Markets Through Virtual Communities*. Boston, MA: Harvard Business School Press.

Hughes, A. (1999). Web response – modern 1:1 marketing. Database Marketing Institute article (www.dbmarketing.com/articles/Art196.htm).

Nielsen, J. (2000). Mailing list usability. *UseIT Alertbox*, August (www.useit.com).

Parker, R. (2000). *Relationship Marketing on the Web*. Adams Streetwise publication.

Reicheld, F. and Sasser, W. (1990). Zero defections: quality comes to services. *Harvard Bus. Rev.*, September/October, 105–11.

Reicheld, F. and Schefter, P. (2000). E-loyalty, your secret weapon. *Harvard Bus. Rev.*, July/August, 105–13.

Rigby, D., Bavega, S., Rastoi, S., Zook, C. and Hancock, S. (2000). The value of customer loyalty and how you can capture it. Bain and Company/Mainspring Whitepaper, 17 March 2000 (published at www.mainspring.com).

Sargeant, A. and West, D. (2001). *Direct and Interactive Marketing*. Oxford: Oxford University Press.

Wyman, T. (1999). *eTailing and the 5Cs*. JP Morgan Industry Analysis, 9th December.

WEB LINKS

E-zine Tips (ezine-tips.com)
List Central (now List Universe) (www.list-universe.com)
Liszt (now Topica) (http://www.liszt.com)

Chapter

6

Crafting e-mail creative

Overview

This is a practical chapter which highlights the different options for developing e-mail creative from the e-mail attributes (headers), through the structure, style and tone of the message body, to its form (HTML and text).

Chapter objectives

By the end of this chapter you will be able to:

- evaluate the effectiveness of e-mail headers (From, To, Subject line and date)

- assess the suitability of e-mail structure and content

- discuss specific design issues for e-newsletters.

Chapter structure

- Introduction
- E-mail usage constraints
- The HTML versus text decision
- E-mail structure
- E-mail headers
- E-mail style and personality
- E-mail body content
- Copywriting
- Calls-to-action
- Landing pages
- Testing creative
- E-newsletter design
- How not to do it

INTRODUCTION

Producing e-mail creative presents a new challenge for direct marketers. But many of the challenges are not new: the limited time to achieve an action is not new; the need for a powerful opening and an appealing offer is not new; constraints of cost and space are not new. However, there are some major differences in the delivery platform that make significant differences, in that we are talking virtual and not physical. How long does it take to assess and discard a direct e-mail compared with a direct mailer? How many other direct e-mails are we competing with? According to a 2002 DTI survey (Parenting suffers in e-mail overload, Monday 20 May 2002, http://news.bbc.co.uk/1/hi/sci/tech/1998334.stm) the average UK employee spends 49 minutes per day wading through e-mail messages. In this time, they may well delete many messages, some after evaluating them for just seconds. So, competition for the recipients' time is fiercer and we have limited means at our disposal to get our message across. What can we offer to avoid our e-mail being ruthlessly deleted? Consider Figure 6.1: we have fewer than 30 characters in the subject line to attract interest and so to stop our message being deleted. Perhaps the reader will get no further than the first word of the subject line, or perhaps no further than the From address, which they will see first as they scan from left to right. Some e-mail readers prefer to use a preview pane to view e-mails. Figure 6.2 shows this arrangement. Here, the recipient will make their decision according to the combination of text plus graphics if it is an HTML e-mail, so we have more scope to achieve a favourable outcome.

In this chapter we will look at how to develop e-mail creative that maximises the likelihood for action. We will focus on promotional e-mails to achieve action. Most of the observations tend to apply to promotional campaigns rather than e-newsletters, which have their own structure and copy. However, many of the principles are similar.

E-MAIL USAGE CONSTRAINTS

Before going on to look at best practice, let us look at the constraints under which we operate. There are two main issues to bear in mind when designing e-mails. First, there are technological constraints. To the majority these are boring technical issues, but we cannot unleash our creative talents without knowing the limits of the technology. These are imposed by recipients using a range of e-mail readers and selecting different options for their configurations. The location of access may also differ: download speeds and display platforms differ between those at home and at work,

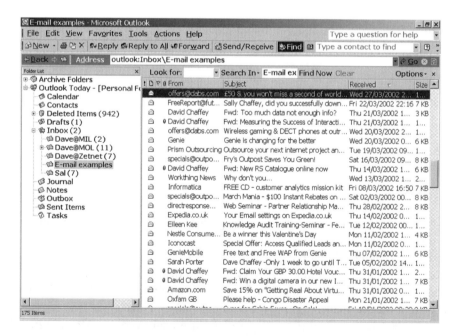

Figure 6.1 The challenge: Microsoft Outlook Inbox *without* preview pane

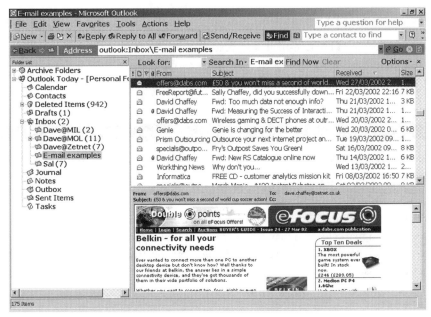

Figure 6.2 The challenge: Microsoft Outlook Inbox *with* preview pane

and between handheld devices, phones and digital TVs. Secondly, there are behavioural constraints. We have to consider the different ways in which e-mail users process and evaluate their e-mails.

Technological constraints

Many of the technological constraints that affect the way in which an e-mail is displayed are most relevant when HTML e-mails are being used. However, some also apply to text e-mails, so we will also highlight where this applies.

A general constraint on both HTML and e-mail is the resolution of the screen. This may be selected by the user, or they may be using default factory settings. It is common for designers to use high resolutions of 1280 by 1024 pixels (dots) or 1064 by 768 pixels. An e-mail that looks good at this resolution may not all fit within the viewable area when it is being read at the lower resolution favoured by many consumers, such as 800 by 600 pixels or 640 by 480 pixels. The amount displayed also depends on the size of window that is used for viewing e-mails. The implication is that designers should decide on an acceptable lowest common denominator, i.e. 640 by 480, and design for this resolution. When reviewing alternatives with designers, ask to see them displayed at a range of resolutions. For HTML e-mail it is advised that a width of 600 pixels is used. Also review messages with the preview pane (Figure 6.2) and with the first three lines of the message displayed.

E-MAIL MARKETING INSIGHT

Insist that e-mails are tested against a representative range of screen resolutions.

THE HTML VERSUS TEXT DECISION

Deciding between using HTML e-mail and text formats in an e-mail campaign is not at all straightforward. The best action you can take is to avoid making this decision by asking the recipient for their preference when they first register for opt-in e-mail.

E-MAIL MARKETING INSIGHT

Always ask customers for their HTML or text format preferences when they first register.

We will see that the decision is difficult for a range of reasons. Some users may prefer HTML to text, or vice versa. As a marketer you may feel that the creative opportunities that HTML gives will enable you to achieve better results; however, technological constraints may frustrate this ambition. Let us look at these issues in turn.

User preference

For many business people, and an increasing number of home Internet users, corresponding by e-mail is an established habit of 2, 5 or 10 years or more. The first e-mail was sent in 1972, pre-dating use of the web by nearly 20 years. Most Internet users still exclusively use plain text e-mail for business and personal correspondence. Initially this was because it was the only option, but we rarely format our business e-mails. Spending time formatting our personal e-mails destroys the immediacy of our correspondence and it makes information transfer less efficient. The implication of this is that for some applications, business-to-business (B2B) in particular, text format may be better. Think of the great Internet marketing newsletters such as the Nua survey digest (www.-nua.com/surveys), Marketing Sherpa (www.marketingsherpa.com), UK Netmarketing (www.-chinwag.com) or Searchenginewatch (www.searchenginewatch.com). These use text because it is the most efficient way of transmitting information to their time-poor readers. Links through to fuller articles available on the web site are available if required, with the newsletter providing an index. There are some other good B2B HTML newsletters, such as Iconocast (www.iconocast.com) and Avantmarketer (www.avantmarketer.com), but I think most would agree that they transfer less information. OK, you may be saying, but these are newsletters: what about promotional B2B e-mails. Well, yes, HTML e-mails may be more appropriate here to achieve an impact and could achieve a higher open rate for those who receive them: we will see below that some company firewalls may stop HTML e-mails. But it depends on who the recipient is: a marketing manager may be more influenced by a well-designed HTML e-mail than a colleague in IT or finance who 'just wants the facts'. Consider another situation, that of a consumer prize draw to win a car, a holiday or a large quantity of alcohol. Would you want your colleagues looking over your shoulder while you are viewing pictures of cars or beaches? This again indicates the importance of choice of format on registration.

Creative opportunities

What does HTML bring that text lacks? Well, a great deal: colour, animation, emphasis, more advanced layout options such as headers, footers and columns, and different sized proportional fonts. This gives the opportunity to deliver much more; for example, it would be impossible to deliver the information contained within the e-mail of Figure 6.3 without HTML formatting. Here, we are taking the web site to the reader. How can you leverage your brand identity and brand values without colour and images? You are limited to the name and creative copy only. HTML also enables us to highlight and emphasise in a more co-ordinated way. The theme of the offer can also be stressed. Differentiating yourself becomes easier.

Given all of these factors, some research points to HTML giving response rates that are, on average, 1.4 to 1.7 times higher than for text (Doubleclick, 2002).

A final, but relatively minor benefit is that with HTML e-mails we can measure the open rate which, as we saw in Chapter 4, lets us assess how well the subject line is working.

Technological constraints

The user may be using a variety of e-mail readers in which the e-mail may be displayed. An indication of the wide range of choices is given in the article by Grossman (2002) which reports on a survey of Internet.com users which showed that there were 12 main e-mail readers. Each of these different readers may display HTML in a different way. The degree of support for HTML may also vary. While Outlook Express and Netscape Communicator have good support for HTML e-mail, older versions of readers such as Eudora, AOL and Lotus Notes may have no or limited support for HTML. So, you may be excluding 10% or more of your potential audience if you only use HTML e-mails. Although 90% of your target audience may be able to read HTML e-mails in theory because they have HTML-compatible browsers, the reality could be lower. This figure could be smaller in some situations such as a B2B campaign where a high proportion of recipients are using Lotus Notes. We will look at solutions for this later. Furthermore, many companies using a firewall may have it set up to remove possible security threats, and since HTML e-mails could contain malevolent scripts, the HTML or the scripting components may be removed by the firewall, possibly leaving a blank e-mail for the recipient. A similar argument applies for e-mails containing Flash animations. For users accessing the e-mails at home via a dial-up connection, if they read their e-mails offline, as many do, then they will often not be able to see the graphic components of HTML e-mails.

One solution to eliminate the problem of HTML not being rendered is simply to ask the user, on opt-in, whether they wish to receive text or HTML. Since 'HTML' will be meaningless to many, it is best to ask: 'Text or HTML (pictures)?' Another approach is to use Multipart or Multimedia Encoding (MIME). MIME is a standard method of formatting your e-mail with an HTML and a text component such that when received, the e-mail client automatically detects whether it can display the HTML version. If it can't the text form is displayed. While this will work successfully in many cases it is not foolproof. In B2B environments, software such as Lotus Notes or Groupwise will not render correctly. In this case the recipient will see a combination of text and ugly HTML tags at the bottom of the e-mail. A further alternative is to use 'sniffer' software, which seeks to detect the type of e-mail that can be read. For example, Lyris List Manager Pro can identify which recipients can read HTML messages. If graphics contained within an HTML are never down-loaded from the server to a particular recipient, this would also indicate that text messages are best for that recipient.

Figure 6.3 Weekly e-mail newsletter from dabs.com

Location of access

The majority of home users use a temporary dial-up connection, although a permanent broadband connection is becoming more common. This means that they will typically download and upload their e-mails for a couple of minutes, automatically disconnect from the Internet and then read them offline. This is an important consideration in campaigns using HTML e-mails. The reason is that the pictures that make up the design may not be downloaded. They will only be downloaded if an individual e-mail is open and the computer is connected to the Internet. This means that, if the e-mail is not carefully designed to take this into consideration, the e-mail will appear as shown in Figure 6.4. This is annoying for the user and ineffective from the marketer's point of view for two main reasons. First, the content of the message is not clear since the images are not displayed. Secondly, the connection window will pop up once for each graphic in the e-mail and this will annoy the user. Two actions are possible to ameliorate this effect. First, the HTML <IMG> tag can be used so that the offer in the e-mail is still evident by alternative text (ALT="text"). This is straightforward. The example in Figure 6.5 shows an HTML e-mail where the offer is evident, even though the user has not downloaded the images. Secondly, the HTML e-mail can be encoded such that the pictures are downloaded as part of the message. This is a seamless process for the user, the only differences are that the pictures are all downloaded and the download of the message will take longer. This is sometimes referred to as 'tagging and bagging'. This approach is used by some e-tailers such as Jungle.com, who are aware of this problem, but the approach is not commonly used. This could be because it results in a longer download time, but this is not significant for the small images used in most e-mails. Alternatively, it could be because not all designers are aware of this solution, which is slightly more complex to implement.

To summarise this section, see Table 6.1. It is an honourable draw at four pros and four cons each. Returning to where we started, this emphasises the importance of asking the user and then dispatching the appropriate e-mail accordingly.

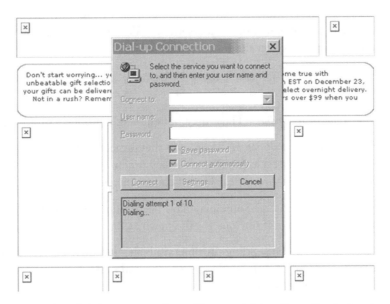

Figure 6.4 HTML e-mail and dial-up connection, offer not visible, alternative text not used

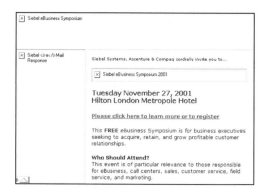

(a) With graphics downloaded

(b) Offline – no graphics

```
Siebel Systems, the world's leading provider of eBusiness applications software, presents:
Partner Relationship Management:
Maximising Revenue Through Channel Partners and Agents

http://www.siebel.com/register.htm

Thursday, March 14, 2002
2:00 p.m.–3:00 p.m. GMT
```

(c) Text – if reader can't read HTML and MIME encoded

Figure 6.5 Three different views of the same e-mail: (a) HTML with graphics downloaded; (b) HTML without graphics downloaded, alternative text used; and (c) text

Behavioural constraints

It is often said that to write good direct mail copy, you need to write for the reader, in other words to imagine the person who is reading your carefully crafted words. But to do this, we need to remember the different positions that our readers are in. Write down how their backgrounds vary. These are some of the variables you should consider:

- *How well do the recipients know your company?* Are they prospects, customers or first-time customers?

- *How well do they know your products?* Have they bought single products or a range of products?

- *What style of communications will appeal?* What will they expect from previous interactions with your brand? Do they like a direct approach or do they prefer a more involved dialogue? What is their age? They may prefer more or less formal communications accordingly.

- *How technologically literate are they?* Some may have been using e-mail and web sites for 5 years, others for only 5 weeks. Make it obvious for the newbies, but avoid patronising the old hands.

- *Do they scan or do they read?* Depending on time available, and their character, some recipients will just scan the e-mail body, whereas others prefer to read more carefully. You need to provide copy and design that works for both.

Table 6.1   Comparison of the benefits of using text and HTML e-mail

Issue	Text	HTML	Comment
Ease/cost of creation	Best	Worst	Graphic designers and HTML coders are not needed for text e-mails
Speed of download	Best	Worst	HTML e-mails are only significantly slower if they contain graphics that are not optimised for download
Ease of reading offline	Best	Worst	If the HTML e-mail has not been set up for the images to download with the e-mail (and they commonly have not) then the graphics will not be viewable when home users are not connected to the Internet
Receipt rates	Best	Worst	Corporate firewalls will stop some HTML messages; some corporate software, such as Lotus Notes, is not good at interpreting and displaying such messages
Differentiation	Worst	Best	Images and design can be used to distinguish and for branding, although the subject line is the same for each
Content	Worst	Best	More detailed content can be displayed in the same area
Response rates	Worst	Best	Research suggests that average response rates are highest for HTML e-mails
Monitoring open rates	Worst	Best	Only possible through HTML e-mails where one can assess the graphics downloading
User preference	?	?	This depends on the individual, so ask them!

By asking such questions you will build a picture of the range of people for whom you are writing. If it is not practical to write for such a wide range consider separating your mailing, for example into recently acquired customers and established customers.

Taking these factors together, develop three or four thumbnails of different types of people to whom you are looking to appeal.

To improve the effectiveness of our campaigns, it also helps to know about the different ways in which users manage their e-mail. Since e-mail is relatively new, compared with direct marketing, little research has been undertaken on this form of communication.

Some insights are evident from the following posts to the BBC web site. Think about how your e-mail design could be changed to accommodate these, or maybe whether you could process your e-mail more efficiently. These e-mail management habits are characteristic of processing e-mail at work:

> *I work on many projects at once. Each e-mail that is project-related has the project code in the header. I have a folder for each job number that I'm working on, as well as*

folders for general admin, personal, humour etc. When I'm very busy, e-mails just get dragged unread to the appropriate folder. Then at some point during the day I will make time to read all e-mails related to each subject.

I basically scan through the sender and subject information, if I don't recognise either then I delete it without thinking. I just don't have the time to read all the spam offering me low rate mortgages or Viagra online!'

I receive approximately two to three hundred e-mails a day. I cannot expect to read every one I receive, so I will read what I can when I have the time to do so, the rest I will never read. Any urgent matter should be dealt with in the traditional method: the telephone!'

I only read e-mail twice a day. Once at the start of the day, once at the end. Anything else more urgent can be dealt with in person or by phone.

It can be seen that there are different types of behaviour:

- 'Categorisers' will put items in folders to be dealt with later
- 'Deleters' ruthlessly delete e-mail if the subject line suggests no relevance to their work
- 'Scanners' skim read most e-mails for relevance
- 'Readers' will carefully read most e-mails since they don't want to miss out on some information.

Clearly, the behaviour will vary according to the volume of e-mail received, how busy the recipient is, the type of e-mail and their interest in it.

E-MAIL STRUCTURE

All e-mails are made up of the message header and the message body. The message header gives the basic properties or characteristics of the e-mail contained in different header fields. These header fields are displayed in the inbox and at the top of the message when opened. The two most important header fields are the From address and the subject line. These are most important, since these will determine whether the recipient decides to open the e-mail. We consider best practice for creating these below. Other fields include CC (carbon copy). This should always be blank for commercial e-mail campaigns. If you disclose the e-mail addresses of other recipients you are breaking their trust. The final header information is the date and time when the message was sent. The actual time and day of week the e-mail was sent can affect the open rate, as was discussed in Chapter 3. The message body is the main content of the e-mail which is viewed once the recipient clicks on the message. It is also visible in the preview pane if this is open (Figure 6.2).

E-MAIL HEADERS

We begin our detailed exploration of best practice for e-mail design by looking at the information in the e-mail headers. This includes the basic attributes of the e-mail which are displayed in the inbox, including From, To, subject line and date/time.

First impressions: From

Many concentrate on the subject line, but you should not neglect 'From', which is an indication of the sender. Figure 6.1 shows that as the recipients scan through their inbox, reading from left to right, their eyes will alight on 'From' before the subject line. In these days of SPAM, the From line should reassure the recipient that they know this person or company. They will be asking themselves whether they know the sender. If they do not they may delete the message straight away. For this reason it is often best that the company name is included in the 'From' address (see Oxfam and Informatica in Table 6.2). This may not be the case if you have decided to send an e-mail from the CEO using their name, which may not be known to all customers. For rented lists the From address is typically the name of the list owner, since it is important to indicate to the recipient that their name has been provided as part of an opt-in to a known company. For house lists there is slightly more flexibility on what can be used.

If the From address contains an '@' symbol, the recipient will mainly be looking at what is after the @ symbol. However, some companies also make use of the part of the address before the @ symbol. Figure 6.1 shows that some companies put a description of the offer before the @ symbol, such as 'offers@dabs.com' or 'Specials@Outpost.com'.

It is not essential to have the @ symbol in the 'From' column, since the 'From' part of the e-mail consists of two parts, the name associated with the address e.g. 'Dave Chaffey' and actual address 'dave.chaffey@marketing-insights.co.uk'. It is the name part of the address that is actually shown in the inbox in the 'From' column, so this can be set to anything. Table 6.2 shows that some e-mails just have the name of the company, whereas others use a campaign-specific address: 'Whatareyouworth' is actually from Workthing. This should intrigue the recipient (who is this from; what is it about?), even if the sender is not known. However, the teaser may be thought to be SPAM.

For regular e-mails such as newsletters it is probably best to have a standard address such as 'offers@dabs.com' or the name of the newsletter editor, but for campaigns it may be better that the sender is personalised, to suggest that the e-mail is from a person, not a machine. Some e-mails are sent from 'Webmaster', who the recipient is unlikely to know, so this is not a good idea. What about using the managing director or CEO? Well maybe, if the managing director is a well-known brand icon such as Richard Branson, Larry Ellison or Stelios Hajionu, but only if the e-mail conceivably involved them. If it is unlikely that they have drafted an e-mail about a special offer, then this

Table 6.2 Some examples of 'From' addresses and subject lines

From	Subject line
Workthing News	That was the year that was . . .
Whatareyouworth	Whatareyouworth?
Oxfam GB	Win a dream holiday in Oxfam's online raffle
Informatica	FREE CD – Guide to integrated mainframe data
g12816@china.com	NEED A DISASTER RECOVERY PLAN!
Directresponse@siebel.com	Free Call Center Web Seminar
offers@dabs.com	Wireless Gaming and Dect Phones at . . .
Specials@outpost.com	Exclusive Deals on Windows XP from Outpost

type of personalisation is false. Another alternative, which could be called semi-personalised, is to send the e-mail from a team such 'as 'The Loyalty Card Team' or the '<Company name> Team'.

Changing the 'From' address may be worthwhile for different campaigns to show that the e-mail is not just 'more of the same'. Being creative can help your e-mail to stand out from the others in the inbox.

A final point on the 'From' address is that this is the address that handles bounces and returns. It must be a valid e-mail address that can be accessed to view any queries, complaints or unsubscribe requests. There may be many replies from a large broadcast, so if you have used the CEOs e-mail, make sure that it is not their main account! However, make it look as if there could be a human at the other end of the line: directresponse@siebel.com does not fit into this category.

Gaining attention: the subject line

The importance of the subject line is self-evident. Think about what we are trying to achieve. For many years those that have developed adverts and direct mail have used the AIDA framework as they try to achieve Attention, Interest, Desire and Action. Where do you think the e-mail subject line fits in here? Certainly we are trying to attract attention, since the e-mail is competing for attention with many other e-mails. Furthermore, we have to stimulate interest and desire in order for the recipient to open the e-mail. The initial action is opening the e-mail, but through the subject line we are conditioning the recipient to take the ultimate action of clicking on a link.

Remember that the first two or three words of the subject line are most important as a user scans through the inbox. Remember also that you have a limited number of characters to get your message across (see Figure 6.1). The subject line should be designed for 30 characters (6 or 7 words), or at least you should be aware that beyond this characters can be deleted.

Approaches to devising the subject line

The subject line can use a number of techniques to gain attention. Common techniques are:

1. *The teaser*: this is intended to intrigue. It says 'read me'. It is often combined with a question. The first two questions in Table 6.2, both from Workthing, are teasers.

2. *The question*: this will usually allude to the benefits. It will work on a need or a problem that the customer may be facing, such as financial or time-based problems.

3. *The event tie-in*: this relates to different types of event, which may be annual holidays or company type events. The JD Edwards campaign in Chapter 6 is related to Valentine's Day. Although the service has no direct relationship to Valentine's Day, an indirect link has been found. 3M Health Care developed an acquisition campaign based on a product centenary.

4. *The direct approach*: we clearly state the offer or benefits, without trying to be intriguing or humorous.

5. *Personalised*: the name of the recipient can be incorporated into the start of the subject line. This is good for gaining attention since this approach is not commonly used. However, this may be for good reason, since it can lead to false sincerity: 'Special offers for Dave Chaffey', for example. The subject line can also be personalised according to particular product interest if a customer has previously purchased a similar product.

In many cases a combination of techniques is used within any one subject line. Look at the examples from my inbox (Table 6.2). Which technique(s) does each subject line use?

What to avoid in the subject line

This is a checklist of things to avoid in the subject line:

1. Make sure the subject line is not too long. If you leave the best to last, the offer may be truncated.

2. SHOUTING!!! Shouting is using capitals. It looks unprofessional. Worse still, it is often associated with SPAM, and SPAM filters stop e-mails with too many capitals in the subject line. Exclamation marks are not a good idea for similar reasons!!!

3. All SPAM characteristics. These are many and various, but some are deeply worrying to marketers; some SPAM filters remove any message with 'FREE' in the subject line. Messages starting with 'RE:', suggesting a response to an e-mail, are used by spammers, but are not likely to be filtered since they could be a valid e-mail. Other filters, which are described in more detail in Chapter 8 are perhaps less obvious. One bank that was offering preferential discounts to under 18s was filtered by SPAM filters looking for X-rated content.

Look at the examples from my inbox (Table 6.2). Spot the SPAM! It has the characteristic, dubious 'From address', SHOUTING and exclamation mark, and does not seem to know whether it is a question or not.

E-MAIL STYLE AND PERSONALITY

Farris and Langendorf (1999) note that since messages are likely to be interpreted literally, you should keep them straight, that is, to adopt a professional tone. E-mail is an informal medium, which lies somewhere between informal phone or face-to-face conversation and formal written communications. However, it is still a written medium and its informality is often reserved for well-known friends and colleagues. So 'instant familiarity' which involves adopting too casual a tone with someone you do not know will be inappropriate for many recipients. You have to earn informality. However, for some brands, such as Kangol (see Figure 6.6), a friendly, casual, conversational tone is right for the brand and the medium. For B2B communications a more direct, formal tone works best (see Figure 6.8).

We explore the tone of e-mail further in the checklist on copy (see Question 3: Is it natural?).

E-MAIL BODY CONTENT

The body of the e-mail typically contains the following elements, many of which are shared with direct mail pieces:

- header
- salutation or greeting to recipient
- lead or introduction
- main copy

- close, including call-to-action

- signature

- unsubscribe

- privacy statement or link.

Each of these is now considered in more detail.

Body headers (headlines)

Distinct from the message header described above, this is the first part of an e-mail body. Headers in the body are almost exclusively used in HTML e-mails since they cannot really fulfil the same function in text e-mails. The function of headers is partly to reassure, partly to inform and partly to offer more. To achieve this, the header is made up of different parts. Part of it is branding in the form of logo and name which will reassure the recipient if it is a well-known brand or credible organisation (Figure 6.6). The header can also give more information about what is on offer through a title to reinforce what is in the subject line. Finally, parts of the header can be clickable. For example, in a newsletter, a special offer can be highlighted by a banner advert in the header.

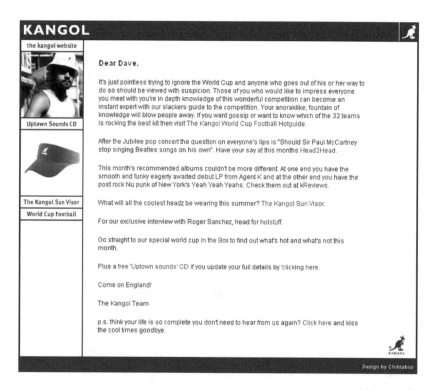

Figure 6.6 Kangol e-mail newsletter (www.kangol.com) (Source: David Hughes, E-mail Vision, www.emailvision.com)

Salutation

The initial greeting to the recipient is not the most important part of the e-mail in determining response rates, but it is one of the first things that will form an impression on the reader. It can set the tone of the e-mail as formal or fun. An appropriate salutation will vary according to the individual's preferences, but we can generalise that an older audience would prefer the more formal approach of Dear Mrs Smith or Dear Mr Smith. A younger audience may prefer Dear John or Joan, but this can suggest false intimacy, which may annoy some. The preferred salutation can be prompted for when a prospect first registers for opt-in, but it is probably one question too many.

Lead copy or introduction

After the header and salutation, you probably will not have much space left above the 'fold', the space for opening copy before the reader needs to scroll down (if they bother). So, think a maximum of two or three snappy sentences for the lead. In this space we need to develop the initial interest to encourage the user to scroll down to find more and click that call-to-action. Better still, if you can manage it, put the call-to-action 'above the fold', in or immediately below the lead. This way, if the prospect has decided to act, you will not delay them. This is successfully achieved in Figure 6.6, where a headline is used for the lead. Rather than encouraging scrolling down for more information, this e-mail encourages clickthrough to the web site for more information. The lead should flow smoothly from the subject line: there should not be a disconnect. You should not, however, repeat the subject line: think about how it can be modified to express the offer in a different way that helps to convince the recipient to click.

E-MAIL MARKETING INSIGHT

Make sure there is not a disconnect between the subject line and the lead, and that the lead reinforces rather than repeats the subject line.

What should the copy of these two or three snappy sentences contain? Typically, you will be expanding on the initial offer made in the subject line. Since your subject line is so short you will need to repeat the basic offer, but provide additional description of the features or benefits involved in the offer. You also need to reinforce the credibility of your company to deliver. Why is this offer better coming from you? A statement summarising the positioning of the company can help here.

Main copy

The main copy is for those readers who want to know more: those who have not lost interest and those who have not already clicked the initial call-to-action. So, the person who gets this far is likely to want detail and reassurance. Since we have a fair amount of detail here, this is often the place to use bullets with bold headings so that the detail can also be taken in by readers who are scanning (Figure 6.7 uses this approach). So, the main copy should include:

- A detailed description of the offer features. If the offer is for a holiday, what specifically is on offer? If the offer is for a seminar, what are the topics, what is the track-record of the speakers?

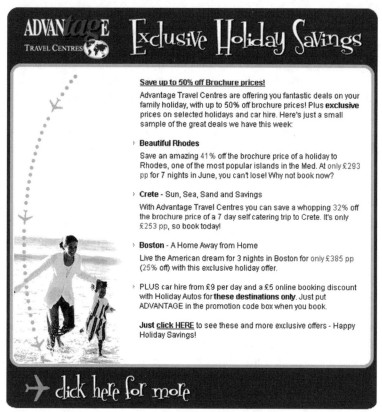

Figure 6.7 Advantage Travel Centres newsletter (www.advantage4travel.com) (Source: David Mill, MediaCo, www.media.co.uk)

- A detailed description of the offer benefits. In the case of the seminar, what benefits will those attending the seminar receive? You can combine features and benefits by adding 'which mean that ...' after each feature.

- Clear instructions about what to do next to receive the offer.

- A description of how the process for fulfilling the offer works.

Close

The main aim of the final part of the copy should be to achieve action. So, a link to execute the action should always be included with the close. The section on achieving the call-to-action below explains the best form for this. The reader will often have had to scroll down to get this far, and it may be worthwhile briefly repeating what has been said to date, in particular the offer.

Signature

This is the sign off. It describes who the e-mail is from. It should be consistent with the 'From' field of the e-mail address header. The form of sign off should be consistent with the remainder of the e-mail. These are some signatures for the e-mails in Table 6.2:

Workthing News

If you would prefer not to receive further messages from us, please follow these instructions:

1. Click on the Reply button.

2. Replace the Subject field with the word REMOVE.

3. Click the Send button.

You will receive one additional e-mail message confirming your removal.

Oxfam GB

If you do not wish to receive future emails, or you have received this message in error, simply reply to this mail with the word "unsubscribe" in the subject line. You'll be promptly removed.

Informatica

If you do not want to receive further e-mails from Informatica then please click below and we will automatically add you to our suppression database.

dabs.com

Unsubscribe information

Thank you for reading our newsletter. You have received this email as a customer of dabs.com and having been through our email preferences screen and requested further information of updates from dabs.com. However we respect your privacy and if you would like to unsubscribe from future updates please click on the UNSUBSCRIBE link below, or click on MODIFY to change your preference to receive a text only version.

Unsubscribe

This is simply an instruction. It should be reasonably prominent and straightforward if you believe in permission marketing. The instruction will usually take the form of typing Unsubscribe into the subject line of the reply or clicking on a link. You do not have to be formal here; Kangol use this 'cool' approach for the unsubscribe to their newsletter:

> *ps think your life is so complete you don't need to hear from us again? Click here and kiss the cool times goodbye.*

This is so 'cool' that it would stop me unsubscribing. Using 'update profile' is preferable.

Privacy statement or link

Since it is undesirable to have a full privacy statement in the e-mail body, this is usually a link back to the privacy statement on the web site. The required contents for privacy statements were covered in Chapter 4.

Related to privacy statement is a 'statement of origination' which explains who has sent the e-mail and why. The importance of this is also described in Chapter 4.

COPYWRITING

Smith and Chaffey (2002) use the acronym CRABS to describe how to write effective web-page copy. This is even more appropriate to e-mail copy, since we have less space to communicate. CRABS stands for:

- *Chunking*: chunking means that paragraphs must be shorter than in paper copy. Think one or two sentences only. This helps scannability.

- *Relevance*: with limited space, we have no room for fillers. Stick with what matters: the details of the offer and how to receive it.

- *Accuracy*: do not get carried away with your copy; do not set expectations so high that you overpromise and cannot deliver something you offer.

- *Brevity*: brevity goes with chunking and scannability. Write your copy, reduce the word count and then reduce it again. Give yourself targets and beat them without sacrificing good English and understanding.

- *Scannability*: this is reading without reading every word, just picking up the sense of each paragraph from the keywords. The eye will pick out words at the start of paragraphs and those emphasised in bold.

The title of Steve Krug's book on web usability gives a useful guideline for copywriting for e-mail: 'Don't make me think'. He also suggests that you should consider the amount of copy you have, halve it and halve it again.

If you have produced copy that follows the CRABS guidelines, you are only a small way there, since there are many issues of style to make successful copy. Check these six key copy questions against the B2B and business-to-consumer (B2C) examples from Figures 6.7 and 6.8 to see how these guidelines apply.

E-MAIL CAMPAIGN CHECKLIST

Six key copy questions

Question 1: Does it excite?

You have a great offer: have you supported the offer by writing enthusiastically to appeal to the reader's emotions? For the consumer you are offering riches, dreams and experiences. For the business person you are offering time, knowledge and control. Does the style of writing enthuse about these benefits? Does it have an initial impact?

Question 2: Does it convince?

You may believe that your service or your offer sells itself on its features, but the recipient is less likely to be a believer: they have neither your interest nor your knowledge. Have you backed up your promise with enough detail to convince the reader that the offer is worthwhile? Is the unique selling point clear?

Question 3: Is it natural?

E-mail is a social medium: we mainly use it to chat to friends or communicate to colleagues. So we want to avoid our e-mail reading as if it were written by a machine. If you can make it conversational, write at the level of your audience and make it flow naturally, then you will get closer to the reader and predispose them to what you are offering. However, do not overdo the informality; you are not writing to a close friend!

Which of the following styles is most natural and likely to achieve results: copy that is:

> **'Selling, slick, clever, funny, creative'**

or

> **'Informative, believable, memorable and persuasive'?**

Question 4: Is the length right?

Looking at the extremes, which is better: short copy or long copy? There can be no right answer because it depends on purpose. In many cases the reader does not want to read your carefully crafted words, just WIFM: 'What's in it for me?' My view is that you can combine short and long copy in one e-mail. For those who are more likely to respond to short copy you use the introduction and the start of the main copy which is above the fold. For the 'scanners', who scan through the whole e-mail, you may impress with detail, provided that detail stands out. For the 'readers', who read every word and want details, you need the long copy. The e-mail cannot be too long if it is relevant and entertaining and the call-to-action is not only included right at the end.

Question 5: Did you repeat yourself?

This is a difficult one. Direct mail wisdom says repeat to reinforce. E-mail wisdom says the reader does not have the time to see information repeated. However, I think some repetition is desirable. We need to repeat what is available in the subject line in the introduction. Then, because the reader has scrolled, repeating the offer in the final call-to-action makes sense.

Question 6: What stands out?

You have satisfied yourself that you can answer the other questions, but now, looking at the big picture, what will the scanner notice? What techniques have you used to *emphasise* the key points in your e-mail? The next section on emphasis reviews your options.

What not to include

We have said that brevity is key, so what do you not include? Jennings (2002) suggests that you should focus copy on what the 'readers want to know, need to know or both'. She suggests you put yourself in the readers' shoes and focus on answering their questions, rather than expounding on

Figure 6.8 E-mail creative from Croner publishers (www.croner.co.uk) (Source: David Mill, MediaCo, www.media.co.uk)

details of the company and its achievements that you are proud of. So, ask whether the reader will be influenced by copy; if not, leave it out.

EMPHASIS!

Think about how you can achieve emphasis of offers, benefits and calls-to-action for those scanning. Think about how you can use:

- CAPITALISATION, particularly in text e-mails, but don't overuse it

- the   space   before and after words and between lines: this is powerful in highlighting offers or calls-to-action

- bullets: asterisks work best in text e-mails to highlight the features or benefits of your offer

- chunking: short paragraphs of one or two sentences

- bold or larger font sizes in HTML e-mails, including in headings: the scanners' and skimmers' eyes especially are drawn towards these

- hyperlinks: blue underlined hyperlinks attract the eye online.

Many of these forms of emphasis are familiar from direct mail, but there are some that you should be wary of online. Using underlining should be avoided since the reader may think it is a hyperlink and will be annoyed if they cannot click on it. Italics are difficult to read online, but can be used in short paragraphs for testimonials. Use of exclamation marks should be limited to humour or for something outstanding.

Fonts

For text e-mails the e-mail will be displayed using the default, non-proportional font such as courier: you have no control.

For HTML e-mails, you have a choice of serif fonts such as Times or sanserif fonts such as Arial. Reading sanserif fonts is easier online and looks neater to most people (Figure 6.6). This is the reverse of the offline world, where most print publications use serif fonts. Look in your own inbox: almost all of the commercial HTML e-mails will be sanserif. You will often find that HTML spam uses serif fonts, so avoid this. However, you might use a serif font in an e-mail if you wanted to be distinctive and appeal to an older audience (Figure 5.8).

CALLS-TO-ACTION

I have called this subsection 'calls-to-action' since you should always consider multiple calls-to-action in your e-mail. There should be at least two calls-to-action because of the limited screen area in which the e-mail is being read. In addition, different recipients may want to click at different times. If one person likes the offer, they will click on it impulsively at the top of the e-mail, but another person may want to scroll down for the details and will then click if the offer suits. So, what we want to achieve ideally is a call-to-action that is viewable and clickable when the e-mail is first opened, and each time the recipient scrolls down using the 'page down' key. There should be a call-to-action at the end of piece, but also near the middle or top, even if they are the same link.

E-MAIL MARKETING INSIGHT

Use multiple calls-to-action.

You will also need to decide how focused to keep your calls-to-action. For specific campaigns, it is best to have a single landing page with multiple calls-to-action leading through to this. What you do not want is a hyperlink leading to a general page giving more detail about the company. However, for a newsletter, multiple links to different areas of the web site are more acceptable, provided they are not too prominent and do not distract from the main offers.

Call-to-action copy

The call-to-action should reiterate the offer and explain the benefits that the recipient will receive by clicking on the link. To encourage action a secondary offer may have been introduced in the earlier copy. This can also be restated at this point.

When devising your call-to-action, remember that you are not simply trying to get the recipient to act, rather you are trying to get them to act now. We have seen that the majority of responses to an e-mail campaign are received within the first 36 hours. This suggests that if we cannot achieve that immediate response on impulse we are unlikely ever to get it. A simple way of achieving immediate action is to give an instruction 'Click now'. This may persuade a small number of people to clickthrough. Better still, think about how you can make it a time-limited offer. Give a date or number of days the offer is open for. A week is probably too long; recipients will forget about the e-mail. What about a 2 or 3 day offer? Alternatively, the offer can be limited by number of entries, although this may exclude those who think they do not have a chance.

For example, this e-mail from Data Warehouse supplier Informatica has the subject line:

> *FREE CD - INFORMATICA'S GUIDE TO HIGH-PERFORMANCE DATA WAREHOUSING*

This offer will be sufficient for some recipients to want to click immediately, for example, if they are an IS manager currently evaluating this area. The opening copy repeats the offer in the subject line, with the call-to-action:

> *Dear <named recipient>,*
>
> *Get all the information you need to take your data up to the next level on one FREE interactive CD!*
>
> *CLICK HERE FOR YOUR FREE CD*
>
> *Your details will be automatically displayed on screen. Simply answer the 3 short questions and click the request button.*
>
> *Your FREE CD will then be despatched to you shortly.*

Details are then provided for those who want to know a little more before clicking:

> *Informatica's interactive CD Guide to high-performance data warehousing contains essential reading for IT strategists. On one FREE CD, you'll find detailed case studies from some of the world's largest companies, important white papers and an extensive range of datasheets and product brochures.*

The call-to-action is then repeated with alternative copy:

> *CLICK HERE TO TAKE YOUR DATA UP TO THE NEXT LEVEL … AND BEYOND*

Call-to-action hyperlinks

Clicking on the hyperlinks within an e-mail will take the recipient to the landing page. The form of the hyperlinks will vary according to the format of the e-mail. We look at text e-mails first, then HTML. In text e-mails, the call-to-action must be the physical address of the landing page, such as:

http://www.company.com/landing_page.htm?id=testing_tags

Try to keep this address as short and simple as possible, although this may be difficult if you are coding the response with testing tags. We showed in Chapter 3 that the different calls-to-action can be tagged so that when we look at the web-site statistics, we can see which was the most effective call-to-action. You will not want to use the text 'testing tags' in your e-mail. If you find that the banner at the head of an HTML e-mail or the first link 'above the fold' works best, then this is where you should concentrate your creative efforts in future. For example, if you have two links in your e-mail to the same landing page you might test them as follows:

http://www.company.com/landing_page.htm?id="top"

and

http://www.company.com/landing_page.htm?id="bottom"

To highlight the call-to-action the link should be separated on a different line and a clear instruction made to click on it. CAPS work in both text and HTML e-mails. For example, a company selling solutions to IT managers to reduce their costs may use this approach:

Click below to receive your complimentary guide to reducing Total Cost of Ownership.

http://www.company.com/TCOguide

Sign Off

Note that in this case we have made the address slightly simpler by creating a directory on the web server 'TCOguide' which contains a landing page 'index.htm'. This page will be automatically opened when the link is clicked on.

For HTML e-mails we do not have to include the daunting full URL in the title. Consider our options for the example above. Four options include changing the copy to:

A. Click below to receive your complimentary guide to reducing Total Cost of Ownership:

FREE guide to reducing TCO

Sign Off

B. Click here to receive your complimentary guide to reducing Total Cost of Ownership

C. To receive your complimentary guide to reducing Total Cost of Ownership, click here

D. To help you lower the costs of running your IT infrastructure we have a prepared a complimentary guide to reducing Total Cost of Ownership

A is an equivalent of the call-to-action for the text e-mail. It is less appropriate here. Although separating out the hyperlink on to a separate line does increase its prominence it spoils the flow of the copy. The other approaches are more common in HTML e-mails.

I prefer B to C since it is more direct and the eye will be more naturally drawn towards the underlined hyperlink at the start of the sentence within the copy as a whole. Design practice for web pages would favour approach D, which makes the call-to-action part of the copy. This may work best for web pages where we are not seeking the hard-sell. For simplicity and encouraging action approach B is best.

Think carefully about the colour of the hyperlink. On the majority of web pages, Yahoo! and Amazon, for example, users are used to seeing a blue hyperlink on a white background. You will get a higher response with this combination because of familiarity. If a white background is inconsistent with your brand or the theme, then it is important to ensure that the call-to-action has good contrast. I have received e-mails with a blue hyperlink on a red background. Sometimes hyperlinks are not underlined because of the branding. Being partially colour blind, like a fair few people, I cannot see link text such as that at the end of the sentences in Figure 6.6. You may also want to use slightly larger text for the call-to-action for this reason. I would argue that you should never, for aesthetic reasons, change the link so that it is not underlined. Put simply, fewer recipients will click on it.

As a reminder of the main points in this section on copy, see the guidelines by David Mill below.

E-MAIL MARKETING EXCELLENCE

Best practice for e-mail copy

David Mill of specialist e-marketing agency MediaCo (www.media.co.uk) gives these best practice guidelines for e-mail copy.

Body content

You have some 10 seconds to grab the attention of the recipient after they have opened the message. Therefore, the content should:

- *be relevant and focused*: the more it appeals to your audience, the better the results

- *make the objective obvious*: for example, 'Enter our competition to win' or 'Here is the latest news on . . .'. In addition, it's often good practice to take an early opportunity to tell the recipient why they are receiving the email. For example: 'You have received this newsletter because . . .'.

With regard to the message itself, it should:

- *be clear and concise*

- *be written in plain language*

- *avoid jargon*: no buzzwords, jargon, funky phrases or punctuation unless expected by the target market

- *be kept short*: short copy delivers results but, if it must be long, a synopsis or content list should be provided at the outset. HTML versions that can be viewed in one screen are also most effective. If they are longer, key elements should be viewable above the fold

- *be immediately of interest*, having the key points and main clickthrough links in the immediately viewable area

- *be creative*, so it stands out from the crowd.

Generally speaking, the content should:

- be compelling active voice and action verbs
- talk about THEM not you
- place them in the action
- stress benefits not features
- build real and perceived value
- have personality ... so you and the recipient connect.

A newsletter is most effective when it does one of two things:

- It reflects the typical reader's personality; it appeals to the reader at another level, i.e. be a personality the reader can both recognise and accept within the context of the newsletter.
- This personality also adds to the human element of the newsletter and boosts the one-to-one characteristic of e-mail marketing, bearing in mind it is not an audience that is being addressed; it is an individual sitting alone in front of a screen.

E-mail disclaimers

These are mainly relevant to interpersonal e-mails, but if your company does not use these, then e-commerce lawyer Jo Brook who works for Sprecher Grier Halberstam suggests that disclaimers should inform the recipient that (*IT Week*, 2002):

- The message is intended for the named individual. If it is transmitted incorrectly, it should be deleted.

- The message received may not be the view of the organisation, but is the view of the individual.

- If the e-mail is forwarded for someone's attention the whole e-mail should be forwarded.

- Their response e-mails may be monitored or stored.

For full legal force, the e-mail disclaimer should be at the start of the e-mail, but for practical reasons, most disclaimers are found at the foot of e-mails.

LANDING PAGES

The attributes of achieving conversion through landing pages were described in Chapter 4. There should be a specific landing page for each campaign, which is not the home page. The landing page should:

- support the tone of the campaign

- include a summary of the offer, but not too much detail unless this was not possible in the original e-mail

- provide more detailed information

- not ask for too much information or too many fields

- not give too many links to elsewhere in the site: do not include a complete menu template to all other parts of the site

- be tested for attrition, unless you have run similar campaigns before

- include privacy statements.

TESTING CREATIVE

In the last part of Chapter 4, we described approaches to testing the different components of a campaign. A common problem with testing the creative is that there is a wide variety of options. To avoid the need to test all options Mercer Management Consulting recommends using an experimental design. Mercer MC (2001) gives the example of campaign testing for Crayola using Mercer Management's Nexperiment methodology. To evaluate a combination of three different salutations, five offers and six price points would have required 360 test e-mails. However, Nexperiment uses a subset of the combinations. This helped to identify a combination of creative that was more than three times more effective than the worst combination in generating a response. An indication of the approaches is shown in Table 6.3.

E-NEWSLETTER DESIGN

Many of the principles of effective design covered above apply equally to all types of e-mail campaign, whether e-promotions or regular e-newsletters. However, there are some specific issues

Table 6.3 Combinations of creative elements for Crayola.com e-mail test from Mercer MC (2001) with changes in response rates compared with worst case shown

Creative element	Worst combination	Best e-mail script
Subject line	Help us to help you (0%)	Crayola.com survey (7.5%)
Salutation	Greetings (0%)	User name (3.4%)
Call-to-action	As Crayola.com grows . . . (0%)	Because you are . . . (3.5%)
Offer	No offer (0%)	$25 Amazon gift certificate drawing (5.2%)
Close	Crayola.com (0%)	Editor: Crayola.com (1.2%)
Overall response	9.7%	33.7%

for e-newsletters as a result of their format. In Chapter 5, we looked at 12 different issues concerned with e-newsletters such as audience, proposition, frequency and length. Here we will look briefly at some of the issues of newsletter layout and design.

We will mainly look at HTML newsletter design, since this gives many more options for layout, but first, a quick look at text e-newsletters.

Text e-newsletters

Using rules and space helps to divide content. This is from the excellent Nua newsletter (www.nua.com/surveys):

NEWS STORIES START HERE

ACCESS DEVICES

Archives: http://www.nua.com/surveys/index.cgi?f=FS&cat_id=26

Detica: 3G services gets the thumbs up

Over 77 percent of respondents who undertook a demonstration trial of 3G services in the UK, found the individual services either 'appealing' or 'highly appealing'.

http://www.nua.com/surveys/index.cgi?f=VS&art_id=905358111&rel=true

Most text newsletters start with a clear header to highlight the newsletter proposition and issue. This is from Nua:

NUA INTERNET SURVEYS NUA INTERNET SURVEYS NUA INTERNET SURVEYS Free weekly email on the latest Internet trends and statistics

Email: surveys@nua.com Web: http://www.nua.com/surveys/

July 1, 2002 Published by: ComputerScope Ltd Volume 7 Number 23

A summary of the contents then follows, possibly with an editorial or introduction before the articles start. Some newsletters use a 'less is more' approach and offer insights on a single topic; for example, the BRMBi Bytesize has a single topic such as 'Attitudes to online advertising' or 'The Evolving use of the web'.

After the article(s) a standard footer includes the unsubscribe, copyright and other legal details. It can also link to the web site for further information, perhaps about new product launches or promotions, if the main purpose of the newsletter is to inform rather than to sell.

HTML e-newsletters

When we move to HTML e-newsletters the amount of information that can be communicated increases dramatically, but with this the complexity of design and the costs also increase. I am often asked whether companies should use a fixed e-newsletter structure. This can be answered by looking at printed publications. Most newspapers and magazines only modify their page layouts and overall structure when they need rejuvenation, not every issue. Agreeing on a standard format or template will also help to crank out the e-newsletters each month. Figure 6.9 illustrates a generic newsletter layout which gives a checklist of the type of content you may want to use.

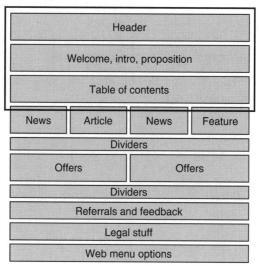

Figure 6.9 Generic e-mail newsletter layout showing different components

The header is an area that is used to brand the e-mail and can also be used as a navigation element. Sometimes menu options will link to headings further down the piece (an underused feature). Sometimes these menu headings will link back to the web site. If they are to the site, highlighting this may prevent confusion. Offers can be highlighted in the header, which is the case in Figure 6.10. If the newsletter is long, with a number of news items or articles, it is conventional to have a table of contents, although since this can use up a lot of space above the fold, it is not always used. Below this, articles, features and promotions can be included in standard positions. A two- or three-column layout such as in Figure 6.10 maximises the use of space as for print, with the number of columns varying, but not too much, throughout the newsletter. For shorter e-newsletters such as in Figures 5.5 or 6.7 which have more focus, a single- or two-column layout can be most effective.

Figure 6.10 shows the layout for a newsletter annotated to show good features. The use of vertical and horizontal rules within this newsletter is effective.

Getting recipients to open e-newsletters: the message header

How do we get the recipient to open the newsletter, given, as we said in Chapter 5, that they may receive several each day? First and foremost, we do not want the subject line to be the same each month, for example 'Company name newsletter for June'. We can make much more use of the subject line if it contains information about the contents, theme or primary offer. These are some examples from the dabs.com newsletter:

- Broadband Britain – the economical way to ride the ADSL wave

- HP put their money where their mouth is!

- Bid now for cut price car audio & more!

- More tools to make your life easier . . .

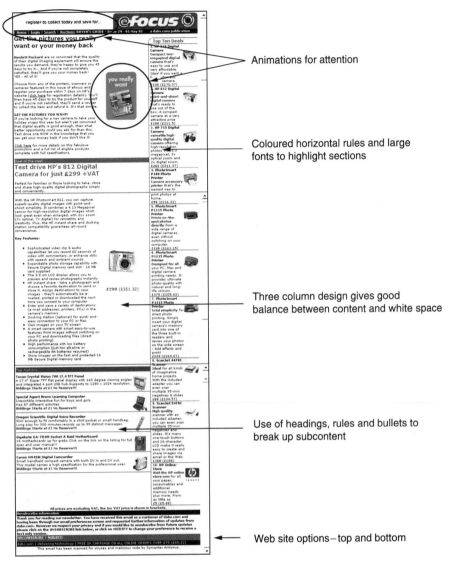

Animations for attention

Coloured horizontal rules and large fonts to highlight sections

Three column design gives good balance between content and white space

Use of headings, rules and bullets to break up subcontent

Web site options–top and bottom

Figure 6.10 A dabs.com newsletter showing the content possible using a three-column layout

These highlight the theme for each week and have a good variety to catch the eye. The Dr EBiz newsletter also highlights different topics in the subject line and adds the first name to grab attention and adds a date for reference:

- Dave, Dr Ebiz: Forums, Surveys, Affiliate Tracking, Titles

- Dave, Newsletters, Banner Sales, Leases, SE Submission, 7/3/02

- Dave, Dr Ebiz: Copyright Permissions, URL Changes, Sponsors, 4/3/02

Some newsletters highlight the main topic in each newsletter, for example a subject line from the quarterly 'Visitor Intelligence News' newsletter from web analytics provider Site Intelligence is: 'How to track visitors who leave the website'.

Remember not to waste the From address. Often, this duplicates the name of the newsletter, as in: 'From: ICONOCAST, Subject: ICONOCAST: Say goodbye to guesswork. Get smarter. but – Don't waste it'. So, use the From for the name of the newsletter.

Newsletter content and copy

As we said in Chapter 5, a key trick with e-newsletters is getting the balance right between sell and inform. This balance depends on how the newsletter is positioned. Figure 6.10 is overtly about selling and this is what it does. However, many newsletters for B2B customers are offered as an information source. In this case, the sell/inform balance should favour informing.

Many of the comments made earlier about copy tone and style also apply to e-newsletters, but an added factor is whether there should be an editor. If there is an editor, preferably pictured, as for the ClickZ newsletters, this helps to develop a connection between the writer and the reader. The

Figure 6.11   Best practice: E-mail newsletter from Stanfords (www.stanfords.co.uk) (Source: David Mill, MediaCo, www.media.co.uk)

editor can develop his or her own style and idiosyncracies, which will become familiar to the reader. However, this approach may not be true in all cases. A useful question to ask about your newsletters is 'Should the personality reflect the reader's personality, the writer's personality or your brand?' The typical answer to this question is that it must reflect the brand, but should also show some degree of the writer's personality, and that this should generally match that of the reader.

Figure 6.11 illustrates a monthly HTML e-newsletter from Stanfords. Some of the principles of good newsletter design it highlights are:

- a themed approach for the month
- an index to access detailed content
- a 'tell a friend' viral element
- a combination of two- and three-column design
- an archive option.

HOW NOT TO DO IT

We end this chapter by looking at how not to do it. eMarketer (2002) reported on a survey of 1250 US e-mail users and asked them about the most annoying features of permission e-mail marketing. The most annoying features mentioned, from highest to lowest (including multiple responses), were:

- Suspect that the company is sharing your address (74%)
- Tried unsubscribing in vain (69%)
- Messages too frequent (66%)
- Nothing of value being sent (59%)
- Too much e-mail in general (53%)
- Messages not targeted to interests (53%)
- Product you seldom buy (46%)
- Not good price (43%)
- E-mails do not affect purchase decisions (37%)
- Messages too 'hard-sell' (36%)
- No longer interested in topic (27%)
- E-mails use 'rich media' (15%)
- E-mails use HTML (7%)

So, the design and style of the creative is not what bugs people; rather, it is when the targeting, timing, relevance and offer are wrong. All of these factors have to be right before we even start on the creative.

REFERENCES

Doubleclick (2002). Q2 E-mail Trend Report. Published at www.doubleclick.net.

eMarketer (2002). Consumers want more from e-mail marketing. eStatNews from eMarketer, 20 May.

Farris, J. and Langendorf, L. (1999). Engaging customers in e-business, how to build sales, relationships and results with e-mail. Whitepaper (www.e2software.com).

Grossman, E. (2002). Real-World Email Client Usage: The Hard Data. http://www.clickz.com/em_mkt/infra/article.php/1428551, 19 July 2002.

IT Week (2002). Keeping e-mail woes at bay. *IT Week*, 15 April.

Jennings, J. (2002). *Evaluating your e-mail campaign, Part 2*. Clickz, 28 February (www.clickz.com).

Mercer MC (2001). Making CRM make money. A Mercer Management Consulting commentary (www.mercermc.com).

Smith, PR and Chaffey, D. (2002). *eMarketing eXcellence: The Heart of eBusiness*. Oxford: Butterworth-Heinemann.

7

E-mail marketing management

CHAPTER AT A GLANCE

Overview

This chapter is about making it happen. We will look at the best way to implement your plans by discussing how to resource e-mail marketing in terms of using partners, purchasing software and managing inbound enquiries.

Chapter objectives

By the end of this chapter you will be able to:

● assess the best approach for resourcing your e-mail marketing

● develop a strategy for managing inbound e-mail.

Chapter structure

● Introduction

● Selecting solution providers

● Managing a campaign

● Choosing e-mail management software

● List servers

● Desktop e-mail management software

● Application service provider model

● Managing the house list

● Managing inbound e-mail

SELECTING SOLUTION PROVIDERS

An important part of your e-mail marketing strategy, although perhaps a mundane part, is the development of a resourcing strategy. This involves identifying the best partners for helping to develop acquisition and retention campaigns. This can be a complex decision since different suppliers will often be selected for different aspects of e-mail marketing. So, you may decide that one agency manages your e-mail promotion campaigns and another your e-newsletter. You may also have different suppliers managing your web site and customer data. In addition, who you use will change through time. You may start by outsourcing your e-newsletter development since you do not have experience in this and want to learn through your supplier. If you are unhappy with the supplier you may change, later perhaps bringing the e-newsletter in-house, by which time you have the necessary experience and skills to manage this at a lower cost.

Then there are the options for resourcing different aspects of each campaign. A typical sequence of activities is strategy, creative design, media buying, e-mail creative execution, web-site design and hosting, data management and e-mail broadcasting. In-house skills may be available for some of these activities, but not for others. Perhaps the skills are available, but time is not. Where there is a resource shortage in terms of skills or time, or if it is thought that outsourcing may be cheaper, then the outsourcing option will be explored. There are two main outsourcing options: a specialist full-service e-mail marketing agency or a traditional marketing/direct marketing agency. Since e-mail marketing is still relatively new there is a strong argument for using the specialist e-mail marketing agency since they will be likely to have experience of most types of campaign, so they have experimented and tested, and will know what works and what does not work. They will also be able to participate in all aspects of the campaign. Unless more traditional agencies have recruited expertise their staff will be learning as they complete your job.

Figure 7.1 summarises the main options for resourcing e-mail campaigns. The client can complete all of the work themselves or they can work with a variety of partners. They may decide on a single 'one-stop shop' or 'full-service' partner to manage all aspects of the campaign; often this will be a specialist e-mail or web marketing agency, or increasingly it could be e-mail and e-marketing specialists within a traditional marketing agency. This agency will manage the strategy and design of the campaign and this work will usually be done internally, although other specialists with HTML or graphic design skills may be brought in. If an acquisition campaign is being run, the client or their agency has the choice of approaching a list owner such as a magazine publisher direct, or they may go through a specialist list broker. Acquisition centres offer a further option for acquiring consumer e-mail addresses, as described in Chapter 4. Finally, the agency or client may broadcast the list themselves or this can be managed through an e-mail broadcaster.

Application service providers (ASPs)

As well as the in-house and outsourced options, there is the application service provider (ASP) option, which lies somewhere between the two. An ASP provides a web-based service that can be used by the client to manage their e-mail activities. Rather than buying software that you host and manage on your server, the software is effectively used on a subscription basis and runs on another company's server. In other words, it provides the technical infrastructure that is needed to run the campaign: this could include the web hosting of the microsite or landing page, the broadcast tools for dispatching the e-mails and the database containing the prospect or customer profiles. For example, you could use a list server ASP which hosts your newsletter archive, manages the subscriber list and broadcasts the newsletter each month. However, you may still do some of the work.

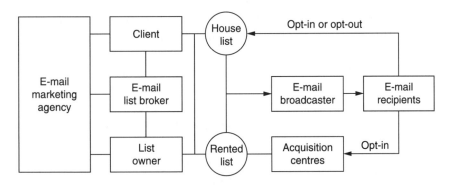

Figure 7.1   Structure of the e-mail marketing industry

For the e-newsletter you will probably create the content each month and upload it to the ASP service for dispatch.

The Aberdeen Group (2000) identifies differences from purchasing licensed software. According to them, with licensed software, the customer must:

- develop and support the IT infrastructure of the application

- make a large capital investment in acquiring and installing the software. For this reason, licensed software is relatively difficult to trial

- develop considerable internal expertise in the use of the software to realise its full potential

- cope with regular software upgrades, bug fixes and version releases.

The ASP model removes many of these problems. It offers:

- reduction or elimination of many of the up-front capital expenses associated with implementing new software systems and databases

- access to skilled IT professionals. The ASP has to pay good rates, perhaps more than you can afford, to deliver a world-class service

- a guarantee of a specific and agreed-on service level

- reduced deployment time

- the potential to reduce systems integration expenses.

The Aberdeen Group (2000) distinguishes between two different types of ASP. First, there is the ASP that is just providing a software service to dispatch and monitor e-mails. Secondly, there is a service that can also deliver strategy, creative design and testing: a service bureau. Aberdeen refers to these as Internet business solutions providers (IBSPs).

MANAGING A CAMPAIGN

In Chapter 3 we looked at key issues in developing a campaign such as the targeting, offer, creative and timing. In detail, there are many more activities that need to be managed within the campaign. Figure 7.2 summarises the tasks under three main headings of A: Design, B: Obtain list and C: Deploy. All of the tasks in stages A and B can happen at a similar time once objectives have been agreed, but stage C is dependent on the other two stages. All of these tasks are either handled internally or shared between the client and their agency. Figure 7.2 shows the tasks where client input is required in italics. Note that if the client is busy with other projects, then these are potential bottlenecks since all hand-offs between one group of people and another will create delay. If the whole project is in-house, then it could take place in less than 24 hours with dedicated staff and simple creative. More often, though, it will take days or even weeks. Entering a time against each of the tasks in A and B and displaying them on a Gantt chart can certainly help to keep the tasks under control.

The process in Figure 7.2 will be swifter if the first two stages are efficient. The clearer the brief produced by the client and the proposal received from the selected consultant, the quicker the overall process. What then should go in the brief? Some general guidelines are given below.

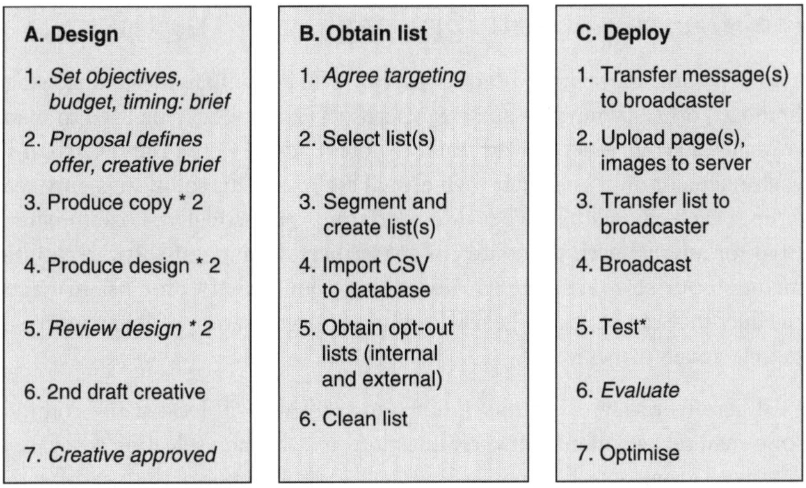

A. Design	B. Obtain list	C. Deploy
1. *Set objectives, budget, timing: brief*	1. *Agree targeting*	1. Transfer message(s) to broadcaster
2. *Proposal defines offer, creative brief*	2. Select list(s)	2. Upload page(s), images to server
3. Produce copy * 2	3. Segment and create list(s)	3. Transfer list to broadcaster
4. Produce design * 2	4. Import CSV to database	4. Broadcast
5. *Review design * 2*	5. Obtain opt-out lists (internal and external)	5. Test*
6. 2nd draft creative	6. Clean list	6. *Evaluate*
7. *Creative approved*		7. Optimise

Figure 7.2   A three-stage campaign plan

E-MAIL CAMPAIGN CHECKLIST

What goes in a campaign brief?

1. Describe how the required campaign fits into the overall marketing strategy and communications strategy, including targeting marketing and differentiation strategy.

2. Clearly state the success criteria or objectives for the campaign.

3. The brief should not be too prescriptive about the form of the execution. Briefs often describe the exact media and offer to use. By being too prescriptive, creativity is stifled; however, this may be more practical if time is tight.

4. Detail the nature of the target audience(s). This should include psychographics as well as demographics. Agencies will often not know the psychographics of the recipients. Thumbnail profiles that show how they live and what appeals to them can help here.

5. Outline competitors and how they differentiate their services.

6. Specify the testing required before the campaign and how the campaign will be modified (if needed) mid-campaign.

7. Provide brand guidelines, including tone, style and personality, for consistency with other campaigns.

8. Specify constraints in time and money.

CHOOSING E-MAIL MANAGEMENT SOFTWARE

We now turn to software that can be used as part of e-mail campaign planning stages B and C (Figure 7.2). Standard office groupware such as Microsoft Outlook may be used to manage mailing lists. To send e-mails, a group is set up with each recipient added to the Blind Carbon Copy (BCC) field, so that each recipient only sees their own e-mail address. This solution is only really practical for a small list, since each contact has to be added and removed manually. To automate this process, which is essential for any list with thousands of subscribers, a range of software solutions is available. These include both software that you install on your own PC for list management and a server-based product that can be located elsewhere in the organisation or by an external ASP and is usually accessed via a web browser.

It is not practical here to review all of the options; instead, we will look at the common functions and structure of e-mail management software, questions to ask when selecting software and some of the more widely used products. The options we will look at support the use of e-mail both for individual campaigns and for e-newsletters.

Figure 7.3 highlights the main components of e-mail management software. The inbound module is used to manage the subscription and unsubscription process. It will decipher an e-mail sent from an HTML form that will contain fields from the form, such as email=first.lastname@company.com or Postcode=LA991PD, and will add these to a database of contact details. This list can be either a text file maintained by the e-mail software, or a separate relational database such as SQL Server or MySQL. This module will also send out a confirmation e-mail (autoresponse) that the subscriber has been added to the list. This module usually also manages hard bounces from campaigns and is able to remove the e-mail from the list. Note that the functions of this module can also be built in to the web site itself. If the site is built using a tool such as Cold Fusion or Active Server Pages, the contact details from the HTML form can be added directly to a database and a confirmation message sent. This has the benefit that information collected from the web can be integrated

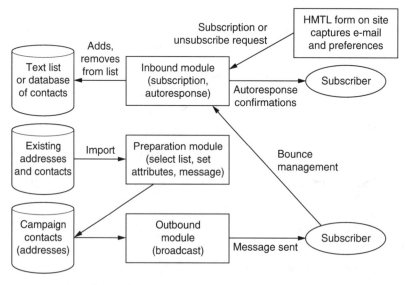

Figure 7.3 Components of e-mail management software

with existing databases. For small-scale sites, however, it may be easier to use a separate list in the format provided by the software.

The preparation module is used to prepare the e-mail to send. First, the members of the list that you want to define have to be selected. For example, if you only want to send the e-mail to female subscribers from the last 2 months it will be possible to select these. This creates a separate campaign contacts list which is then broadcast by the outbound module. This module also enables the message header to be specified (i.e. the From, To and Subject line fields). Finally, the content and type of the e-mail (text or HTML) associated with the campaign will be assigned.

The outbound module is for broadcasting the e-mails. It simply processes the list of recipients and sends the appropriate message to each (text, HTML or MIME) via the SMTP mail server of the Internet Service Provider (ISP) or organisation. If the message is not received (a bounce), it will usually also record this and the SMTP server will continue trying to send it for a specified period. If it is not received (a hard bounce), the recipient can be removed from the list.

When selecting software for e-mail management there are many issues to consider. Here are some of the main ones:

- Does the software support all three modules described above?

- Do the inbound module and preparation module integrate directly with a relational database using defined fields, or is it necessary to export from the database and then import into the mailer software format?

- Is it easy to add e-mails and details captured offline? Can they be added as a batch from a text file, or entered manually via a form?

- Does the preparation module enable multiple selects, i.e. how many fields can be used to select the members of the list you require?

- Do the preparation and broadcast module support a mixture of text, HTML and MIME e-mails for sending?

- Is an additional programme required for designing HTML e-mails? Is a preview of the message shown when selecting the message to be sent?

- Can you include test records, which you sent to your own test addresses both before and during the main mailing?

- Can configuration settings be saved to make multimessage campaigns easier?

- Does it readily support multiple newsletters based on users' preference selected from the form?

- Can database fields be placed (merged) on the subject line such as name or product interest for personalisation?

- Can the body of the message be personalised, by placing merge fields such as 'Dear <First Name>' or 'As a purchaser of <Product name>'?

- How well does it support recovery from a failure part way through a mailing (if, for example, the connection is lost)?

- How are bounces handled? Are the hard bounce addresses automatically removed from the list?

- Can conditional statements be used to tailor the e-mail body? For example:

> *IF product category = TV THEN*
>
> *Insert Text Block*
>
> *ELSEIF product category = HIFI THEN*
>
> *Insert Text Block*
>
> *ELSE*
>
> *No insertion*
>
> *ENDIF*

- Does broadcasting support multithreading, being able to send more than one message at a time for speed?

- What reporting options are available for monitoring bounces, clickthroughs, subscriptions and unsubscribes?

- What are the error handling features of the different modules?

- Is the documentation easy to follow and what support is there when things go wrong?

Finally, if it fulfils all the other criteria satisfactorily, look at price.

We will now look at some of the more widely used solutions for managing e-mail. We start by looking at the List server products, which are usually hosted by ASPs, and then look at desktop software.

LIST SERVERS

List servers are software tools, hosted on a server computer, which are used for managing e-mail communications. They are well-established tools; the first version of Listserv was introduced in 1981. Many list servers are ASPs that are used by many companies worldwide. An idea of the scale of these list servers is indicated by SparkLIST.com. This company announced in 2002 that it delivers 750 million e-mails a month (9 billion a year) to over 50 million e-mail list members, which it manages on behalf of its e-mail list hosting clients.

List servers are used for broadcasting e-mails, but also manage the addition and removal of subscribers to and from an e-mail list. Adding and removing subscribers was traditionally carried out by e-mail subscribe and unsubscribe messages, but these may be confusing for novice users, so in selecting a list server, the option to be able to use a web form to add or remove a subscriber from the list is essential for commercial organisations. They are most typically used for managing e-mail newsletters, but can also be used for promotional e-mail campaigns. The mailing lists they are used for can be one-way, which is the case with a standard newsletter, or two-way where they are used for a discussion mailing list which is usually a moderated forum about a particular topic. Such discussion mailing lists such as UK NetMarketing (www.chinwag.com) may involve tens of messages or 'posts' each day, so list servers offer two different methods of e-mail delivery. The first is where single messages are delivered as soon as they have been posted and the second is digest delivery, which contains all the messages for a day or week in a single message. A further option to consider for such mailing lists is whether web-based delivery is possible. This allows subscribers or non-subscribers to view current or archived messages.

The names of the main list servers that are available reflect their 'techie' heritage. The summary below is based on more detailed information available at ServerWatch (www.serverwatch.internet.com). Note that the list servers are usually purchased outright with an annual maintenance fee. An increasingly popular option is to use the list server on an ASP basis, where management of the list is outsourced. The main options for list servers are:

- *ListProc* (www.listproc.net): the most common users of this package are educational organisations, for which the fee is waived.

- *Majordomo* (www.greatcircle.com/majordomo): according to ServerWatch this is the most popular list server since it is free. It is a modular package that includes some graphical subscription and viewing interfaces, which may make installation lengthy and complex.

- *Listserv* (www.lsoft.com): based on development of the original List Server, this package is available for both Microsoft Windows and UNIX-based servers. There is an advanced web-based interface for subscribers and list managers. L-Soft, the supplier of Listserv, provides an outsourcing service which involves hosting the list. The list is then managed remotely in the company using web-based tools. The cost of hosting the list varies according to the number of lists and subscribers.

- *Lyris List Manager* (www.lyris.com): this recently established list manager was developed as a commercial product from the outset. This means that the architecture and services are arguably more rational. As with Listserv there is an advanced web-based interface for subscribers and list managers. The product is designed to not be suitable for spammers, so by default has a double opt-in mechanism, where subscribers have to reply to a confirmation e-mail after the initial opt-in. Like L-Soft, Lyris also offers an ASP or outsourcing service. SparkList (www.sparklist.com) is based on the Lyris List Manager and is also a popular list server.

DESKTOP E-MAIL MANAGEMENT SOFTWARE

Mailloop 5.0 (www.marketingtips.com/mailloop)

Mailloop is software that can be used for managing both inbound and outbound e-mail. It has three main modules: an incoming e-mail processor used for autoresponding to subscription and unsubscribe requests arriving from e-mails generated by an HTML-driven form, a list processor used for setting up lists for mailings such as selecting which records you want to send, and an outgoing e-mail processor for mailing to a list. The list processor works with text file-based lists, which must be exported from a database rather than integrating directly with a database. This enables selects to be achieved according to different fields, but each select requires a different filter operation. It readily supports multiple newsletters since it identifies keywords in incoming e-mails generated from an HTML subscription form such as 'Frequency = Monthly' and then sets up the appropriate subscription.

ProAutoResponder (http://scc.proautoresponder.com/)

Like Mailloop, ProAutoresponder can also be used to manage a newsletter list. It enables e-mails to be sent in text, HTML or MIME format. It also enables a sequence of e-mail messages to be sent as multistage e-mails (see Chapter 4). For instance, it will send a standard message on sign-up, then another on day 10, on day 20, and so on.

Infacta Group Mail (www.infacta.com)

As the name suggests, Group Mail is designed for sending to an unlimited number of groups, each with unlimited recipients. It enables personalisation and is more sophisticated than other products in its integration with other information sources (e.g. file-based records, databases or address books).

Gammadyne Mailer (www.gammadyne.com/mmail.htm)

Gammadyne Mailer (Figure 7.4) is one of the most widely used e-mail packages. It has the standard features described above, but its main distinguishing feature is that it enables integration with a range of databases (ODBC compliant). This may be too complex for some needs since it does not work with its own text-based list as do products such as Mailloop. It is has a wide range of options to enable personalisation, but this makes it more complex than some other packages.

APPLICATION SERVICE PROVIDER MODEL

The following services use an ASP model. Practically speaking, this means that the user has to configure their campaign via selecting options within a web browser while connected to the ISP. The list of e-mails to be sent is uploaded to the ASP before dispatch. Some ASPs can also install the software on a company's server.

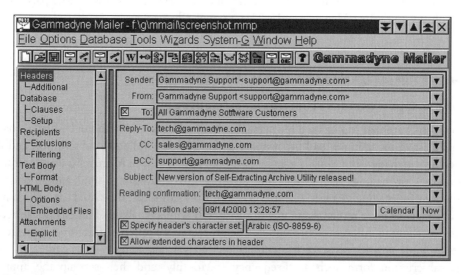

Figure 7.4   Setting the e-mail attributes using Gammadyne Mailer

messageREACH (www.messagereach.com)

messageREACH is part of xPedite, an established direct-marketing organisation. It manages secure broadcasts for many large companies, including financial services. Its e-mail management service can be managed by the company's staff, or there is an option for customers to manage a broadcast directly.

E-mail Vision (www.emailvision.com)

E-mail Vision is an e-mail specialist based in France and operating throughout Europe. Like messageREACH, they offer client services to manage all aspects of a campaign, or clients can manage their own campaign. Their advanced reporting product e-mail Commander is widely used.

e2Communications IonMail (www.e2communications.com)

e2Communications is a well-established US-based e-mail service company. Their IonMail service, which mainly targets large organisations, can either be based in-house or use an ASP model.

iMailer (www.emailtools.co.uk/iMailer.htm)

This tool, which can be managed remotely, offers standard tools for managing subscribe/unsubscribe requests and bounces are automatically removed. It offers message personalisation, but this is not as sophisticated as some packages. It includes options for multistage messages (follow-ups).

GravityMail (www.gravitymail.com)

This is a web-based solution similar to iMailer. It differs in that it has templates for building e-newsletters.

MANAGING THE HOUSE LIST

As noted in Chapters 4 and 5, there will be a high turnover of e-mail addresses, or 'gone-aways' in traditional direct mail speak. Research by Mercer MC (2001) showed that on average 20% of customers in a typical database will change their contact information over the course of a year. This varies from 16% for an address and 17% for a job, to 25% for an e-mail address and 33% for a cell-phone. Furthermore, they estimate that the cost of updating or reconsenting to these databases can run into tens of millions of dollars for a large database, not to mention the opportunity costs from lost customers. These figures highlight the importance of creating measures to capture these changes. Worse still, the permission provided for contact may change with time, since you will have asked different questions about how personal data will be used to market to the customer. Options for managing this change include:

- periodic checks by call-centre staff and at other touchpoints

- a 'Change personal details' option on the web site (this is required by data protection laws in some countries)

- e-mail or telesales campaigns aimed at updating data (the Corpdata case study in Chapter 4 shows how this process works).

E-MAIL MARKETING EXCELLENCE

FreshAddress guidelines on keeping a list fresh

Austin Bliss, CEO of specialist e-mail change-of-address company FreshAddress Inc. (www.freshaddress.com/biz), suggests that these are the most common methods for updating addresses:

1. *Identification of addresses that should be removed from your list.* These may be addresses that match a list of suspicious addresses (e.g. 'abuse@aol.com', 'none@none.com', etc.), match a block list, are unrecoverable bounces, or are duplicates. Some services can also catch different addresses belonging to the same person, so that you don't double-message these people.

2. *Flagging of addresses that should be manually reviewed.* These might be addresses that meet certain rules maintained by the provider, or simply violate standard guidelines for email addresses (e.g. containing unusual characters, etc.).

3. *Correction of typos.* Using tables of known typos as well as heuristic rules, your provider can help you recover customers lost to 'dead' addresses as a result of thousands of typos and syntax errors, including every typo example presented earlier. Some providers even offer recursive processing, which can intelligently correct multiple typos in one pass.

4. *Updating of old addresses.* All true NCOA for Email providers operate popular consumer websites designed for individuals to use when their email addresses change. These updated addresses, in addition to across the board domain changes, are then made available to you.

Typical vendors offer pay for performance pricing. On average, this works out to less than fifty cents per recovered address. Depending on the type and quality of your list, initial match rates will vary from very small to over ten percent. Your relationship with a vendor may be a simple one-time run, or a contract-based relationship where they will help you keep your list fresh over time.

A further issue is acting on information received about changes of address and unsubscribes. One of the main complaints about permission e-mail marketing is that unsubscribes are not acted on. When hard bounces are received, indicating that an e-mail address is no longer valid, some companies will use the facilities of the software mentioned in the previous section to remove the e-mail address automatically. Instead, a more proactive approach can be taken for business-to-business (B2B) addresses, perhaps a flag to a sales representative that the address has changed and tasking them with finding the new address or understanding this change.

In addition to the approaches discussed here, standard database-cleaning approaches can be used to remove duplicates resulting from joining databases (merge–purge).

MANAGING INBOUND E-MAIL

Inbound e-mail is all incoming e-mail to the organisation. Here, we focus on managing e-mail enquiries from customers. There are two conflicting concerns in managing inbound e-mail that will determine the inbound customer contact strategies: customer service quality and cost. Customer contact strategies are a compromise between delivering quality customer service, with the emphasis on customer choice, and minimising the cost of customer contacts. Typical operational objectives that should drive the strategies and measure their effectiveness are:

- to minimise average response time per e-mail and range of response time from slowest to fastest. This should form the basis of an advertised service quality level

- to minimise clear-up (resolution) time, e.g. number of contacts and elapsed time to resolution

- to maximise customer satisfaction ratings with response

- to minimise average staff time and cost per e-mail response.

Now let us look at cost. Farris and Langendorf's (1999) survey found that the cost of manually managing each inbound e-mail averages $2.75. By using automation to manage the inbound e-mails, they suggest the cost can be reduced to less than 25 cents. How many e-mails does your organisation receive that are processed manually? Multiply that number by £2. Is this a cost that you would like to reduce? If so, this section explains some techniques used to reduce costs by companies that receive hundreds of thousands of e-mails.

E-MAIL MARKETING EXCELLENCE

Managing e-mail costs at Travelocity

Travelocity is the Internet's largest online travel site, with more than 33 million members. Travelocity make extensive use of e-mail to communicate real-time information such as price changes and details of offers among the 700 airlines, 55 000 hotels and 50 rental car companies with which the company works.

Each month, Travelocity sends some 1.2 million itinerary e-mails, 4.4 million 'Fare Watcher' messages and 6 million 'Real Deals' newsletters. The travel site currently sends more than 2 million e-mails per day and the numbers are projected to grow to 12 million messages per day. With such high volumes, paying external companies on a per-message basis is clearly expensive.

Travelocity decided to bring e-mail marketing in-house by using Accucast Enterprise from Socketware. Iconocast (2002) reported that according to the Vice President of Systems, Richard Pendergast, this decision was based on the scalability, capacity and ability of the system to interface with the customer database which helps e-mail preferences. He estimates that by bringing e-mail marketing in-house, Travelocity saved around $10 000 per month.

Source: Iconocast (2002).

Customer contact strategies for integrating web and e-mail support into existing contact-centre operations usually incorporate elements of both of the following options:

1. *Customer preferred channel*: the company uses a customer-led approach where customers use their preferred channel for enquiry, whether it is phone callback, e-mail or live chat. Little attempt is made to influence the customer as to which is the preferable channel. Note that while this approach may give good customer satisfaction ratings, it is not usually the most cost-effective approach, since the cost of phone support will be higher than customer self-service on the web or an e-mail enquiry.

2. *Company preferred channel*: the company will seek to influence the customer on the medium used for contact. For example, easyJet encourages customers to use online channels rather than using voice contact to the call centre for both ordering and customer service. Customer choice is still available, but the company uses the web site to influence the choice of channel. Visit the easyJet web site (www.easyjet.com) and view the box to see how this is achieved.

Other management options for contact management strategy that concern resourcing include:

- *Call-centre staff multiskilling or separate web contact centre*: many companies start with a separate web contact centre and then move to multiskilling. Multiskilling is the best way of effectively answering queries from customers whose support query may refer to a combination of online or offline activities. Multiskilling also reduces hand-offs and can increase variety for contact-centre staff.

- *Balance between automation and manual processes*: automated responses, intelligent routeing and autosuggestion are all techniques described in the next section which can be used to reduce the number of queries handled by human operators. If the automated approach fails, however, then inappropriate responses may be received by customers.

- *Insourcing or outsourcing*: software, hardware and staff can be deployed internally or can be out-sourced to an ASP who will work according to a service level agreement to achieve quality standards.

Developing a plan for managing inbound e-mail

To develop a plan for managing inbound e-mail, the best approach is to consider the typical stages by which an e-mail is received and responded to (Figure 7.5).

The five stages are as follows.

Stage 1: Customer defines support query

The first stage starts before the customer has even sent the e-mail, since if we are concerned with reducing cost, we want to minimise the number of e-mails that need to be responded to. Provided the customer does not have to spend too much time seeking out an answer, this can also give rise to better customer service. As the box below shows, easyJet encourage users to view the frequently asked questions (FAQ) first, before giving them the option to e-mail or phone.

So, to reduce costs, we need self-service tools on the web site that help customers to find answers to their query. Many sites have FAQ, which have usually been compiled without too much thought as

Best practice

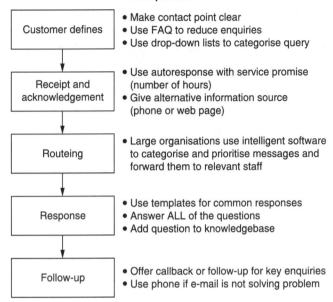

Customer defines	• Make contact point clear • Use FAQ to reduce enquiries • Use drop-down lists to categorise query
Receipt and acknowledgement	• Use autoresponse with service promise (number of hours) • Give alternative information source (phone or web page)
Routeing	• Large organisations use intelligent software to categorise and prioritise messages and forward them to relevant staff
Response	• Use templates for common responses • Answer ALL of the questions • Add question to knowledgebase
Follow-up	• Offer callback or follow-up for key enquiries • Use phone if e-mail is not solving problem

Figure 7.5 Stages in managing inbound e-mail

to what customers are actually asking. Start by moving from a brief list of FAQ to a more extensive, researched and structured list of FAQ. This can be compiled based on questions already fielded from customers. If you supply complex products such as hardware or software, then FAQ will probably not be enough. A knowledgebase can be used here. The most used knowledgebase is probably the Microsoft knowledgebase, which contains articles written by engineers in response to customers' questions. To be effective the knowledgebase requires suitable query tools that offer both keyword-based search and restricted searches in particular categories, such as the product type and problem type. Some knowledgebases contain specific responses to individual customers, but the Microsoft approach of writing a more detailed article gives a better quality of response and avoids duplication.

Another approach that can be used for some products is an automated diagnostic tool, which steps the user through their problem by asking a series of questions and then offering appropriate solutions. Epson (www.epson.co.uk) provides an online tool to diagnose problems with printers and suggest solutions.

E-MAIL MARKETING EXCELLENCE

easyJet manage e-mail volume (www.easyJet.com)

If an easyJet customer selects the 'Contact Us' option, rather than listing phone numbers and e-mail addresses, the customer is led through the three steps shown below which are intended to reduce the need for them to call the contact centre:

Step 1. Links or FAQ. These are based on careful analysis of phone calls and e-mails received by the contact centre. Examples include questions concerning use of the site and booking online, fares, availability, pricing, airports, check-in and travel information.

Step 2. E-mail enquiry through web form completion. Examples include technical queries relating to the site, customer service, route feedback and general feedback, for comments and suggestions (these e-mails are categorised to help prioritisation and routeing to the right person).

Step 3. Telephone numbers. Phone contact is only encouraged at the final stage. As easyJet explain, 'We've tried to make the FAQ and email service as simple and efficient as possible in order to keep the cost down and provide you with a good service, but if you're really stuck then, of course, you can call us'.

Companies should also consider how easily the customer can find contact points and compose a support request on site. Best practice is easy-to-find e-mail support options. Finding contact and support information on a web site is often surprisingly difficult. Standardised terminology on a web site is 'Contact Us' or 'Support'. Options should be available for the customer to specify the type of query on a web form, or alternative e-mail addresses such as products@company.com or returns@company.com should be provided on-site, or in offline communications such as a catalogue. Utilities provider Servista (www.servista.com) provides a good example of such a form.

When the site visitor finally comes to complete the support form, it is vital to have a field on the form that identifies the type of query, for example: 'Product fault', 'Delivery enquiry', 'Product information required' or 'other'. This is best achieved with the aid of a drop-down product list box from which the customer chooses an option. This can help in assigning the e-mail to someone who can answer the problem, since there is a restricted range of options.

Finally, the web site should determine expectations about the level of service quality. For example, inform the customer that 'your enquiry will be responded to within 24 hours'.

Stage 2: Receipt of e-mail and acknowledgement

Best practice is that automatic message acknowledgement occurs. This is usually provided by autoresponder software. While many autoresponders only provide a simple acknowledgement, more sophisticated responses can reassure the customer about when the response will occur and highlight other sources of information. Blackstar (www.blackstar.co.uk) provides a good example of best practice:

> *Thanks for emailing blackstar.co.uk.*
>
> *There are currently 51 emails in the queue in front of yours, so our expected response time is approximately 1 hour, 10 minutes.*

Don't forget that you can track your order status on line at: http://www.blackstar.co.uk/circle/order_status (where you can also cancel your order if you've made a mistake, or have just changed your mind).

Many other common questions are also answered in our help section: click on the big question mark in the header bar or go direct to http://www.blackstar.co.uk/help/

Stage 3: Routeing of e-mail

Best practice involves automated routeing or workflow. Routeing the e-mail to the right person is made easier if the type of query has been categorised at stage 1. It is also possible to use pattern recognition to identify the type of enquiry. For example, Nationwide (www.nationwide.co.uk) uses Brightware's 'skill-based message routeing' so that messages are sent to a specialist adviser, to whom specific enquiries are made. Such software can also be used at stage 1 to give an autoresponse appropriate to the enquiry. Using this approach, Mark Cromack says that 40% of messages no longer reach the advisors.

Stage 4: Compose response

Best practice is to use a library of pre-prepared templates for different types of query. These can then be tailored and personalised by the contact centre employee as appropriate. The right type of template can again be selected automatically using the software referred to in stage 2. By using such autosuggestion, the Nationwide has seen e-mail handling times reduced by 25% for messages requiring advisor intervention. Sony Europe identifies all new support issues and adds them, with the appropriate response, to a central knowledgebase.

Stage 5: Follow-up

Best practice is that if the employee does not successfully answer the first response, then the e-mail should suggest a phone call-back from an employee or a live chat. Indeed, to avoid the problem of 'e-mail ping-pong', where several e-mails may be exchanged, the company may want to phone the customer proactively to increase the speed of problem resolution, and so solve the problem. Finally, the e-mail follow-up may provide the opportunity for outbound contact and marketing, perhaps enquiring whether there are any further queries while advising about complementary products or offers.

E-MAIL MARKETING EXCELLENCE

Customer service at the Nationwide

The Nationwide is a financial services organisation which has been active in using the Internet as a customer service tool. Bicknell (2002) reports that the volume of customer service is as follows:

900 000 registrants on site with 2.4 million visits to the site in August 2001. Of the 1.2 million who entered the online bank, 900 000 made transactions resulting in 60 000 online contacts which require customer service.

These figures highlight the number of transactions that will have reduced customer contacts in real-world branches and by phone, but this still leaves 60 000 online contacts. The Nationwide believed that customers should expect service to be fast and accurate. Mark Cromack, operations manager, said:

> *There was a huge demand for more and more information and an explosion in the level of information that people wanted. That had implications for staff morale. What we needed was an autoresponse facility which provided quality, compliant and consistent answers.*

To reduce the volume of calls, FAQ was not sufficient. Nationwide purchased two products from Firepond to improve service. *Concierge* is provided on the home page to provide a facility with natural language searching to help customers to find the answers to their queries more rapidly. *Answer* is an automated message routeing tool that provides automated answers to simple questions, which can be reviewed by contact-centre staff before dispatch and yet is able to spot the phrasing of more complex queries for completion by call-centre operators.

Using these solutions, the quality of answers improved to give a first-time resolution rate of 94%. With the reduced staff time involved, the cost per contact has been reduced from £4 to £2.

REFERENCES

Aberdeen (2000). e-Marketing: to outsource or not to outsource – that is the question. Executive white paper, The Aberdeen Group, November.

Bicknell, D. (2002). Banking on customer service. *e.Businessreview*, January, 21–2.

Farris, J. and Langendorf, L. (1999). *Engaging Customers in e-Business*. e2 whitepaper (www.e2software.com).

Iconocast (2002). Travelocity relies on Accucast to help save money. *Iconocast*, 17 April (www.iconocast.com).

Mercer MC (2001). Making CRM make money. A Mercer Management Consulting commentary (www.mercermc.com).

WEB LINKS

List servers

ListProc (www.listproc.net)
Listserv (www.lsoft.com)
Lyris List Manager (www.lyris.com)
Majordomo (www.greatcircle.com/majordomo)
ServerWatch (www.serverwatch.internet.com)

Personal e-mail software

Gammadyne Mailer (www.gammadyne.com/mmail.htm)
Infacta Group Mail (www.infacta.com)
Mailloop 5.0 (www.marketingtips.com/mailloop)
ProAutoResponder (http://scc.proautoresponder.com/)

ASP-based e-mail management software

E-mail Vision (www.emailvision.com)
GravityMail (www.gravitymail.com)
iMailer (www.emailtools.co.uk/iMailer.htm)
messageREACH (www.messagereach.com)

Chapter **8**

E-mail marketing innovation

Overview

This chapter looks at a variety of issues that will affect the future of e-mail marketing. These include the rise of SPAM and the battle against it, the use of wireless access devices such as PDAs and mobiles, and the new opportunities for rich media such as video streaming provided by increased bandwidth.

Chapter objectives

By the end of this chapter you will be able to:

- assess different approaches being developed to control SPAM.
- evaluate the relevance of rich media e-mails.
- identify the options for e-mail using wireless access devices.

Chapter structure

- Solving the SPAM problem
- Rich media e-mails
- Messaging through mobile or wireless access devices
- Picture messaging

SOLVING THE SPAM PROBLEM

Newmediazero (2002) reported that according to a new Forrester report the 'spam flood will drown e-mail marketing'. We all see the evidence of this in our inboxes, unless we are enlightened enough to have taken action using the techniques described later in the chapter. According to Forrester, 70% of all online consumers believe that they receive too many e-mail offers and promotions, compared with just 44% two years ago. Meanwhile, business users receive more e-mail than all other forms of communication.

Forrester believes that all attempts by Internet service providers (ISPs) to filter SPAM and efforts by governments to legislate against SPAM will be ineffective. Forrester suggests that it is the responsibility of marketers to manage their campaigns such that consumers receive relevant e-mails at the right frequency.

I don't think that the picture is that negative. SPAM filters such as SPAMcop (www.spamcop.net) and SPAM Assassin (www.spamassassin.org) are effective in cutting out a large proportion of SPAM, although they can certainly prevent some wanted e-mail getting through. Users can quickly recognise SPAM and delete it. Another argument is that there is an increasing volume of permission e-mail. This, however, is less of a problem than SPAM since e-mail recipients always have the option of unsubscribing. If your unsubscribe rate remains less than your subscribe rate then there is no great problem. If marketers can devise e-mails that are targeted, appeal to their audience and are read regularly, then these are still preferable to direct mail.

Reducing the volume of SPAM

ISPs and company IS managers are active in deploying technology to reduce the volume of SPAM; after all, not only does SPAM decrease their users' productivity, but it also costs money to store and archive SPAM on servers. Where ISPs are not active, many knowledgeable home and business users are battling SPAM unsupported.

The current methods of reducing SPAM are mainly based on blocking and filtering (Figure 8.1b). Blocking works by checking each incoming e-mail against a 'blacklist' of known SPAM addresses or senders. If there is a match, the message is bounced back to the sender. Filtering works through software tools that check the subject line, From address, and optionally the content for characteristics of SPAM; if you like, for the degree of 'spamminess'. We all know these tell-tale signs: using ALL CAPS, overuse of exclamation marks and so on. Check whether your e-mails may inadvertently use some of the excluded words used by Microsoft Outlook – see the E-mail Campaign Checklist below. The problem is that to be effective, not all these lists are published, and e-mails from legitimate marketers may be excluded. Take the example of the estate agent in Sussex, informing clients about new houses in the county: their e-mails may be intercepted because of the use of 'sex' in the subject line.

E-MAIL CAMPAIGN CHECKLIST

Words excluded by Microsoft Outlook

Rules from Microsoft Outlook 2002 file 'filters.txt' used to identify SPAM. Check that your campaigns do not include these – for example, a financial services provider might use the terms 'money back' or 'over 18'.

From is blank
Subject contains "advertisement"
Body contains "money back"
Body contains "cards accepted"
Body contains "removal instructions"
Body contains "extra income"
Subject contains "!" AND Subject contains "$"
Subject contains "!" AND Subject contains "free"
Body contains ",000" AND Body contains "!!" AND Body contains "$"
Body contains "for free?"
Body contains "for free!"
Body contains "Guarantee" AND (Body contains "satisfaction" OR Body contains "absolute")
Body contains "more info" AND Body contains "visit" AND Body contains "$"
Body contains "SPECIAL PROMOTION"
Body contains "one-time mail"
Subject contains "$$"
Body contains "$$$"
Body contains "order today"

Body contains "order now!"
Body contains "money-back guarantee"
Body contains "100% satisfied"
To contains "friend@"
To contains "public@"
To contains "success@"
From contains "sales@"
From contains "success."
From contains "success@"
From contains "mail@"
From contains "@public"
From contains "@savvy"
From contains "profits@"
From contains "hello@"
Body contains " mlm"
Body contains "@mlm"
Body contains "////////////////"
Body contains "check or money order"
Adult Content Filter:
Subject contains "xxx"
Subject contains "over 18"
Subject contains "over 21"
Subject contains "adults"
Subject contains "adults only"
Subject contains "be 18"
Subject contains "18+"
Body contains "over 18"
Body contains "over 21"
Body contains "must be 18"
Body contains "adults only"
Body contains "adult web"
Body contains "must be 21"
Body contains "adult en"
Body contains "18+"
Subject contains "erotic"
Subject contains "adult en"
Subject contains "sex"
Body contains "xxx "
Body contains "xxx!"
Subject contains "free" AND Subject contains "adult"
Subject contains "free" AND Subject contains "sex"

Brightmail offers an application service provider (ASP)-based SPAM filtering system that is based on a network of hundreds of thousands of dummy e-mail addresses. SPAM received to these addresses is used to build rules to identify SPAM and can also be used to filter out new attacks by blocking the address before SPAM is sent to the entire list.

Mailwasher software (www.mailwasher.net) provides an alternative approach for individuals to combat SPAM. This tool enables you to monitor and delete e-mail before it is downloaded from the mail server, and categorises it into different risk categories. It can even bounce messages to suggest that the e-mail address is invalid, and so reduce the chance of further SPAM. SpamKiller (www.spamkiller.com) is a similar product that has recently been purchased by McAfee, which shows that such programs will soon become mainstream.

The new approach will be based on accepting e-mail from trusted sources that are on a 'whitelist'. Only preaccepted e-mails will be delivered. Organisations and ISPs will maintain a list of valid addresses on behalf of each user (a whitelist, see Figure 8.1c). This approach has been suggested by, among others, Dvorak (2001), who likens the approach to instant messaging where you cannot get your message through unless you are on a list of approved senders. The onus will be on the user to keep this list updated. Initially, the process is likely to be clunky. Say a business person sees a newsletter to which they would like to subscribe; they would have to inform the IS department, or fill in a form on an in-house system adding this e-mail address to the list of authorised senders. Note that addresses are not usually advertised on subscription, so this will need to change. In the future, an automated system may be possible using public and private certificates. The user will be able to register on a web site and the security certificates of the client and subscriber will be exchanged automatically. Such schemes have, however, proved difficult to sell to consumers or

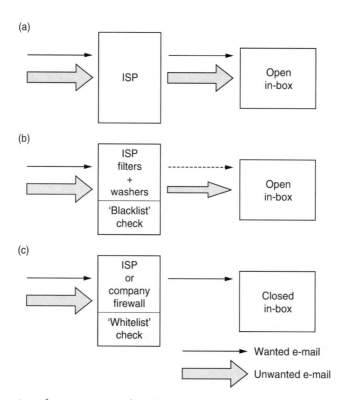

Figure 8.1 Progression of attempts to reduce SPAM

Figure 8.2   Bonded sender (www.bondedsender.com)

businesses for e-commerce. Many trusted certificate authorities (CAs) for e-commerce have not proved successful where the customer has to register proactively with the CA. One can foresee a situation where it will be worth paying subscribers to put them on their accepted e-mail list.

Many individuals already use such an approach with a primary e-mail address that is only given to trusted friends, colleagues and business contacts. They will use other addresses for less well-trusted sources or for opting in to newsletters. You should also try to avoid 'mail to' e-mail addresses being put on the web since spammers use harvesting programs to build their lists from these sources.

One approach is the concept of a 'bonded sender', developed in the USA by Ironport (www.bondedsender.com). Senders of opt-in e-mail post a financial bond to prove they are a reputable company. Senders of SPAM would not be able to afford to pay the bond. Recipients who feel they have received an unsolicited e-mail from a bonded sender can complain to their ISP, IT manager or Ironport and a financial charge is debited from the bond. For senders of e-mail the benefit of using this service is that their e-mails will not be blocked by SPAM filters such as those of Brightware or Hotmail, since the filters will identify the e-mail as coming from a trusted source.

E-MAIL MARKETING INSIGHT

Rosalind Resnick on the future of e-mail marketing

In this article, Resnick describes Internet users as being 'e-mailed to death' and acknowledges that this is disappointing since early adopters of permission marketing expected this to decrease the amount of SPAM. The reality is that in the face of ever-increasing volumes of SPAM some users are 'tuning out' of commercial e-mail completely, whether it is solicited or unsolicited. In this interview, the issue of declining clickthrough rates is also addressed. Resnick's view is that while it may be disappointing not to be able to emulate the historical 5–15% clickthrough rates of acquisition e-mail, a 1–2% clickthrough will still give a profitable acquisition cost and compares with traditional direct mail. She also believes that clickthrough rates for permission e-mails will not drop as low as banner adverts, since the prospect has shown interest in the product. Asked about the role that e-mail can play in the overall marketing mix, Resnick makes the analogy of an e-mail being the envelope and the web site the letter. Expanding on this, she says that the aim of the e-mail is not to close the sale in a single message, but to drive people to the web site to get them to act; e-mail by itself is simply a powerful lead generation tool. Ten years in the future she foresees e-mail becoming an integral part of the communications mix, with routine coverage of customer e-mails and e-mail seamlessly integrated with direct mail and advertising. She does not see rich media e-mails replacing advertising as a branding tool. Finally, looking at multichannel marketing, Resnick foresees a great future for e-mail marketing. The example is given of a magazine publisher sending out a renewal notice by postal mail and then following that up with three, four or even five e-mail reminders. What makes e-mail powerful is the very low cost of doing an additional 'e-mail blast'.

Source: AvantMarketer (2002).

The future of e-newsletters

Nielsen (2000) says he hopes that mailing lists will not have much of a future. In the long term he believes:

> *we need to remove everything from e-mail that is not in the nature of personal correspondence. Users are suffering under overflowing inboxes that combine many disparate types of information.*

He envisages that the services currently provided by mailing lists should be:

> *shown in a communications control panel that would monitor all the things the user is interested in on the Internet. Areas that are hot or have news would be highlighted and an agent in the user's computer would prioritise the most important one and give them most real estate.*

According to David Hughes, Group Account Director or E-mail Vision, client retention campaigns have average open rates of 44% and clickthrough rates of over 10%, while acquisition campaigns have open rates of 26% and clickthrough rates of less than 5%.

Spam Assassin, *http://www.spamassassin.org/*, uses rules to classify e-mails according to their degree of SPAM.

MailWasher can be used to filter and bounce SPAM before an e-mail is downloaded.

Where the ISP or IS department of an organisation does not provide the anti-SPAM tools, the user may also take their own measures by subscribing to services such as MailWasher or SPAMcop. Dvorak (2001) postulates that anti-virus software may offer options for deleting SPAM. It will identify SPAM signatures in much the same way as virus signatures are identified and then warn the user of likely SPAM.

RICH MEDIA E-MAILS

Rich media e-mails go one step beyond the use of static or animated graphics in HTML e-mails and give a richer experience through more complex animation, video and/or sound. Some refer to HTML as rich media, but more commonly the term is used to refer to more dynamic or interactive content. The video or the Flash package is streamed when the user opens the e-mail, or the message is displayed in the preview pane, and downloaded and displayed in real-time. Messagizer (www.messagizer.co.uk) has already done a number of video e-mail campaigns for clients such as Columbia Tristar and Pathe films. Their Videomail product streams video content directly into the e-mail without the need for any plug-ins. A further example is SAAB, which has included TV adverts in its e-mail campaigns. Alternatively, graphics and animations can be sent as attachments, but these are likely to be removed by some company firewalls. Companies such as Digital Outlook (www.digital-outlook.com) are increasingly using Java-based streaming since this does not require format specific decoding, i.e. recipients do not need to rely on having the right version of the Real or Windows media player and the right plug-ins installed, since most computers have Java capabilities. Posting to the UK Net Marketing forum (www.chinwag.com), Glen Collins of Digital Outlook points out there are still disadvantages with video streaming. He says:

> *With video streaming you will probably have to pay on a per view basis, so if the video spreads virally you could end up with a huge bill or having to turn off the stream. With downloads you pay once.*

Even with new encoding techniques, if you are a home user video streaming can be very poor quality. If your video is quite dark and fast moving (like the Spiderman trailer), this will not come across very well on a dial up connection. If your video is light, with slow moving block colours (like the telly tubbies) you could get away with it.

My advice is, if your objectives are to get the home user to watch a video, send them an e-mail directing them to a site where they can download it, this way you're not blocking up their inbox with large files and they have the choice to download it or not. If you are looking at hitting a broadband or office network user, video streaming is the way forward.

Some very successful viral campaigns from the likes of Ikea and MTV have used the video form of rich media to shock, thrill or entertain. Rich media will make a bigger impact and have better recall than static e-mails, but this all depends on the user actually seeing the rich media. You can imagine that all the constraints of receiving HTML will be magnified. Take Flash. Here, the user will need to have the appropriate plug-in installed already and be using an e-mail reader with the capability to detect and then display Flash content. Flash comes in different versions, and if you choose the latest, currently Flash MX, not all of your audience will be able to play the animation. You cannot assume that users will wait many minutes to download multimegabytes to view your rich media. So, lower grade alternatives based on .GIF animations should be provided for those who cannot play, or will not wait for the rich media.

E-MAIL MARKETING EXCELLENCE

Rich media streaming

Posting to the UK Net Marketing forum (www.chinwag.com), Derek Mansfield of Bold Endeavours has this advice:

> *We're using vmail marketing on a regular basis – but it's still trial and error. It's reasonably easy to do a viral – when people forward it to friends. Make a video using sex, violence and black humour and it works – at least with men aged 18–35. You'll lose your female audience of course but from what we've seen many companies haven't understood this yet. They see the raw numbers and are apparently happy. We've tried 5 types of encoding and have settled on Java encoding because the viewer doesn't have to download or have a player installed. With vmails you can't sniff the player in advance so you must use Java. There is a problem over the horizon as XP installations grow but it isn't with us (completely) yet.*
>
> *We get between 60% and 85% of vmails being read and we can track who opens what and when and where they go on the site – if they go to the site. We're finding it's in the detail – for example all of our vmails are personalised but there is a different response when you use Hi <name> or Hello <name> in the subject line. There's a big difference in openings and response levels – and unsubscribes – according to the time of day, day of week and frequency of mailings too. We're also discovering that you need to sell a different benefit in each vmail ... you can't send the same mail umpteen times. Companies are using vmails – but the time when you could send your TV commercial out or show your TV commercial on the web is ending ... it's no longer novel in itself. Today (for us anyway) we're learning that it's about creative approach, production values (it shows even in a tiny screen), tracking response and testing, testing, testing. I think there was a brief period when the marketing director could get his home video camera out, film himself talking and plonking it on the website. Bit like when the world was designing brochures using Word. Now you need real skills and kit. One other major plus is that video, unlike Flash, will sit happily on the web site and can be surrounded by words so you don't lose your SE rankings.*

Figure 8.3 Rich media e-mail example

MESSAGING THROUGH MOBILE OR WIRELESS ACCESS DEVICES

Mobile technologies are not new; it has been possible for many years to access the Internet for e-mail using a laptop connected via a modem. However, the need for large portable devices directly connected to the Internet has now been overcome with the development of personal digital assistants (PDAs) such as the Palm Computing Palm VII or Psion and mobile phones. We are now seeing a range of hybrid devices combining PDA features such as calendar, address list, task list and office tools with phone features. The forerunner was the Nokia 9210 Communicator, which was large and earned the epithet related to house building. While the 9210 has been enhanced, there is now a range of phone-PDAs, of which the Treo and XDA were the latest at the time of writing.

The importance of mobile access devices is evident from Figure 8.4. This shows that, in the UK, the usage of mobile phones far exceeds that of the fixed Internet. This pattern is repeated throughout the world. What does this mean for e-mail marketing? First and foremost, messaging to mobile devices offers greater reach than Internet-based e-mail marketing. However, messaging to mobile devices brings a host of new technical and ethical issues. The main form of messaging to mobile phones is now short message service (SMS) text messaging, which we explore below. Since the mobile phone is arguably a more personal device than the

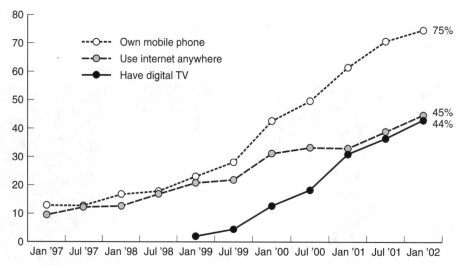

Figure 8.4 UK rate of adoption of different new media, December 2001 (Source: e-MORI, 2002)

fixed PC, companies can be even more unpopular if they are perceived to have delivered SPAM. There is also the constraint of the limited space for communicating by SMS (limited to 128 characters). How do you explain your offer and proposition in this space without recourse to a landing page for the direct response? Although these current limitations are significant, they will be swept away in the future by the advent of new-generation phones which use the wireless Internet to access e-mails using conventional inboxes such as Outlook Express. Many users already access their e-mails on their mobile through Yahoo!, but the limited, largely text-based user interface offers limited potential for marketing. The new technologies such as WAP, GPRS and 3G have been much criticised for their disappointing speed and the cost of the licences. But the technology will be widely adopted, worldwide; it is only a matter of when. Research suggests that technology such as 3G may not become mainstream technology until after 2005, but in the meantime, users will be accessing rich e-mail through large-screen mobile PDAs.

The proposition of wireless Internet access is suggested by the supposedly idyllic image used in many adverts of a user accessing the Internet via a laptop or phone from a beach or mountaintop. Wireless devices provide ubiquity (can be accessed from anywhere), reachability (their users can be reached when not in their normal location) and convenience (it is not necessary to have access to a power supply or fixed-line connection). In addition to these obvious benefits, there are less obvious additional benefits: they provide security (each user can be authenticated since each wireless device has a unique identification code), their location can be used to tailor content, and they provide more privacy than a desktop PC: looking for jobs on a wireless device may be better than under your boss's gaze. A further advantage that is now available is that of instant access or 'always on'; here there is no need to dial-up a wireless connection. Table 8.1 provides a summary of the mobile or wireless Internet access proposition. There are considerable advantages over PC-based Internet access, but this is currently limited by the display limitations such as small screen size and limited graphics.

Table 8.1   Summary of mobile or wireless Internet access consumer proposition

Element of proposition	Evaluation
Not fixed location	The user is freed from the need to access via the desktop, making access possible when commuting, for example
Location-based services	Mobiles can be used to provide geographically based services, e.g. an offer in a particular shopping centre. Future mobiles will have global positioning system services integrated
Instant access/convenience	The latest GPRS and 3G services are always on, avoiding the need for lengthy connection
Privacy	Mobiles are more private than desktop access, making them more suitable for social use or for certain activities such as an alert service for looking for a new job
Personalisation	As with PC access, personal information and services can be requested by the user, although these often need to be set up via PC access
Security	In the future mobiles may become a form of wallet, but thefts of mobiles make this a source of concern

Short message service (SMS)

Using mobile phones for text-based communication has become incredibly popular, courtesy of the SMS. This is a simple form of e-mail that enables messages to be transferred between mobile phones. The main use of SMS is for personal messages between phone users, but voicemail notifications, alerts about news and transactions have also become popular. According to MobileCommerceWorld (2002), 1.3 billion text messages were sent in December 2001, bringing the total number of messages sent in 2001 in the UK to 12.2 billion. This suggests an average of nearly 300 messages per person annually and a much higher figure for some users.

SMS messaging can be effectively used as a direct response medium where users' mobile numbers and names can be collected. This works in a similar way to e-mail marketing, with an offer being used to encourage the user to reply with their details. Rather than personal details being provided through a web page, however, the phone user simply types in their details and texts them to a published number. *The Guardian* (2002) gives the example of FlyTxt (www.flytxt.com), a mobile marketing agency, offering a prize draw entry for a flight to Australia and then sending text messages offering further chances to win, in this case Australian champagne and discounts on using the company's services. A great benefit of text messaging is that to help convert the prospect to a customer you have access to a phone number on which to call them. It is harder work to find a phone number to follow up a prospect from a business-to-business (B2B) e-mail campaign. The same company also ran an SMS campaign for Cadbury, where the number to text was included on wrappers for different chocolate bars in return for the chance to win cash and Sony Playstations. Such campaigns often also require the user to text a promotional code, which is used to track the different forms of advertising.

The immediacy of mobile communications can also be used to advantage. For example, messages can be sent out at a particular time of day, perhaps Friday afternoon, to encourage people in a certain area to attend a particular club.

WAP and 3G

In 1999 the first of a new generation of mobile phones, such as the Nokia 7110, was introduced that offered the opportunity to access the Internet. These are known as wireless application protocol or WAP phones, or in plainer language, web-enabled or Internet phones. These phones offer the facility to access information on web sites that has been specially tailored for display on the small screens of mobile phones. There was a tremendous amount of hype about these phones since they offered all the benefits that have been provided by the World Wide Web, but in a mobile form. This hype, however, ignored the limitations of the devices in terms of screen size and colour, and bandwidth or access speeds. These limitations were so great that most users sought out fixed Internet access or made do with other media.

As a consequence, levels of product purchase by mobile phone have proved very low in comparison with the Internet, even for standardised products such as books and CDs. Many m-commerce providers such as Sweden's M-box went into receivership. However, analysts expect that with new access platforms, such as 3G, this will change. Taking the example of travel, this is the leading e-commerce category in Europe by revenue for the fixed Internet. Analysts IDC (2002) estimate that by 2005, 23 million Europeans will buy travel products and services using their mobile phones. Mobile-based messaging will be important for reaching these consumers.

Despite the lack of m-commerce success for mobiles, they are increasingly being used for e-mail by those who do not have ready access to a fixed PC; they are popular with students for this reason. Figure 8.5 illustrates a campaign showing how WAP-enabled devices allow the user to read and reply to e-mails hosted through online e-mail services such as Yahoo! The Vodafone campaign also highlights that its services enable e-mails to be accessed by any phones through SMS.

The Japanese experience with i-Mode suggests that with suitable access devices that support colour images, the impact of 3G could be significant. MobileCommerceWorld (2001) reports that Japanese i-mode users spend an average of 2614 yen (US $21.60) each month on wireless content and m-commerce. Mobile phone ringtones and other music downloads are the most popular i-mode purchase, followed by other paid-for information services. The strength of the proposition is indicated by over 30 million Japanese people using this service despite a launch less than 2 years previously.

In 2001 new services became available on General Packet Radio Service (GPRS). This is approximately five times faster than GSM and is an 'always-on' service which is charged according to usage. Display is still largely text based and based on WAP. Over the next one to three years different telecoms providers will introduce new services. A completely new generation (3G) of services will become available by UMTS; with this the delivery of sound and images should be possible, enabling instant access or 'always on'. In the UK auctions for the licence to operate on this frequency have exceeded £20 billion, such is the perceived importance of these services by the telecommunications companies. Many commentators now believe that it will be difficult for the telecommunications companies to recoup this money and this has resulted in large falls in their share prices.

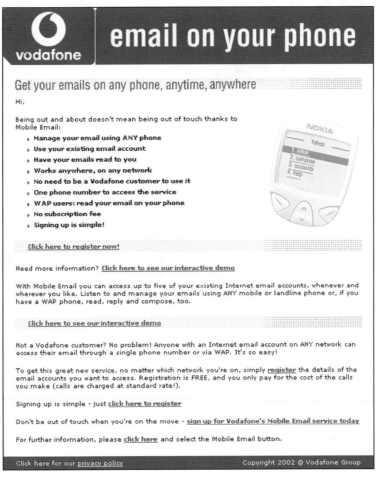

Figure 8.5 E-mail campaign to promote e-mail access from mobile phones (Source: David Mill, MediaCo, www.media.co.uk)

Figure 8.6 shows the potential form of 3G devices that will integrate PDA, phone and office tools. While these devices will undoubtedly become popular with time, it is clear from their form that they will coexist alongside fixed PC-based Internet access.

PICTURE MESSAGING

Wray (2002) reported in *The Guardian* that there will be fierce competition for picture messaging services. Technically, picture messaging is known as multimedia messaging service (MMS). T-Mobile plans to launch the UK's first wireless picture messaging service for Christmas 2002. All four of the main UK networks also plan to have a service operational by Christmas. Such services are expected to prove popular for two main reasons. First, the market for personalised ringtones and images for mobiles has experienced massive growth in all developed countries. Secondly, early adopters of picture messaging such as the i-MODE system in Japan have been successful and it is

Figure 8.6 Prototype 3G device (www.nokia.com)

also a revenue generator. Based on these factors, *The Guardian* reported that analyst Ovum estimates that mobile users in the UK will send over 35 billion multimedia messages during 2007 and the market will be worth over $5 billion. However, the service will be of most relevance to users with a handset that can take pictures and this will require new handsets to be purchased. It will, however, also be possible to load messages via the fixed Internet. Forecasts for new mobile commerce technologies from all analysts have proved wildly optimistic in the past.

REFERENCES

AvantMarketer (2002). NetCreations' Rosalind Resnick on permission email. *Avantmarketer E-mail Newsletter*, 17 June (www.avantmarketer.com).

Dvorak (2001). The modernisation of e-mail. *PC Magazine*, 3 April.

e-MORI (2002). Technology Tracker, January 2002. Available online at: www.e-mori.co.uk/tracker.shtml.

The Guardian (2002). Getting the message across. *The Guardian*, 2 May.

IDC (2002). Online Travel Services Set to Boost Mobile Commerce. IDC Research press release, 23 January 2002. www.idc.com.

MobileCommerceWorld (2001). i-Mode users spending more on content. Press release 26 November 2001 based on data from Infocom. http://www.mobilecommerceworld.com.

MobileCommerceWorld (2002). British SMS records smashed in December. Press release 24 January 2002 based on data from the mobile data association. http://www.mobilecommerce-world.com.

Newmediazero (2002). E-mail marketing warning. *NewMediaAge*, April.

Nielsen, J. (2000). Mailing list usability. *UseIT Alertbox*, August (www.useit.com).
Wray, R. (2002). Mobile set for price war. *The Guardian*, 6 June.

WEB LINKS

AudioBanner (http://www.audiobanner.com): rich media
Digital Outlook (www.digital-outlook.com)
Dynamics Direct (http://www.dynamicsdirect.com)
Eyewonder (http://www.eyewonder.com): video
InChorus (http://www.inchorus.com): Flash
Ironport (www.bondedsender.com)
MailWasher (www.mailwasher.net)
Messagizer (www.messagizer.co.uk)
MindArrow (http://www.mindarrow.com): comes in as attachments and HTML
Mobile Marketing Association (www.wirelessmarketing.org.uk)
SPAM Assassin (www.spamassassin.org)
SPAMcop (www.spamcop.net)
TMX (http://www.tmxinteractive.com): Flash

Index